# RABBINIC LITERATURE & THE NEW TESTAMENT

# RABBINIC LITERATURE & THE NEW TESTAMENT

## WHAT WE CANNOT SHOW, WE DO NOT KNOW

## JACOB NEUSNER

*Wipf & Stock*
PUBLISHERS
*Eugene, Oregon*

Wipf and Stock Publishers
199 West 8th Avenue, Suite 3
Eugene, Oregon 97401

Rabbinic Literature and the New Testament
What We Cannot Show, We Do Not Know
By Neusner, Jacob
Copyright©1994 by Neusner, Jacob
ISBN: 1-59244-519-5
Publication date 1/30/2004
Previously published by Trinity Press International, 1994

FOR

H. E. JOSEPH CARDINAL RATZINGER,
WHO TEACHES THE SIMPLE BUT GOVERNING TRUTH
THAT HERMENEUTICS IS THE CHILD OF THEOLOGY,
AND EXEGESIS, THE GRANDCHILD

# Contents

**PART   THREE**
**Differences of Opinion on How Rabbinic Literature**
**Should Be Used for Historical Purposes**

**PART   FOUR**
**What We Can Show**
**and What We Want to Know**

# Preface

Scholars of the New Testament, including not only professors in universities and seminaries, ministers in pulpits and priests in parishes, but also engaged lay people, generally realize that rabbinic literature, produced in the same centuries as the formative writings of Christianity, portrays the beginnings of the Judaism as we know it. They rightly take for granted that rabbinic literature illuminates the world in which earliest Christianity took shape, and, of course, since Jesus was born, lived, and died a Jew, as did his mother and his disciples, it is quite natural to them to suppose that what the ancient rabbis tell us may clarify the life and teachings of Jesus, his apostles, Paul, and the other earliest figures of Christianity.

In this book I mean to explain enough of the character of rabbinic literature to call into question the rather facile use made of it by some New Testament scholarship and point to ways in which that literature has been misused. That is because many scholars imagine that, while the New Testament has to be subjected to the most astringent and incredulous inspection applied to any book of faith, the rabbinic literature is to be believed at face value as inerrant.

My argument is not negative or destructive. I do not maintain that we cannot learn historical information relevant to New Testament studies in rabbinic literature. To the contrary, we learn much in rabbinic literature that is quite relevant to the understanding of the New Testament in general and even to the exegesis of the Gospels in particular. The problem I raise is: what in particular is relevant to those tasks, and how do we know the relevant from the irrelevant?

So my argument is a different one. I invoke the principle: what we cannot show, we do not know. To adduce in evidence a story or saying in rabbinic literature to clarify problems of New Testament history and exegesis, we first must show that the story or saying provides facts about the first century in particular, things really said and done in the time of Jesus. If we can show this, we should use that evidence along with all other evidence subjected to the same criterion of verification and falsification. On that basis I call into question errors, not of fact but of method, that render historically useless scholarship on New Testament history and exegesis that calls uncritically upon rabbinic literature. That means, of course, most scholarship that appeals to rabbinic literature at all.

In these pages, by way of reply, I conduct four simple operations. First, I spell out the characteristics of rabbinic literature, showing why it is not easily used for the kind of history — facts about what really happened, opinion really held, thoughts really put forth, in particular in the first half of the first century in a province of the Land of Israel named Galilee — that New Testament scholarship proposes to produce. Then I show how various scholars misuse the literature, quoting what they say and raising questions about whether from that literature we know what they assume we know. Third, I go over important differences with critics of mine. Finally, I end by repaying the New Testament field for all it has taught me by telling the field to abandon its principal interest. The reason is (so it seems to me) that in the study of New Testament history and exegesis we are dealing with theology — theology that appeals for validation of its claims to facts that it alleges derive merely from critical history. My point throughout is simple: what we cannot show, we do not know. So let us find out what we really can show to have been fact and allow theological truth to take its own course.

I hope that by framing issues within the setting of New Testament history and exegesis I may persuade New Testament scholars to reconsider how and whether scholarly salvation really is of the Jews after all. Up to now rabbinic literature has not been used for New Testament history and exegesis in accord with the canons and conventions of critical learning that otherwise characterize New Testament studies. It would therefore probably be best to stop talking about "Judaism," if the basis for discourse remains as presently set forth, and start a new line of inquiry altogether.

Before proceeding, it remains to address one sensitive point. My quite negative, indeed dismissive reading in chapter 6 of Professor E. P. Sanders's *Judaism* should not be misconstrued as a statement of disrespect for the man and his mission. To the contrary, Sanders takes up subjects with a virulent anti-Semitic tradition, and he has devoted his life to presenting Judaism in such a way as to help Christians overcome their ancient heritage of Jew-hatred and contempt for Judaism. This he has done not through apologetics for the Christian tradition of anti-Semitism and anti-Judaism — he never says blatant anti-Semitism is anything other than what it is — but through a positive reading of the Judaism of the time and place of Jesus. Sanders addresses not merely entrenched bigotry, but also bigotry perpetrated and perpetuated by reputable scholars in our own days. For example, as he says, "I have had to argue at length against the prevailing views, which are enshrined in volume 2 of Schürer's *History of the Jewish People* (now revised and updated by Geza Vermes, Fergus Millar and others)."

No scholar in our time, then, has done more in his chosen, important field to prevent a future Holocaust involving Christianity's inspiration and, in some countries, institutional complicity — not renegades like Hitler but priests and bishops, German Christians and their pastors, professors of theology in the German universities, for instance — as did the one that took place in our own day. Many exemplary Christians from Pope John XXIII onward have joined in the task of the rehabilitation of Christianity in the aftermath of the Holocaust. So my remarks about Professor Sanders represent a genuine appreciation of a great labor. He has done more to help Protestant Christianity rid itself of its loathing of Judaism and Jews than any other scholar of our time.

Since some of Professor Sanders's writings may reflect a level of personal animosity toward me, it is important to say in so many words that I do not in any measure reciprocate. To the contrary, I publicly state my admiration for what I believe is his sacred and life-affirming goal, one that embodies in our day the love for the other that Christianity's founder professed. I do say in so many words that his is not the way to accomplish so worthy a goal. But if a single word in the pages that follow suggests a different attitude from one of appreciation for this man's life's work and respect, if not for his results and methods, then for his motivation and the goals of his scholarly career, I apologize for it. My publisher and I have made every effort to convey just the opposite: the respect expressed through sustained and rigorous criticism, that alone.

That Sanders and I publish through Trinity Press International pays eloquent tribute to yet another Christian. This book could only have been written for and with and published by that one publisher, Dr. Harold Rast. In many ways that I should have wanted for these papers either Trinity Press International or no publisher at all pays to him the kind of tribute the entire academic world of religious studies owe to him and to those in his model. It is characteristic of Protestant Christian academic publishing and also important figures in American secular academic publishing that E. P. Sanders and I should publish through the same firm. It is a tribute to American and Christian academic publishing in general but in particular to that firm, its integrity, its professionalism, its honesty to the academic ideal of free and open exchange of ideas and opinions. That people who disagree so radically as we do should find ourselves at home with the same publisher tells us all we need to know about the state of virtue and honesty in the American academy and in Christian academic publishing. Trinity Press International makes certain that all viewpoints have a proper hearing.

Free exchange of ideas, rather than boycott, suppression, and character assassination, serves the interest of all parties. That is why I wrote *Judaic Law from Jesus to the Mishnah: A Systematic Reply to Professor E. P. Sanders*,[1] *Why There Never Was a "Talmud of Caesarea": Saul Lieberman's Mistakes*,[2] and also *Are There Really Tannaitic Parallels to the Gospels? A Refutation of Morton Smith*[3] — not to mention *A Rabbi Talks with Jesus: An Intermillennial, Interfaith Exchange*.[4] Argument is an act of respect and ultimate seriousness in relationships.

With much pleasure I express my continuing thanks to the University of South Florida for providing ideal conditions — including a generous research expense fund — in which to pursue my research, and to my colleagues in the Department of Religious Studies and in other departments and colleges of the university for their ongoing friendship and stimulating conversation. They have shown me the true meaning of the word "collegiality": honesty, generosity, sincerity, engagement.

JACOB NEUSNER

---

1. South Florida Studies in the History of Judaism (Atlanta: Scholars Press, 1993).

2. South Florida Studies in the History of Judaism (Atlanta: Scholars Press, 1994).

3. South Florida Studies in the History of Judaism (Atlanta: Scholars Press, 1994).

4. New York: Doubleday, 1993.

*Introduction*

# What Do I Have to Know about Rabbinic Literature to Study the New Testament?

In the past, I had always assumed the question posed in the title of this chapter was reversed: what do I have to know about New Testament studies to work on rabbinic literature? For me, the path led from New Testament studies to the study of rabbinic literature, not the other way around. I had no other model of critical study, interesting study, study of important questions with answers of consequence. Rabbinic literature had never cared to make statements of general intelligibility. A literature of enormous human interest, it was in the hands of ghetto-minds who converted learning into a blood-sport but hunted small game — rabbits, not elephants.

So I had always seen New Testament studies as a field from which, in my work on the history of Judaism, I learned important methods and interesting ideas. I had always understood the New Testament to form, along with the writings of Josephus and some other odds and ends, the single best evidence on first-century life in the Land of Israel ("Palestine"). Since my work focused on rabbinic literature, beginning with the Mishnah (a philosophical law code generally held to have reached closure at ca. 200 C.E., ending with the Talmud of Babylonia), which I found to be history's most successful and absorbing piece of religious literature of the social order, I never took for granted that I had much to tell colleagues in a neighboring field. And all of the other writings on which I was working came later than that time.

1

For my work, moreover, I had for decades found in the New Testament scholarship of our own century, both at home and in Britain and Europe, methods for adaptation, ideas for exploration, guides, signposts, warnings — and admirable results. When I read Bultmann's *History of the Synoptic Tradition*, for example, I said to myself, "I'd like to do that for the Talmud." True, I could not have said just what "that" might be. But I knew I was in the presence of acumen, wit, imagination, and profound understanding.

I have also been astonished that people did not know the answer to the question this chapter raises, which is, "not a whole lot." After all, or so I thought, I had answered that question — indeed, I assumed I had made a rather substantial statement in response to it since: (1) I have re-presented the entirety of rabbinic literature in antiquity, so I have shown how I think it should be read, and that has included not only translating nearly everything, but also writing systematic introductions to each of the documents. I have made the entire rabbinic literature available in English in form-analytical translation. People now have access to everything and do not have to go off and consult their local rabbis about what Jesus ate for breakfast or what Saul (who became Paul) learned in *heder,* that is, grammar school. (2) I have also provided an introduction to each document, identifying its indicative traits of rhetoric (form), logic of coherent discourse, and topic and proposition. We therefore confront not just a mass of undifferentiated sayings and stories but well-crafted documents, each of which we can understand in its own terms. That work of thirty years is now all in print. So I supposed I had already told people about the character and uses of the canon of Judaism with the result that New Testament scholars could form their own judgment on what this literature said and how it might be used in solving their historical and exegetical problems, to the degree that it might be used at all.

As I shall explain in Part One of this book, I do not think that the bulk of that literature can serve the narrow purpose of telling us precisely how things were in the first century in the Land of Israel. In some isolated instances, I think some points of clarification may emerge, but overall I do not see how the rabbinic literature, which reached closure for its first document two hundred years after the beginning of Christianity, can serve in the way people seem to want to use it, that is, as a handbook of New Testament exegesis.

Most informed New Testament scholars understand that fact

and regard with amusement the slavish consultation of Billerbeck and his imitators, not taking seriously the gullible and ignorant resort to much later sources in explaining what Jesus really said or really meant. The updating of Billerbeck by Samuel T. Lachs in his virtually unintelligible *A Rabbinic Commentary on the New Testament: The Gospels of Matthew, Mark, and Luke*[1] has won remarkably slight interest; no reviewer has pronounced it the final solution to the problem of the historical Jesus. Most reviewers have remarked about its gullible premises and uncritical acceptance, as evidence on first-century matters, of whatever a rabbinic document says — early, later, or medieval. So the field today is far more sophisticated about rabbinic literature than it was when people would quote a medieval midrash-compilation to explain a statement of Paul in his letter to the Corinthians a thousand or fourteen hundred years earlier. That stands for progress.

But there is a second reason I had no ready answer: I thought I had already replied. I have addressed the world of New Testament scholarship in particular. No one has accused me of publishing too little or not repeating my message quite systematically and very energetically, each time to a distinct, natural audience for my ideas. I have worked hard to speak directly to colleagues in New Testament, because I have owed them so much and have tried to learn their language and to speak it with them. Bilingual, if with a distinctive accent, I had long engaged in dialogue — two-sided conversation — with the New Testament world, regarding in particular what that world contributed to the study of Judaism, whether little or much. I counted as my nearest colleagues New Testament specialists. And I always found understanding, appreciation, and respect among them that generally were denied among the folk who ought to have grasped what I was proposing to accomplish. Only in the world of modern Orthodox Judaic scholarship, both in universities and yeshivas, in the United States, Canada, and Britain, have I found a hearing equivalent to what New Testament scholarship throughout the world has accorded.

This sustained address of scholarly results relevant to the New Testament field, to be sure, was in work published a decade or more earlier, when I compared problems of scholarship in that area with the counterpart problems in this. Some of the work I report on here was done in the 1970s, some in the 1980s. In 1979 I was asked to address the Society of Biblical Literature. There, in

---

1. New York: Ktav Publishing House, 1991.

an address that in revised form serves as chapter 1 of this book, I spelled out the character of rabbinic literature and the problems of doing history with it by translating the traits of that literature into Christian counterparts. That is to say, if the writings of early Christianity reached us in the form and condition in which those of Judaism of the same general period come down to us, and Christianity were written down in the way in which Judaism is, what should we know about Christianity, and how should we know it?

I can think of no better way of explaining to people what is strange to them than by translating the strange into the familiar. That address in the language of the study of early Christianity, a bilingual talk for the diverse academy, directly spoke to the concerns of New Testament scholarship. It had a massive audience. Admittedly, I doubt that it got heard. The only person in the room (so it seemed to me then) who got my point was Morton Smith, with whom I had written my doctoral dissertation two decades earlier. In the middle of the lecture, from a seat prominent in a front row of a section in the center of a crowded ball room, he got up and slowly meandered out — and never spoke to me again.

Smith had made his career by being the bilingual interpreter, from his *Tannaitic Parallels to the Gospels* (1953), telling New Testament scholars how to solve their problems by parallels in rabbinic writings. I, of course, was engaged in a massive project that would in the end set aside as no longer relevant his first and, I think, best book. These results that show Smith quite wrong on every major point are summarized in my *Are There Really Tannaitic Parallels to the Gospels?: A Reply to Morton Smith*.[2] Acting on his own results, of course, from that point he had used rabbinic literature as a mass of information on how things really were in the first century, believing what he chose and ignoring the rest, like many others, but superior in his knowledge of rabbinic literature.

My address called into question the Judaic foundations of Smith's and others' work. I made the point that it is much more difficult than people seem to realize to utilize rabbinic literature for the study of first-century Christian writings, and much of the use of that evidence ignores the critical methods that supposedly define Gospels research, particularly on the life and teachings of Jesus. In its use of rabbinic literature, Smith's *Jesus the Magician* represented the satanic counterpart to the angelic historical Jesuses

---

2. South Florida Studies in the History of Judaism (Atlanta: Scholars Press, 1993).

(and they are many). He chose to believe everything bad he could about Jesus, perhaps making up what he could not read into the sources. Since I had done my dissertation with him, I bore a special responsibility to say that that was what I thought. So, when I published that lecture, I said so in footnote 18 (the number eighteen standing for *life* in its Hebrew character).

What I wished to advance was not a new theory of criticism but the application of an established theory of criticism to rabbinic literature from which, except in my work and that of a handful of disciples of mine, it simply is absent. That was what was at stake in my SBL address and, unhappily, remains a vital issue in chapter 1. If a life of Jesus appealed to the Gospels with the pure gullibility that characterizes the use of rabbinic stories about, e.g., Hillel, the generality of New Testament scholarship would simply ignore that "life" as uncritical or condemn it as "fundamentalist." But the same scholars who would do so (I give heavyweight examples in Part Two of this book) confidently tell us about the historical Hillel and the historical Pharisees and ask us to believe that we can make sense of sayings "attributed to" Jesus by appeal to sayings that "Hillel said..." or "that day" and find the correct setting for interpreting the career of Jesus in the world of "Pharisaic-rabbinic Judaism."

New Testament scholarship, then, has long taken for granted that in the resources of Judaism, meaning in the rabbinic literature, we have a virtual handbook for New Testament history and exegesis. Line-by-line handbooks cite rabbinic sayings deemed parallel or at least pertinent to the exegesis of New Testament documents, sentence by sentence. Lachs's is the most systematic and therefore the worst; he supplies footnotes referring to rabbinic literature — often not even quoted, just cited — to verse after verse of the Gospels. But every account of the life and teachings of Jesus told about "Judaism," describing that encompassing religion by appeal to the very writings that I have spent my life to describe, analyze, and interpret. Midrash-compilations of the third through the thirteenth centuries routinely contribute passages for the clarification of New Testament verses on the assumption that there was, or must have been, a single, harmonious, unitary tradition that testifies to the state of "the Jews' views" at any time and in any place — therefore also in the Land of Israel in the first century and, especially, in Galilee.

When scholars today deliberate on what Jesus "really" said or did, picking and choosing among the sayings and stories assigned to him in the Gospels, they constantly appeal to "Judaism." What is Greek is alien and what is demonstrably "Jewish" (by appeal to a single, unitary, incremental "Judaism" attested everywhere and anywhere through time) is authentic; so he really said it. Or he was original, and what is "Jewish" is inauthentic because repetitive; so he really did not say it. Moreover, since Jesus was a "revolutionary" or a "reformer," the "Judaism" that he revolutionized or reformed or rejected likewise is there to be described (and, of course, dismissed through invidious comparisons). These and other fixed formulas — labor-saving devices, really — rested on the premise that the rabbinic literature, in whole or in part, tells us what we need to know about Judaism in the first century in the Land of Israel.

To be sure, there are things to be learned from rabbinic literature for New Testament studies. But every time I have tried to make a contribution, I wondered whether, in the end, it was worth the effort; the work was much, the result uncertain. My reading of the documents of rabbinic Judaism concerned the history of the formation of that Judaism, and, in general, I had long since concluded that that Judaism, with roots in the first century, reached the form in which we now know it only much later on. The first century does not form the principal arena of those documents or, therefore, of my studies. I worked on first-century problems when the rabbinic writings on which I concentrated referred to the first century; then I moved onward, now spending my time on the sixth and seventh centuries.

Some topics on which the Gospels and rabbinic literature intersect — for instance, the Pharisees of the period in which Jesus flourished — of course again and again had drawn my attention to Gospels research, and the attention of Gospels scholars to mine. The ferocity of criticism directed to my results is always joined by curses and imprecations, which suggests that the generality of New Testament scholarship has understood and in the main accepted my results. Otherwise, why so much animosity and why such sustained effort not merely to refute my results but, in some instances, to discredit me personally? In my *Judaic Law from Jesus to the Mishnah,* I reply to E. P. Sanders's *Jewish Law from Jesus to the Mishnah,* bringing together all my studies both constructive and critical that respond to his writings on Judaism. I go over my reviews of his three books on Judaism, my reply to his criticism of my work, but also my positive results on the history of Jewish law as the Mishnah conveys that history, on the one side, and the meaning of "covenantal nomism," a term of Sanders's that I find quite felicitous, on the other. Though we concur on more matters than he seems willing to concede, Sanders makes much of the small differences.

Now, to be sure, I understood that the Mishnah and successor documents did not begin on the day they reached closure; they contained materials formulated prior to the final conclusion, and they not only refer to, but also may well draw upon, sayings over a long if indeterminate period of time. I devoted much energy to devising methods to show how the Mishnah preserved evidence of ideas held long before its closure and how the Talmuds also utilized materials completed before they were finished. But I have produced only limited results relevant to the first century, and few of these intersected with New Testament studies in particular. My principal point is that here and there, there are points of interest, but viewed as documents, these writings talk about what interests them, and the vivid issues of the New Testament are only rarely illuminated in rabbinic literature. Where the writings do intersect, it is on what is systemically inert for both sets of writers.

True, the documents themselves made a claim not to be dismissed out of hand, since they persistently set forth stories about persons and events back to Abraham and Moses; they assigned sayings to holy people from Adam onward. But how am I supposed to know which stories are invented and which record something that really happened? And which sayings were authentic to the person to whom they are attributed? If I reject out of hand that in rabbinic literature Abraham is portrayed as he really was, how do I know that what a late antique or medieval compilation attributes to a rabbi seven or ten centuries earlier represents an authentic tradition, to be cited in studying that figure's times and places and even personal views? These questions are perfectly routine. They require us to work hard to answer, why this, not that? — and to tell others how we know.

The "Herr Professor" who passes his opinion without fearing any public laughter will tell us, "This certainly has the ring of truth," but he rarely goes so far as to say how he knows and, more important, why we should know too. A commonplace sentiment in German and Israeli scholarship in this area, submissive as it is to authority and politics, confirms the professor's certainty of the historical facticity of the opinion he formed that morning. The "Herr Professors" tend to make things up as they go along and call the result eternal truth, from of old. So they pronounce judgment. They posit "oral tradition" without identifying institutional evidence (e.g., schools for professional memorizers, a class of memorizers, a status assigned to what was memorized) pertinent to the first century; there is ample evidence for the third and fourth centuries that should serve as a model. The work of picking and choosing what to believe is "very early" and "even back to the time of Jesus" out of the mass of allegations that the whole goes back anyhow to Moses (so why not also to Jesus?) rarely is systematic. Usually it is anecdotal, episodic, and therefore capricious. If subjective opinion makes its way as fact, it is because of the political power of a given professor, not because of the power of persuasion of reasoned and systematic arguments, beginning with hypotheses on the character of the evidence in hand — the documents and how their authors know what they tell us.

When people suppose that these writings served as historical sources to tell us how things really were, not in the early third century, as with the Mishnah, or the early seventh century, as with the Talmud of Babylonia, but in the first century B.C.E., when Hillel lived, or the first century C.E., when Yohanan ben Zakkai flourished, it is equally natural to fall silent: "I'm not entirely sure; I have to work on it." There are other routine and (to the believers) self-evidently valid responses, which would have provided a more satisfying answer than mine. After all, "would our holy rabbis lie?" as an Israeli historian asked! Is it not the fact that "the burden of proof is on the one who doubts the source," as the regnant dean of scholars pleased to call themselves "the Jerusalem school" opined?

But it has still to be demonstrated that rabbinic Judaism, as expressed in its principal and indicative traits, its myths and symbols, its institutions and generative ideas, had yet come into being in the first century. So if we can prove a given idea announced in a sixth-century document also was maintained by someone in the first century, then what we may actually know as fact is that said idea is not originally rabbinic but has been appropriated for their own purposes — where, when, and by whom we do not know — by rabbis later on. If something is early, then it is not rabbinic, unless we can show that the Judaism we call rabbinic was fully worked out in institutions and ideas in the time of Jesus. And if it is rabbinic, then it cannot be early, until it can be shown that it was; but then it is not rabbinic. So we trudge around in circles.

When a New Testament scholar provides evidence that the Judaism of the dual Torah, represented by the Mishnah, Tosefta, two Talmuds, and midrash-compilations belonging in particular to rabbinic authorities, flourished in the early decades of the first century in Galilee, then and only then will the promiscuous citation of those writings in the interpretation of the life and teachings of Judaism prove intellectually legitimate. Otherwise silly arguments about "would our holy rabbis lie?" and "you have to believe it until you can prove it didn't happen" will be seen for what they are. These form Judaic counterparts to the labor-saving devices that ease the work of New Testament scholars: self-evidence in place of plausible proposition, compelling argument, and well-analyzed evidence.

Still, a child of the American academy — quite literally, being the first and, so far, the only scholar of Judaism to hold the presidency of the American Academy of Religion and the only scholar of religious studies ever to serve on the National Council of the National Endowment for the Humanities — I cannot take for granted what the sources tell us is true unless we can prove it is true. The premise of the question — we do not take the sources at face value but have to investigate them in an independent spirit — accounts also for the answer. New Testament scholarship begins with premises other than those of the faithful, and it is that scholarly tradition more than any other that has shaped whatever critical work is done on the rabbinic literature. How, then, am I supposed to respond to a legitimate question provoked in one critical field by appealing to a credulous reading of the sources of neighboring territory? What do I have to know about rabbinic literature to study the New Testament? The answer "everything" — as in, if you want to understand Jesus, you have to know a lot about Judaism and therefore rabbinic literature, which accurately, historically, and normatively represents "Judaism" — proves elusive. And the answer "nothing" would be premature, little work having been done within the critical premises of the questioner.

The Israeli scholars who find satisfying the self-serving answer, "believe it unless you can prove it's wrong," conduct deductive reasoning in a world of inductive inquiry. In so doing, they carry forward a Middle European tradition of philosophy and a kind of deductive historiography that, for British and North American scholarship, wins little respect. For them you can make a rule and solve a problem (and you make the rule so that you can solve the problem in such a way that permits you to do what you want to do anyhow). Within the stated principle, "believe until you can't any more," scholars may shape an academic agenda presupposing that the rabbinic literature serves as a handbook to how things really were long before the documents of the literature reached closure. Not only so, but within that same premise, the various documents that comprise the rabbinic canon may be read uniformly as evidence of how things were everywhere and at any time. No boundaries distinguish one compilation from some other. They all are equally valid evidence, undifferentiated in time and space. After all, go prove otherwise!

In the Anglo-American tradition of pragmatism, I live in a different world: if you can't show it, you don't know it. For us the Israeli rule, "believe unless you have to doubt," is set on its head: doubt until you must affirm (and believe nothing!). In Anglo-American scholarship, moreover, there is no historical a priori. We have a body of knowledge about times past, but not solid evidence to demonstrate it as true. We know only what we can show, and therefore we presuppose only what we demonstrate to be fact. In that context, we have no difficulty insisting that most of the Hebrew scriptures of ancient Israel (the "Old Testament") attest to stories believed and opinions held authoritative in the first century. But which stories and whose opinions? Only the first-century writings themselves can answer that question. So even the Hebrew scriptures themselves present more questions than they settle.

The conception of a historical a priori being hopeless, we are left to answer the correct question "what do I really have to know?" with "I don't know." What we may learn from the Mishnah and midrash-compilations and Talmuds about ages prior to their own always struck me as a question to be investigated, not a premise to be postulated. And that question dictates the only reasonable answer: "what we cannot show, we do not know." To begin with, then, to find it necessary to "know rabbinic literature" for New Testament studies, we have to show that rabbinic literature in general or at some specific point or some concrete passage in New Testament history and exegesis intersects with New Testament studies. That is my message in these pages, and the rest of the book spells out the character of the literature, on the one side, and the uncritical ways in which otherwise reputable scholars wish to utilize that literature in their New Testament studies, on the other.

Much careless work has gone on and the problems before us prove formidable, but that does not mean scholarship on the New Testament and on rabbinic literature may each go its own way.

The stakes of dialogue between these two kindred fields prove very high. The dialogue rests on compelling arguments too: the interchange between New Testament and rabbinic studies is a necessary and legitimate one.

Since scholarship on the New Testament, and especially on the Gospels, had worked on the problem of how we know an incident reported in an ancient document really happened, or a saying really was said by the person to whom it was attributed, I always took for granted that I was a consumer, not a producer, in that field — learning about methods to be adapted to my work, trying to understand ideas and attitudes of mind utterly alien among co-workers of mine on rabbinic literature. Specializing on rabbinic literature, I never thought I knew much about the first century, certainly no facts that would otherwise be unavailable to New Testament learning.

Still, Jesus was a Jew. So am I. Therefore I might know something a gentile might not know. After all, New Testament scholars had learned from the results of three-quarters of a century or more that the Gospels and Paul's letters could not be read without constant reference to rabbinic literature, which served as a key to open most locked doors. From the time of Billerbeck's counterpart to a telephone book — look up the right number, you make your connection — everybody in New Testament scholarship enjoyed free run of the rabbinic literature of late antiquity and medieval times. And from the publication of Moore's *Judaism,* accounts of the condition of "the Judaic background" of Jesus appealed not only to writings prior to the time of Jesus himself, beginning with most of the Old Testament, but also to those writings written down long afterward but deemed to tell us about "Orthodox Judaism" or merely "Judaism" when Jesus lived.

The result was books on Jesus as a rabbi; accounts of "Judaism" in the century before and after the turn of the first century C.E. that simply paraphrased the Mishnah; biographies of Hillel, a contemporary of Jesus, made up of stories first found in the Talmud of Babylonia ca. 600 C.E.; and the like.

But the question remains: "what does the New Testament scholar have to know about rabbinic literature?" In my opinion, these are the traits that would have to characterize rabbinic literature for that literature to serve, as it now serves, New Testament history and exegeses: as a handbook, a collection of facts, a corpus of hard evidence on how things really were when Jesus and the apostles and Paul flourished and their heirs after them.

1. All of rabbinic literature takes place on a level plane, considerations of place and time not pertaining.

2. Rabbinic literature is made up of bits and pieces of writing, the various rabbinic documents collecting and arranging, without much revision, these available bits of writing or oral tradition in fixed form.

3. The components of the documents, the bits of writing, were written down at the time of the events of which they speak or derived from stenographic reports of things really said, produced by responsible observers.

4. Rabbinic literature represents the sole Judaism or the authentic and normative Judaism, which all but a few sectarians or crackpots affirmed. It is "what the Jews believed." It is to be read, where it is silent or contradictory, in light of Orthodox Judaism today.

If these were the things we knew about rabbinic literature, then to study the actual history of the persons and events portrayed in the New Testament, New Testament scholars would have to know pretty much the whole rabbinic canon. They could use the sayings and stories as authenticated facts about what was believed in the first (as much as in the sixth) century. They could compare sayings attributed to Jesus with sayings assigned to rabbis of that time or any later period. Those facts would permit them to determine the position of Jesus vis-à-vis Judaism: if a saying assigned to him formed part of it — Judaism — it would therefore be authentic to Jesus; if it was against it, it would therefore be inauthentic; and so on.

Indeed, if we knew those facts about rabbinic literature, we should frame our scholarly program precisely in response to the kind of information we assume we now have in hand. We would write biographies, or at least intellectual biographies, of rabbis, thus having a Hillel to place into juxtaposition with Jesus. We would produce theologies and exegetical accounts for Judaism, thus comparing and contrasting Judaism with Christianity of the same time and place. We would collect and arrange rabbinic commentaries to the New Testament books, because these commentaries would tell us what Judaism says about the same matter or the language Judaism used in the first century in connection with the same topic or story ("parable") or verse of the Old Testament used in the New. And if we wished to describe "Judaism in the time of Jesus," we would simply open rabbinic literature or some preferred document (e.g., the Mishnah) to provide us with information on how things really were day by day in the first century.

And that belatedly answers the question: what do I have to know about rabbinic literature to study the New Testament?

To have to know rabbinic literature to study the New Testament, then, we should be able to demonstrate these facts:

1. There was a single Judaism

2. attested through sayings preserved by stenographers or disciples and stories written by well-trained, objective reporters,

3. which sayings and stories were then preserved in the very wording they originally were given, through oral formulation and oral transmission, until written down in documents

4. that were merely scrapbooks and that in no way made an impact on their contents.

None of these conditions should surprise colleagues in New Testament studies. To the contrary, it is from them that the handful of us who work in a critical manner in rabbinic literature, history, and religion have learned how to do our work. That is what we have to know. What do we think we know?

1. The various rabbinic documents are to be differentiated from one another, and the compilers of each made choices that expressed the distinctive purposes served by the several documents.

2. Sayings and stories were made up and attributed to prior times or authorities.

3. No single, unitary, orthodox Judaism exercised hegemony in antiquity down to the seventh century.

Therefore if in rabbinic literature we find a saying or a story we think relevant to a passage in the New Testament, our work commences. What do we then have to determine as fact before bringing said fact to the New Testament to tell us how things really were in the first century?

We have to find evidence that the saying or story stands independent of the document in which it occurs and does not serve the larger purpose of the writers who produced the composition and the compilers who used the composition in a larger composite.

Otherwise we have to consider that the saying or story may have been made up for documentary purposes, that is, to help accomplish the goals of the authors of compositions and the compilers of composites of which a given document is made up — and not for what we should call historical purposes.

We have to undertake argument from evidence that points to an origin of said saying or story in the first century. In that case, we must explain how we think the saying or story circulated until it was written down, in original form, in such a way as to find a position in the late document that now contains the saying or story.

We have to demonstrate that the fully spelled out rabbinic Judaism of the canonical writings — from the Mishnah onward for four hundred years — flourished in the first century, so that the comparison and contrast of Jesus' sayings and stories about him to those set forth in the rabbinic literature of the third through seventh centuries is at all apropos. For if we do not know that rabbinic Judaism, as we know it from its literary statements, flourished in the first century, then a saying we can show to represent opinion held in that early period cannot be taken for granted to speak in behalf of that Judaism that we know only later on. If a saying belongs to the first century, it may not stand for the view of "the rabbis" of that period, unless we can show that it did. One proposition that requires attention therefore poses this conundrum: if a saying is early, it is not (originally, distinctively, and emblematically) rabbinic and, if it is indicatively rabbinic, it cannot be early.

To study the New Testament out of the resources of rabbinic literature, therefore, what I have to know is that that literature tells me about things done and opinions held in the first century, in the Land of Israel or among Jews elsewhere in the world in which Jesus and Paul and their disciples and communities flourished. If I do not know that that is so, then that literature will prove only marginally helpful in solving the critical problems of New Testament history and exegesis.

In what follows I spell out the rules for reading rabbinic writing. To make the character of that writing clear, I start in chapter 1, as I explained, by translating Christianity's sources into Judaism's modes of formulation and transmission. In chapters 2 and 3 I proceed to the principal facts of the rabbinic writings that I have now established.

First, documents matter. Each document may be shown to exhibit its indicative traits of rhetoric, topic, and logic of cogent discourse (the literary–critical principles we learn, after all, from ancient philosophy). Therefore everything in a document has to be examined in the context of the document's own interests and program. It follows that we cannot ignore the documentary provenience of a saying but must ask how the interests of the framers of a document, or of the materials collected in that particular document, have intervened in the shaping of a saying. We cannot take sayings out of documentary context but have to read them, to begin with, in the setting in which they occur.

Any claim that a saying speaks about the first century and not about the time of the document in which it occurs and concerning views held at the time of the document in which it occurs, by the framers of that document in particular, has to be substantiated, verified, and also subjected to a test of falsification. Since what we cannot show, we do not know, we cannot take at face value attribution of a saying to a first-century authority as reason to assign that saying to that time. Attributions in rabbinic literature, as in any other of its character, are conventions of an other-than-historical character. The same saying may be assigned to several figures. A saying bearing a name in one document may be given anonymously in another. There are sound logical or doctrinal reasons for such treatment of attributions. But the facts call into question reliance, without solid grounds, upon attributions of sayings for the dating of those sayings, that is, for the positioning of those sayings as typical of one century or country or region rather than some other. Any notion that we can lift sayings out of documentary context and imagine that they had some independent existence "for a long time" before being snatched up and used for the document in which they now occur has to be tested, not merely alleged. Documents count. And that fact changes everything.

Second, people made up sayings and put them into the mouths of long-deceased authorities, or made up stories and claimed they had happened long ago. So we cannot take at face value everything in the rabbinic literature. Since that is demonstrably the fact some of the time, we have to show for any given saying or story that that was not the case, so that that saying or that story may be adduced in evidence of what was thought or done long before the closure of the document that preserves it. Once we realize the character of the rabbinical literature — the processes that gave shape to its components, the rules that governed the formation of the compositions written for it, the composites compiled in it — we enter into the critical age in which New Testament scholarship has flourished for so long and with such remarkable success.

In these ways I say what we do know about rabbinical literature that affects the use of that literature for New Testament studies. I then proceed to examine how, by contrast, people do use that literature. Part Two presents examples of how evidence has been used by entirely reputable scholars, past and present. We deal, first, with how New Testament scholars use rabbinic evidence. Second, we consider how scholars of Judaism purport to instruct Christians on how Jesus was really a Pharisee or a rabbinical wonder-worker. In chapter 6 I point to how the Mishnah is used as a handbook for describing "Judaism" in the most recent book of E. P. Sanders. Alongside, in chapter 7, I show how the premises as to the character of the evidence of rabbinic literature govern the framing of the questions that are brought to that literature.

This is a subtle but fundamental point: if you think you can answer a given question, you ask it. If not, you do not ask it. I therefore point to what I conceive to form the basis for poor work: asking the wrong questions. Here I return to the use of rabbinic literature for historical purposes, now in the context of the study of Judaism, and show how asking questions that presuppose we have information we may or may not have leads to a pretense at critical study where, in fact, there is only the old-time gullibility. So I show how Shaye J. D. Cohen frames what can only be called a pseudocritical agenda: a study based on questions external to the stories he deals with, but resting on the premise that the stories he deals with tell us about things that really were said or done. In this way, an essay by Morton Smith's outstanding disciple Shaye J. D. Cohen is shown to embody the very pretense against which his master, Smith, warned: pseudo-orthodoxy.

Since in print my principal critics have been, besides Professor Sanders, Professor Shaye J. D. Cohen and Mr. Hyam Maccoby, I devote Part Three to the issue of the Mishnah in particular. Here I turn to the general criticism of S. J. D. Cohen and H. Maccoby.

In chapter 9 I address my New Testament colleagues' principal venture, their quest for the historical Jesus. I explain why I regard the "quest" as theological in every way and as historical in none. Dealing with two remarkable examples of the quest at its best, and one of the quest at its most deceitful, I underscore the theological stakes in what is portrayed as historical writing, citing great scholars' own account of the purpose and value of their inquiry. The entire matter — why someone would want to study the rabbinic literature in order to make sense of the history and ex-egesis of the New Testament — begins in a single question: how can I learn about the historical Jesus, as distinct from the Jesus the Christ, God Incarnate, who is portrayed by the Gospels? Therefore I conclude with some unsolicited advice to New Testament scholarship, as represented by Smith's *Secret Gospel,* Meier's *Marginal Jew,* and Crossan's *Historical Jesus,* the latter two being valiant efforts to rehabilitate a field of learning unable to defend itself from what more than a few scholars have concluded was Smith's forgery and fraud.

My admiration for Meier and Crossan — the one the master scholar, the other the elegant and engaging writer — and the field they so admirably embody accordingly leads me to ask: but is this history at all? And why ask history to testify to matters of faith and doctrine? Can theology ever solve its problems through historical study? In asking those questions, of course, I turn matters around. My work on rabbinic literature begins with the principle that these are documents of religion and are to be read as evidence of religion; they may contain some historical facts, but they are, entirely and flawlessly, themselves — all of them — historical facts about religion. And that is how they are to be appreciated, understood, interpreted, and re-presented to the world: for what they are, not for what they are not.

As is clear, in these pages I not only present new writing but systematically re-present earlier statements of mine. In all cases I have recast as needed my results to address the readers of this book. My sense is that my original presentation of matters was insufficiently focused on the issues of immediate concern to New Testament scholarship. Many of the papers appeared in journals that New Testament specialists do not ordinarily read or in books they may not have supposed concerned their interests at all. In these pages, therefore, I redo some of the many writings I have set forth to speak to my neighbors near at hand. In them I mean to speak directly and bluntly to the many New Testament scholars who want to know "what do I have to know about rabbinic literature to study the New Testament?" In a word, my answer is: what we cannot show, we do not know. That means that only with perspective on the rabbinic literature as a whole will the particular critical problems before us take on urgency.

# PART ONE

# THE CHARACTER OF RABBINIC LITERATURE

# 1

# The Gospels and the Mishnah, the Church Fathers and the Talmud: If Christianity Were Written Down by Rabbis...

If Christianity were written down in the way in which Judaism is, what should we know about Christianity, and how should we know it? For New Testament scholars to find out what they need to know about the rabbinic literature in order to use it for their studies, they require a clear picture of the character of the rabbinic literature. What better way to provide such a picture than to translate "Judaic" into "Christian"? As a kind of bilingual interpreter, I mean to give a picture of the kind of evidence scholars of earliest Christianity would face if the New Testament and patristic writings were truly comparable to the Mishnah and rabbinic literature.

I wish to paint a picture of the problem we would have in studying early Christianity if the sources of early Christianity had reached us in the way and in the condition in which those of early rabbinic Judaism come down to us. That is to say, what should we know and how should we know it if the records of early Christianity were like the rabbinic literature of late antiquity?

1. What could we know if all the literature of early Christianity had reached us in a fully homogenized and intellectually seamless form? Not only the New Testament, but all the works of the church fathers, from Justin to Augustine, would be represented as expressions of one communal mind, dismembered and built into

a single harmonious logical structure on various themes. True, these writings would be shown constantly to disagree with one another. But the range of permissible disagreement would define a vast area of consensus on all basic matters, so that a superficial contentiousness would convey something quite different: one mind on most things, beginning to end. The names of the fathers would be attached to some of their utterances. But all would have gone through a second medium of tradents and redactors — the editors of the compendium (the patristic Talmud, so to speak) — and these editors picked and chose what they wanted of Justin, Origen, Tertullian, and Augustine in line with what the editors themselves found interesting. In the end, the picture of the first six centuries of early Christianity would be the creation of people of the sixth century, out of the sherds and remnants of people of the first five. Our work then would be to uncover what happened before the end through studying a document that portrays a timeless world.

Not only would the document be so framed as implicitly to deny historical development of ideas, but the framers would also gloss over diverse and contradictory sources of thought. I do not mean only that Justin, Irenaeus, and Tertullian would be presented as individual authors in a single, timeless continuum. I mean that all Gnostic and Catholic sources would be broken up into sense-units and their fragments rearranged in a structure presented as representative of a single Christianity, with a single, unitary theology. This synthesized ecumenical body of Christian thought would be constructed so as to set out judgments on the principal theological topics of the day, and these judgments would have been accepted as normative from that day to this. So the first thing we must try to imagine is a Christianity that reaches us fully harmonized and whole — a Christianity of Nicaea and Chalcedon, but not of Arians, Nestorians, monophysites, and the rest. So there is no distinctive Justin or Augustine, no Irenaeus and no Gnostics, and surely no Nag Hammadi, but all are one "in Christ Jesus," so to speak.

2. Let me emphasize that this would be not merely a matter of early Christian literature's reaching us without the names of the authors of its individual documents. The thing we must try to imagine is that there would be no individual documents at all. Everything would have gone through a process of formation and redaction that obliterated the marks of individuality. Just as the theology would be one, so would the form and style of the documents that preserved it. Indeed, what would be striking about

this picture of Christianity would not be that the tractate of Mark lacks the name of Mark, but that all of the tractates of the Gospels would be written in precisely the same style and resort to exactly the same rhetorical and redactional devices. Stylistic unity so pervasive as to eliminate all traces of individual authorship, even of most preserved sayings, would now characterize the writings of the first Christians. The sarcasm of Irenaeus, the majesty of Augustine, the exegetical ingenuity of Origen, and the lucid historicism of Aphrahat — all are homogenized. Everyone talks in the same way about the same things.

3. To come to a principal task of the study of early Christianity: what should we know about Jesus, and how should we know it if sayings assigned to Jesus in one book were given to Paul in a second, to John in a third, and to "They said" or "He said to them," in a fourth? Can we imagine trying to discover the historical Jesus on this turf if the provenance of a saying could not be established on the basis of all those to whom it is attributed, or if a single *Vorlage* and *Urtext* could not be postulated? Then what sort of work on the biography and thought of any of the early figures of Christianity would be credible?

4. This brings me to the most difficult act of imagination that I must ask readers to perform: a supererogatory work of social imagination. Can we imagine a corner of the modern world in which this state of interpretation — of total confusion, of harmonies, homologies, homogenies — is not found confusing but reassuring? Can we mentally conjure up a social setting for learning in which differentiation is avoided and credulity rewarded, in which analysis is heresy, dismissed as worthless or attacked as "full of mistakes"? Can we conceive of a world in which repetition in one's own words of what the sources say is labeled scholarship and anthologizing is labeled learning? In New Testament scholarship, we must imagine, the principal task now is to write harmonies of the Gospels, and in patristic studies to align the Catholic with the Gnostic, the second century with the fifth, the Arian and the Athanasian, monophysite and Nestorian.[1] In a word, we speak of

---

1. I wrote this in 1979 and could not foresee that E. P. Sanders would present precisely such a picture of a single, homogeneous Judaism, joining the Judaic counterpart of monophysites and Nestorians into a single conflation. In chapter 6 I show that he has done precisely that. Sanders exhibits an incomplete grasp of the entire critical agenda in the study of the Judaic sources, as an examination of his presentation of them in his *Judaism* and his *Jewish Law from Jesus to the Mishnah* shows. My reply to him is in *Judaic Law from Jesus to the Mishnah: A*

a world in which the Diatessaron is the last word in scholarship and in which contentiousness about trivial things masks a firm and iron consensus. In this imagined world, scholars further hold that all the sources are historical, and merely alluding to them suffices to establish facts of history.

If readers can envision such a state of affairs, then we have entered the world of sources and scholarly orthodoxies confronted by us who study the ancient Judaism emergent from the rabbinic literature. It follows that scholars of New Testament history and exegesis will grasp the fact that rabbinic literature is simply not homologous to the writings on which they work and cannot be used in anything like the same way. Not only so, but that literature deals with different types of problems and answers altogether different questions, with the result that we cannot present to rabbinic literature questions deemed appropriate for address to another kind of writing. A life of Jesus or of Augustine is plausible; a life of Aqiba or Hillel is not. An intellectual biography of Paul and his theology is entirely apropos, the sources answering precisely the questions that are asked. A counterpart picture of Judah the Patriarch, who wrote up the Mishnah, or of Rabbah, Abbaye, or Raba, the greatest geniuses of the Talmud, is not. To use one type of writing to address questions appropriate to another type of writing is surely a dubious operation, or it would be if it were not entirely routine, as the second part of this book will demonstrate.

I can spell out matters now very simply and very rapidly. First, as to the axioms of scholarship, all the rabbinic sources are treated as representatives of a single, seamless world view and as expressions of a single, essentially united group, either the views as a whole or among the enlightened, the rabbis as a group. While some more critical souls concede there may have been distinctions between the first-century rabbis' thought and that of the fourth, the distinctions make no material difference in accounts of "the rabbis" and their thought. Whether anthologies or anthological essays (Moore, Montefiore and Loewe, Bonsirven, Urbach), the rabbis are represented in their views on God, world, and redemption as though all rabbis for seven hundred years had the same thing to say as all others.

Now this representation of the rabbis is subject to an important commonplace qualification. Everyone knows that the Talmuds

*Systematic Reply to Professor E. P. Sanders,* South Florida Studies in the History of Judaism (Atlanta: Scholars Press, 1993).

abound in recognitions of differences between the teachings of different rabbis in different periods on different points in discussions of which traditions or source was followed by the proponent of this or that opinion. But the recorded differences are about particular, trivial points. The talmudic discussion, moreover, is directed normally toward reconciling them. What is particularly lacking in available accounts of "the rabbinic mind" is, first, recognition and delineation of different general positions or basic attitudes and of the characteristic makeup and backgrounds of different schools. Second, what is lacking is anything like adequate reporting of the alteration of teachings over the course of time and in relation to historical changes. Obviously there is plenty of speculation about how an individual or group reacted to a particular historical situation or event. That is how people in "talmudic history" make their living. But these random speculations are unsystematic and appear to be made up for the occasion. So these apparent exceptions to what I say have to be recognized, because they prove the accuracy of my description of the prevailing consensus.

As to the sources, the documents of earlier rabbinic Judaism exhibit an internally uniform quality of style. So the scholars who represent a seamless world accurately replicate the literary traits of the sources of the portrait. It is exceedingly difficult to differentiate on formal or stylistic grounds among the layers of the Mishnah, which is the document of rabbinic Judaism first brought to redaction. The two Talmuds then lay matters out so as to represent themselves as the logical continuity from the Mishnah. They do so by breaking up the Mishnah into minute units and then commenting on those discrete units of thought. Consequently the Mishnah as a document, a document that presents its own world view and its own social system, is not preserved and confronted. Nor do the Talmuds present themselves as successive layers built upon but essentially distinct from the Mishnah. Rather, the Talmuds aim at completely harmonizing their own materials both with the Mishnah and among themselves, despite the self-evidently contradictory character of the materials. Once more, we observe, there are limits to disagreement. The continuing contentiousness of the documents, their preservation of diverse viewpoints on single issues, underline the rigidly protected limits of permissible disagreement. Intense disagreement about trivialities powerfully reinforces basic unities and harmonies. The fact that out there were Jews who decorated synagogues in ways the Talmuds cannot have led us to anticipate is mentioned only in passing, as if it is of no weight or concern. What matters to this literature is not how the Jews lived nor even how they worshiped, but only the discussions of the rabbinical schools and courts. What the documents say is what we are supposed to think, within the range of allowed difference. Consequently the intellectually unitary character of the sources is powerfully reinforced by the total success of the framers and redactors of the sources in securing stylistic unity within documents and in some measure even among them.

These facts have not prevented scholars, myself included, from writing about history, biography, and theology upon the basis of the unanalyzed and unchallenged allegations of the rabbinic sources. Just as people had arguments about what Jesus really said and did before the rise of form-criticism, so the rage and secure contentiousness of scholars in this field mask the uncertainty of their entire structure.[2] It is as if, as in the Talmuds themselves, by arguing on essentially minor points, the colleagues may avoid paying attention to the epistemological abyss beneath them all. And those who — to shift the metaphor — ask where are the emperor's clothes are only rarely asked to make their views known in the forum controlled by the emperor's friends. And the know-nothings, the mediocrities, the unbelieving alumni of yeshivas all compete to please the emperors of the moment, rulers of the corner where politics substitute for persuasion and ad hominem slander for serious scholarship. Only on that basis could the silly notion "believe unless you have to doubt" (or "believe unless you can prove it isn't so" and "would our holy rabbis lie?") gain a hearing.

So there are agreed-upon solutions to the problems of diverse authorities behind the same saying and amplification and variation of details in a single story. These commonly lead to very felicitous conclusions. If the same saying is in three mouths, it is because they agreed to say it. True, "we cannot be sure that they were not talking simultaneously in different places (thanks to the Holy Spirit)." Or if there are three versions of essentially the same story, like the Sermon on the Mount and the Sermon on the Plain, it is because, in the wonderful ways of providence, it happened two times. Every time the text says "one time," that was, indeed, one event.

Finally, as I have already hinted, these serendipitous facts, these happy agreements, these assured and unquestioned results of a

---

2. The utter inability of scholars in rabbinic literature to conduct a civil argument, their insistence that the purpose of scholarly debate is not to refute the position of the other party but to discredit him or her — these testify to the weakness of the existing structure.

hundred years of critical scholarship following upon fifteen hundred years of uncritical scholarship that produced the same results, enjoy the powerful support of the three great communities that read the rabbinical literature at all: Orthodox Jews in yeshivas, scholarly Jews in rabbinical seminaries and Israeli universities, and the generality of Christian scholars of New Testament. To the Orthodox, the rabbinic sources are part of the whole Torah of Moses our rabbi, the revealed word of God. For them "our holy rabbis" cannot deceive. To the scholars in rabbinical schools and Israeli universities, the critical program of scholarship on early Christianity is perceived from a distance. In their books and articles they settle complex questions of literary analysis and historical epistemology with an array of two assumptions, three logical arguments, and four "probative" examples. They do not perceive the immense, detailed work that stands, for example, behind debates on Q and the synoptic problem. Indeed, the work of analysis of sources bores them. Whether work is original or dull, the bulk of it simply dismisses as settled, questions that would be deemed urgent in biblical and patristic literature and in the history of early Christianity. As to the New Testament scholars, their view is that things go better when we read rabbinical literature as a set of facts that speak for themselves, rather than complex problems requiring solutions. For them, the rabbinic literature as it stands, unanalyzed and uncriticized, tells us all about Jerusalem and Galilee in the time of Jesus. Billerbeck is a dictionary of facts and the beginning of sound exegesis. Or, to put matters in a more theological way, in Gospels research, salvation is of the Jews.

Now that I have described the state of the evidence in terms accessible to colleagues in biblical studies, I wish to outline some of the solutions to some of the problems as I have seen them and worked them out. If I dwell on my own work, it is because, in matters of method and theory, there is no other work that in a systematic and fundamental way has addressed the issues of the historical study and use of the rabbinic literature. Others substitute arguments for hard work, examples and anecdotes for systematic and thorough examination of the sources. None has troubled to reread and retranslate (or translate for the first time) entire documents on which historical work is supposedly based. I have reread and translated for the first time, or for the second, every rabbinic document I have adduced in evidence for the study of rabbinic Judaic religion and theology and of the history of the formation of Judaism.

The part of the work of special concern to New Testament scholars defines my focus. Among the many problems of analysis and description left to me by the kindness of earlier scholars, two first attracted my attention. One I solved and one I did not, in the first critical work of the lot, which was *Development of a Legend: Studies on the Traditions concerning Yohanan ben Zakkai.* The first problem was how to deal with diverse versions of a story; the second problem was how to analyze the blatantly formalized character of much of the rabbinic literature. There is a reason for both the success and the failure. The choice of Yohanan ben Zakkai for the first break with the established way of doing things was dictated by the simple fact that, eight years earlier, I had written a biography in the accepted manner, organizing all the stories about and all the sayings attributed to the man in the order and categories indicated by their content. I had further assembled pretty much everything everyone else had said about the same stories and sayings in the same believing spirit, thinking, of course, that was scholarship. Then my friend and teacher, Brevard Childs, asked me: is it possible that you are doing history too soon, and might you be asking the wrong questions? Since I didn't know the answer, I determined to find out.

I thought it best to begin again from my own beginning. Since I had written Yohanan's life without analyzing the sources but, essentially, merely alluding to or just citing them, I realized that the new beginning had to start with the specification, translation, and analysis of all relevant materials. Laying all the cards on the table seemed the right way. That explains *Development of a Legend.* Uncomprehending colleagues ask, why not just paraphrase or summarize? But that is the very point. The source is not the answer but the question, not the solution but the problem. So it is an act of scholarly honesty and responsibility, and I do not mind being criticized for it. These are not sources that people widely know, and those who claim to know them have not analyzed them and made explicit what they believe they understand about them. That accounts for the state of learning today and the necessity for writing this book, as Part Two demonstrates through *ipsissima verba* of people who claim to know how to use these writings for the study of the New Testament. So the paramount trait of my scholarship, beginning with *Development* and onward to the present, was going to be a massive labor of new translation and, of more importance, totally fresh exegesis.

When confronting the same story running through the Mishnah, Tosefta, the Talmuds, and the Tannaitic and other midrashic compilations, I decided to see whether there were fixed relationships as the story moved from one document to another and, if so, how I might account for them. Chapter 3 of this book shows one such study. What made matters difficult was that there is some doubt about the relative priority of the various documents. What I found, to sidestep that difficulty, was that relationships tend to be fixed no matter the priority or posteriority of the documents. The general result is that the simplest version would be the Mishnah's. Then details that had been omitted would be given by Tosefta, usually further enriched by the Palestinian Talmud and, at the end, by the Babylonian one. Since I was able to show that the details added in a given version dealt with questions left open or even generated by another version, I showed that what we have are not several incidents, each of which happened, gaining or losing weight in its peregrinations. So we bid adieu to a rabbinical equivalent of the Sermon on the Mount and the Sermon on the Plain. A second point that struck me was that it was possible to make sense of the sorts of materials that occur in one document and not in some other.

That led me to the issue of forms. I specifically wanted to know whether there really were fixed literary forms and rhetorical devices in the rabbinic literature. What I found was that while there clearly are highly formalized traits attached to sayings and stories of Yohanan ben Zakkai, they form no coherent unit associated distinctively with his name. They conformed to the formal preferences of the documents in which they occur, and that suggests that documents form the basic and definitive literary category, and not the name of a given authority that is tied to a story or saying. So documents, not historical personages or events, formed the first line of inquiry. I had reached the end of the historical road and the beginning of a different path altogether.

At this point I had already reached what I would come to understand as the pivot of all further work, but I did not see it as such. I had stumbled across the simple fact that all analytical and critical work in rabbinical literature must begin in the study of specific documents, their formal traits, redactional preferences, and substantive interests. Before I expand on that simple and obvious proposition, I have to say it did not even occur to me for two more sizable projects, *The Rabbinic Traditions about the Pharisees before 70* and *Eliezer ben Hyrcanus: The Tradition and the Man*. Both of these lengthy projects continued to ask essentially historical questions. That is to say, they continued to treat topics that carried me through the far reaches of diverse collections. The former turned out to be wildly influential, much to my surprise. I dealt in enormous detail with the character of what rabbinic literature had to say about the Pharisees; in volume 3, I made some tentative remarks about who and what the historical Pharisees might have been and in a companion textbook, *From Politics to Piety,* I summarized these results and speculations for a broader readership. The academic statement went into more printings, and the textbook found its way into footnotes in scholarly articles, no less. So people interpreted as historical study what I meant as literary analysis, though admittedly I bear responsibility for making some off-hand remarks along the way — wrong signals of a right course.

What I wanted to know in *Rabbinic Traditions* — as the title of the work said in so many words — was what the later rabbis have to tell us about the Pharisees, how they tell it to us, and whether it is so. What I found out, as distinct from what I wanted to know, was a great deal about the use of form-criticism as a rather sharp tool for literary analysis, about the mnemonic traits of important strata of the rabbinic literature, about the overall shape of the rabbinic traditions about the Pharisees, and about the difficulty of interpreting materials assigned to a given name or set of names when approached totally outside of the documents — that is, the systems — in which they occur.

What I wanted to know about Eliezer ben Hyrcanus was what in fact we can say about the man. What I found out was a great deal about the history of a tradition associated with a given name. Not all of that history called into question the possibility of speaking of the man, as distinct from the tradition about him. But most did, and from that point onward I regarded as a waste of time sustained work on rabbinic biography. In the interim, my students of that period and I had accomplished the examination of the sayings and stories assigned to or told about all the major figures of Yavneh, down to Aqiba. The results proved marginally interesting in the study of the history of traditions since, over all, the kind of materials in a given document about various names proved uniform, different from the kind of materials in other documents about those same various names. That result, achieved with much hard work (we were still imagining at some point biography might be possible), underlined the centrality of the document and the peripherality of attributions in the formation and presentation of the rabbinic literature.

Quite what that meant about documents, how they were to be studied and interpreted, was slowly becoming clear. What was emerging was a new *episteme:* the systematic analysis of documents and their traits, the systems they set forth one by one, on a long path toward the analysis of the writings aimed at a synthesis, properly set forth, of the same writings. That accounted for the title toward which I then aimed and ultimately achieved: *Judaism: The Evidence of the Mishnah.* That meant: what Judaic system is set forth by this document? It did not mean: what was Judaism? But one can always count on some to misread the obvious and botch up their work, and some did. Readers will see much more obtuseness in Part Two of the book than the mere misrepresentation of a perfectly clear program, explicit in the title of that book and its systematic sequels (*Judaism and Scripture: The Evidence of Leviticus Rabbah; Judaism: The Classical Statement, The Evidence of the Bavli; Judaism and Story: The Evidence of the Fathers according to Rabbi Nathan.*).

Three problems in my procedures to this point irritated me. First, I found that I covered a wide range of topics, but each one superficially. By that I mean one thing: I never saw the law in its own terms which, in the nature of things, meant in its literary context; I saw only the law in the episodic setting of this item and that item tied to a particular name. Accordingly I concluded I never really grasped the law in its own terms — but it was to present the law in its own terms that the principal documents were formulated. The counterpart for scholarship on early Christianity would be to read Augustine for everything but his theology, or Aphrahat for everything but his polemic. The inner logic of a given ruling and its place in the unfolding frame of the chapter of law in which it found its place never fully revealed themselves. Consequently I could not find entire satisfaction in my results.

Second, I could not explain even in theory how to deal with sayings lacking attributions. So the state of a law at a given point in time could not be ascertained. The monotonous mantra held, "If it's unattributed, it's old." But I could not grasp and still cannot understand why repeating obscurity yields clarity. First of all, how old? Second, why old at all? To the contrary, in the Mishnah, studded as it is with disputes, we have unattributed sayings alongside contrary sayings assigned to named masters. In the context of the Mishnah, the purpose of leaving a saying without attribution is to signal that it represents the consensus of sages. That is said in so many words in the Talmuds. Further, in the context of the dispute, if the named saying is young and the anonymous saying old, then how is it possible that Meir or Judah should take a position contrary to an old, received legal tradition? The same good folk who repeat the mantra also describe "Judaism" as a tradition, so we are asked to believe that the authorities of the tradition are not traditional. Finally, in the context of a dispute, the unassigned saying and the assigned one match in every respect: form, wording, topic and problematic, and the literary evidence invariably tell us that the sentences, unattributed and attributed, belong to the same authorship, the same period, and so on. How the dogma of the "antiquity" of the unassigned saying got going need not detain us; why people take at face value a claim so utterly at variance with the literary evidence they purport to interpret "historically" leads us out of scholarship and into murky corners of personal preference and private, idiosyncratic belief.

Third, I recognized that, when all was said and done, I relied for my periodization of materials on attributions of sayings to specific figures and on that alone. What I saw in *Eliezer* was that while I did not take for granted that everything in the name of Eliezer really was said by him, I did tend to assume that everything said about Eliezer in the name of some later authority really was said by that later authority. So it was a case of postponing the act of gullibility, not abandoning it. Thus a growing, unsolved dilemma no longer could be avoided. I found myself on that same slippery turf that I had many times thought to have abandoned, because the only grounds I had for assigning a saying to a given man or period was that the sources said he had said so. I had not moved far from the world in which the traditionalists would say that our sages would not lie and in which the modernists would say that they would not have assigned a saying to a given man if they did not have a reason (which is precisely what the old timers were telling us in their quaint way). When I was at work on the history of the Jews in Babylonia, Brevard Childs had told me that I might be asking the historical question too soon. He certainly was right. I now realized, however, that it was not only a premature historical question but also a question meant to precipitate the writing of the wrong kind of history to begin with.

These several irritants goaded me to attempt something other than and preparatory to social and religious history, namely, a fresh look at a single document and its history. I had no difficulty choosing which one. It had to be the first in the rabbinic canon, so it was the Mishnah. But from the Mishnah, I proceeded systematically outward through the rest of the canon of Judaism in antiquity, so that I finally translated every document — the Tosefta, Avot, both Talmuds, all the midrash-compilations, beginning to end. But my original plan (which at the time I assumed would take up the rest of my life and which did yield forty-three volumes) addressed the Mishnah, so let me focus on that.

The work on the Mishnah has several facets, of which four are of widest general interest: exegesis, form, the use of attributions, and the issue of anonymous materials. Each may be briefly stated.

I found that all earlier exegetes took as their problem the placing of the Mishnah's laws into relationship with all other laws, of all documents and all periods, so forming a single, urgent construct: *the* law, *the* halakhah. An account of what the Mishnah means when seen by itself and in its own context could not be expected under such conditions.

To determine the Mishnah's meaning to its original authors, I decided to ask whether the Mishnah's language provided guidance. What I learned is that the Mishnah provides its own first and best commentary through its highly formalized rhetoric and syntax. Analysis of the large-scale formal traits shows, moreover, that forms as we have them are mostly imposed within the processes of redaction. There is little formulation anterior to redaction of the Mishnah itself, and redaction proves in the end to constitute an act — the governing and commanding forms themselves reveal little or no history. Form-history, strictly speaking, is not possible. The thesis of New Testament form-history may be sound, but it cannot find any support whatsoever in the earliest document of Judaism. Since form-historians have commonly invoked Jewish procedures of oral formulation and oral transmission, I have to give them the sad news that these procedures, so far as they are indicated in the Mishnah, do not go back much before 200 C.E. As I said earlier, as is the message of this book, salvation is not of the Jews.

Of what good are attributions? To repeat my mantra: what we cannot show, we do not know. It follows that we have to find out what we can demonstrate so as to define what we can also falsify. Let me define with some precision the problem of attributions. There are in fact two separate questions. One is the question of the reliability of the exact quotation of *ipsissima verba*. I know no way to show that any rabbinic attribution contains *ipsissima verba* of the rabbi to whom the words are assigned. In fact the opposite is the case whenever we can conduct a sustained inquiry.

For it is easy to show that most of what is attributed takes on the formal traits and adheres to the redactional requirement of the document in which the attribution appears. So it is uncommon to have anything like *ipsissima verba.*

The second question, which is much more important, concerns the reliability of an attribution of the essential content of a statement. If we could show that the gist, if not the exact wording, of what is attributed to Hillel actually was said by him, then we should have information on how one person either in the age in which Hillel lived or afterward summed up what Hillel had said, and we should be able to relate what that person thought he had said to what others of roughly the same time and place may have had on their minds. This is the important matter, not the wording of what is assigned. And there has been some progress here. I am able to show whether a fair number of statements belong in the periods in which the men to whom these statements are attributed flourished. Let me now explain.

We can ask whether there are correlations among groups of sayings given in the names of authorities generally supposed to have lived in successive periods, intersecting sayings dealing with a single topic. What I mean is this: if a saying is in the name of an earlier authority, is its principle or conception prior in logic, more primitive in principle or conception than an intersecting saying given in the name of a later authority? If there is a correlation between temporal attribution and traits of logic or conception so that what is claimed in the attribution to be early is shown in the character of what is attributed to be relatively primitive, then that saying may be shown to be prior to another — because a saying may also be shown to be posterior. I did this work for the entire Mishnah and found the results mildly interesting. It ceased to interest me as the full weight of the documentary approach to the study of the rabbinic literature made itself felt. I realized that the history of ideas is yielded by the comparison of documents.

This matter of testing the value of attributions for the study of history, biography, law, and theology brings us to the much-vexed matter of what is not attributed at all. I have already alluded to the matter of the unattributed saying; in this context, only a few words are needed to close the question. In the case of the Mishnah, I was startled to be unable to find the problem. The reason is in two parts.

First, we have to know that a Mishnah-tractate usually is not merely a collection of information but a careful essay about a set of problems concerning a given topic. A ruling lacking an attribution nonetheless finds its place within the intellectual framework of the tractate that contains it. There are very few that are so totally out of context as to be insusceptible to location or situation within an established framework.

Second, when we work with the known, the pericope that can be located and reliably situated, we normally are able to relate the unknown to the known. It follows that an anonymous ruling containing an idea otherwise first attested in named materials is not apt to go back to a time one hundred or two hundred years earlier. In fact, the really interesting thing is not what the tractates of the Mishnah contain but what they assume. I have already described the ideas held by people ultimately represented in the Mishnah at various stages in the Mishnah's history. I have now completed controlled speculation on the origins of some ideas and facts that lie deep in the Mishnah's substructure, and that do not appear in scripture. This controlled speculation I call my method of hypothetical-exegetical-reconstruction through a series of contrastive or analogical processes.

I wish now to specify the single most interesting thing contributed in my history of mishnaic law, that is, to remove the Mishnah from the context of a whole transtemporal legal system and to insist that the document be read as a statement of a single system, a single world view, produced at a given moment by a group of people who addressed a distinct and distinctive set of problems. In this I have corrected what I believe to be the principal error in earlier work, which has been to treat all sayings and all stories wherever they occur as part of a single "rabbinic" corpus of materials, of pretty much identical origin and provenance, all to be handled atomistically and out of documentary context.

Let me explain this point. When the Mishnah is read in a larger framework than the Mishnah, we are prevented from seeing the Mishnah's materials as a coherent corpus on their own. This latter approach to the Mishnah is absolutely opposite to our purpose. For I have stated and historically accounted for the unfolding of the law of the Mishnah in *particular*. If we assume that the Mishnah constitutes a single document — and the internal harmonious formal and intellectual traits of the Mishnah require that we make that assumption — then we have no choice but to honor the limits of the document when attempting to describe and interpret it.

My work has differed from that of earlier exegetes and many

that have come along since then, as we shall see in Part Two. Others in the past read and interpreted the Mishnah in a different context as part of a large, unitary corpus of law, *the halakhah*. It is the purpose of nearly all exegetes to relate each of the parts to the transcendent whole and to force the whole to encompass all of the parts. It is not, as I originally thought, the ahistorical (or antihistorical) and harmonistic purpose of the earlier exegetes that made their Mishnah-commentaries so intellectually prolix, indeed, indifferent and irrelevant to the text under discussion. That is a misunderstanding that has taken me many years to recognize. It is, rather, that the earlier exegetes presuppose something much more profound, much less susceptible to articulation. This is the construct, "Jewish law" or "halakhah." To them the Mishnah constitutes an important component of this construct. In their mind the correct approach to Mishnah's interpretation is to relate its halakhah to other halakhah, that is, to *"the* law." This harmonistic, atomistic, and yet encompassing approach is natural for people who keep the law and who take for granted their audience wants to know *the* law, even though not all of the law of a given document is practical and practiced.

But the point of interest is clear, and it explains to them what is relevant and what is not. Since social context and intellectual framework define what is relevant, their essays — to us, total chaos — to them are orderly and reliable. But the fact remains that in a different world, their language of exegesis is puzzling, just as is ours to them. So, in all, what I contributed in my history of mishnaic law is to state clearly what the Mishnah wishes to say, in its own setting, within the limits of its own redactional framework, upon the subjects chosen by it, and for purposes defined within the mind of those specific people, its authors, who flourished in one concrete social setting. Reading the document by itself in its historical context and therefore outside of its atemporal, halakhic context requires a different approach. That approach is represented, I firmly believe, in the pages of my books.

We have come a long way from that mental experiment I asked us to perform at the outset, to imagine what we should know about the first Christians and how we should know it if New Testament and patristic literature, indeed all of the literary remains of the first five or six Christian centuries, reached us in the form of the talmudic and midrashic literature. So let me turn toward my conclusion by referring once more to the state of the field.

1.  No longer is it possible to treat the diverse corpus of rabbini-

cal literature as a uniform whole. Once one document is shown to bear its distinctive formal and intellectual characteristics, as I have demonstrated in the case of the Mishnah, then all others must be subjected to appropriate analysis to determine the characteristics of each.

2. No longer are the anonymity and the collective character of documents to be allowed to prevent differentiation and discrimination within a document and between documents. The work of harmonization is in ruins. The work of history may begin.

3. No longer are we left to cope with all sayings, whatever document contains them, and to treat each as of equivalent weight to all others. Diverse attributions of a given saying in different documents are to be examined in the context of the preferences and tendencies of the several documents themselves. True, biography of the principal authorities of the Mishnah is not going to yield a rich account of someone's life and thought. The historical Meir is not going to be fully delineated. But the place of an authority such as Meir in the unfolding of the law most assuredly is to be delineated.

To be sure, the institutional supports for what I regard as a credulous and gullible reading and use of the sources remain somewhat more than negligible. But what should be heartening to the enlightened is not the darkness but the light. Most of the work of history, biography, and the law and theology that has been published in this country, Canada, Britain, Germany, and Holland in recent years has taken full and ample account of the program I have outlined. So I think on the whole there has been truly amazing progress even in the institutions and politics of scholarship, a diffusion of new viewpoints far more rapid and complete than anyone could have dreamed ten years ago.

To conclude, I return to the point of departure. At the outset I emphasized the importance of trying to allow the literary and historical situation of early Christianity to serve as a metaphor for the problem of nascent rabbinic Judaism. At the end I must construct the opposite of a simile, for at the foundations the two are essentially opposite to one another.

The work of studying early Christianity requires us to put together distinct individuals, systems of thought, and institutions, and to find out how these diverse expressions of Christian experience form something coherent and say something cogent. In a word, the work of Nicaea and Chalcedon also defines the labor of learning. The task of studying nascent rabbinic Judaism is the opposite. In the Talmuds and midrashic compilations we have the result of centuries of harmonization and cogent construction. But understanding these documents and the world they portray requires us to unpack them and see how they function. It is as if from the Nicene Creed we had to find our way back into the intellectual and theological issues of the earlier generations of Christians.

For in the end, knowing what people thought without understanding the world about which they reflected does not help us either to understand the people who did the thinking or to interpret the result of their reflection. Without such understanding, we may take the results of their thinking — their theology, their exegesis of scripture, and their law — and we may build on it for one purpose or another. But we essentially know nothing of the inner structure of that building which we ourselves propose to construct. Not knowing the points of stress and places of tension in the building, not knowing the main lines of the foundation of the structure, not knowing the places at which the builder put the strongest joints and beams, we add to the building in total ignorance. It is not building. It is destruction — making things up as we go along. To state matters more generally, in front of us is a labor of description and interpretation, establishing context and providing exegesis. We have a sizable corpus of texts that clearly express a world view and propose to create a society and a way of life for a distinctive group of people. To describe that world view and to understand the society and way of life shaped by the ancient rabbis, we have to interpret texts. To interpret those texts, we have to do three things.

First, we have to read the texts one by one, which I have now done, and which not one of my critics has ever done for even a single text in its entirety, as the blatant errors and superficialities of their purported critiques of my work on only one document, the Mishnah, shows for all who care to see.

Second, we have establish context and setting. We have to describe the world in which the texts took shape and to offer a theory of the questions that seemed urgent and compelling to the people who made the texts as they are and not in some other way. So the work of exegesis depends upon establishing the appropriate context of exegesis. At the same time, to describe the context we have to read the texts.

Third, we have to move from description and analysis, now complete so far as I am concerned, to the work of synthesis and interpretation of the whole — in which work I am now engaged.

Once we have read the documents one by one, we have the further task of reading them all together. This should tell us (1) what they take for granted, the Judaism beyond the texts that remains to be critically investigated, and (2) how they fit together, the Judaism that holds the texts together that, in the end, will show us what was truly normative and definitive, and therefore theological.

Just as there is no exegesis out of context, so there is no description of setting without appeal to the evidence of the texts. Yet beyond text and context lies another fact, which is the inner cogency and continuity of the texts beyond their original context. For Judaism as we know it emerges from the documents under study, and its claim from ancient times to the present is to constitute the logically necessary spinning out of the principles contained in the ancient Torah of Moses "our rabbi" and of the rabbis of olden times. That inner logic which precipitates and governs the unfolding of the theology and law of the rabbis has itself to be discerned. There is then this threefold task, a triple cord not to be separated: text, context, inner logic. When we have discerned the threads of the cord and shown how they are interwoven, we shall perceive what holds together and imparts meaning to an ancient world that is yet with us.

If we ask ourselves why people should want to know about these things, we need not fall back upon the bankrupt claim that they merely are intrinsically interesting. Nor do we have to offer historical salvation to scholars of early Christianity and say they cannot understand their subject without also knowing this one. The formation of Judaism by itself is a compelling social and intellectual phenomenon. For among other such phenomena, it teaches us how to describe and interpret the interplay between the historical situation of a distinct society, on the one side, and the world view brought into being to explain and shape that historical situation, on the other. When we can relate the religious world view and way of life of the ancient talmudic rabbis to the society whose vision they chose to shape and whose conduct and institutions they wished to govern, we can report much about what it is that religion, as a mode of constructing reality and explaining the world, is and what religion does.

Here, before our eyes, is the literature made by a particular group of men in a particular time for a particular society. That literature of antiquity defined what would happen for all time. In unpacking the end-product, in taking it apart to see how it works, we can tell our own times more than a few things about this remarkable *thing*. For this was a world view and way of life capable of bringing order to the chaotic world of ancient times, and it remains capable of preserving a stable and enduring world from antiquity to the present. Given the world's potentialities for disorder and the difficulty of holding together any group of people subject to those ongoing disruptive forces affecting any continuing historical society, we should find more than merely interesting the story of Judaism's formative centuries. In a world of disintegration and an age of disorder, we should find urgent that story, indeed any story, of restraint, order, balance, and continuity — all in the name of the sacred.

## 2

# Documents Matter:
# The Case of Comparative Midrash

In chapter 1 I have argued that documents form the principal components of the literature, defining the lines of structure and order. I now have to spell out the implications for the exegesis and history of the New Testament, as rabbinic literature is supposed to facilitate that work of the documentary hypothesis. My task is to frame a concrete question to focus the abstract hypothesis just announced. I do so in terms of comparative midrash. Here the issue is simply put: does the appearance of an exegesis of a verse of the Old Testament in one midrash-compilation rather than some other affect our reading and use of said exegesis (midrash)? Or do midrash-exegeses circulate freely from one place to another, so that the occurrence in a given document of a given exegesis may be treated as inconsequential? Either materials are interchangeable or they are to be interpreted in a documentary context, but both cannot be the case. But the implications of the discussion at hand extend to the entirety of rabbinic literature: its character, therefore its standing as a set of historical sources.

For New Testament scholarship the issue is readily re-presented. If a saying assigned to Jesus occurs in Mark, then do we ask how the viewpoint of Mark's Gospel has shaped the saying? Or may we ignore that question altogether and simply join the saying with others deriving from John, Luke, Matthew, Gnostic gospels — whatever — to form our picture of the teachings of Jesus? When sayings assigned to Hillel are formed into a pastiche of thoughts, without attention to the occurrence of such sayings in one document rather than some other, people assume that documents do not matter. Whatever their date and whatever their viewpoint or polemic, diverse documents make no impact upon their contents. So one thing New Testament scholarship has to know about rabbinic literature is that to use that literature for New Testament studies concerns not only historicity (is a saying or story attested to the first century, the Land of Israel, Galilee, or Nazareth?) but textuality. I dwell on the point because one of my principal contributions, in my view, is to insist on the importance of the documentary components of rabbinic literature — to maintain that the building blocks of the rabbinic literature are not the isolated saying or story but the documents that present sayings or stories in a well-crafted context. In many ways, what follows forms the centerpiece of my reply, therefore, to the question: what do I have to know about rabbinic literature to study the New Testament?

Let me spell out what is at issue and then offer a test case. The issue is this: may we extract a saying or a story from the document that contains it without referring to the documentary locus in which it occurs? Or must we ask about how the framers of a document have selected and arranged materials that they utilize, in which case we cannot promiscuously choose whatever we wish out of diverse documents without regard to the interests of the authors of those documents themselves? A case in point is the exegesis of scripture. Can we compare various exegeses of the same verse of scripture without regard to where those exegeses occur? Or must we take account, in comparing diverse readings of a given verse of scripture, of the documentary provenience in which a particular reading is located? At issue is whether or not the framers of documents — authors of compositions, compilers of composites used therein — shape the contents. If they do not, then the origin of a saying or story in one document rather than in some other does not matter. If they do, then it matters a great deal.

The appearance of a saying or story or exegesis of scripture in a given document will then bear important implications for the use and interpretation of said saying or story or exegesis. We shall have to begin our interpretation of the passage with the question: how has this item been so shaped as to carry out the interests of the authors of the document who have used it? And, more to the point, we shall no longer be able to lift items from hither and yon without regard to the place in which they originate: its date of closure, its program, its forms and logic and propositional interests and the like.

The matter is settled by whether or not documents exhibit distinctive traits. If they do, then we cannot regard them as mere scrapbooks or containers for whatever people wished to toss in them. If they do not, then we shall ignore documentary lines and simply cite what we wish without regard to its point of origin. If the former, then the date of closure of a document will make a difference. The program of the document, the point its compilers or authors wish to make, and the aesthetic choices they have made will all form part of the localization of the selected item to its point of origin. If the latter, then, as I said, everything is as good (or as bad) as everything else; there are no lines of order or structure that follow documentary boundaries. We focus upon scriptural exegesis: do exegeses of verses of the Old Testament float about independent of the documents that present them so that we may use this here, that there, without regard to their point of provenience in a crafted document?

I choose as my test case the matter of midrash and what is called "comparative midrash." Comparison of exegeses of the same verse of scripture under various auspices and in various documents is commonly carried on without the slightest reference to the documentary setting of the data. Now I ask how we should carry on the comparison of scriptural exegesis, or midrash, pertinent to a given verse as treatments of a single verse occur in several documents. A variety of compilations may refer to and comment on the same verse of scripture. How may we compare these comments? Specifically, is it proper — as is nearly universally the case today — to take midrash-comments out of documentary context and treat them as free-standing, available for comparison to other treatments of the same verse without reference to their origin in particular documents or in the circles that produced those documents? Precisely that sort of comparative study engages the attention of scholars of the history of Judaism and of Christianity. In comparative midrash, scholars study Judaic, sometimes also Christian, exegesis of the Old Testament and compare the exegetical results achieved by one group with those produced by another, either within Judaism or deriving from Christianity. Comparative midrash, then, is an exercise in comparison without regard to the documentary context of that which is compared.

In my judgment we start with the definition of the documentary context, the whole of a compilation of exegeses. This rests upon the firmest premise; it is what we know for sure. No speculation whatever leads us to the claim that (1) a given method of exegesis has yielded (2) a given exegetical comment on a verse of scripture, the result of which is now in (3) this particular document. Since we know that wonderfully simple fact, what is found in which document, we can begin the work of describing the traits imparted by that document to the exegetical result of the exegetical method at hand. Traits characteristic of the documentary setting likewise emerge without a trace of speculation. If a document routinely frames matters in accord with one repertoire of formal conventions rather than some other, and if it arranges its formal repertoire of types of units of discourse in one way rather than some other, we can easily identify those traits of the passage under study that derive from the documentary context. Accordingly, we begin with the document because it presents the first solid fact. Everything else takes a position relative to that fact.

What, then, are some of the documentary facts? Here are some: this saying or story occurs here, bears these traits, is used for this larger redactional and programmatic purpose, makes this distinct point in its context (or no point at all). One may readily test these allegations and determine their facticity. These facts define the initial context of interpretation. The facts deriving from the documentary setting define the context in which a given trait is shared or not shared among the two discrete items to be compared.

In laying emphasis on the document as the correct first point of comparison, I exclude as the appropriate point of departure for comparative studies two others, namely, (1) modes of exegesis, hence, comparative hermeneutics, and (2) results of exegesis, hence, comparison of the exegesis of a verse in one document, deriving from one period and group of authorities, with the exegesis of that same verse in some other document, deriving from a completely different sort of authorities and a much earlier or much later period. This latter way commonly describes how the work is done today. In both cases I maintain that the context for comparison is improper, with the result that the work of comparison produces mere information but no insight.

What do we *not* know if at the outset of comparing things we ignore what I regard as the first and fundamental issue, the plan and program of the document in which an item appears? If we ignore as unimportant the characteristic traits of the documentary location(s) of an exegesis of a verse of scripture or of a story occurring in two or more documents, or if we treat as trivial the traits characteristic of those locative points, we do not know the rule governing both items subject to comparison. We establish no context that imparts meaning to the work of comparison. Why not? Because we have no perspective on similarities and differences among the two or more things that are compared with one another. Similarities and differences may prove merely adventitious. But we shall never know. Points of likeness may constitute mere accidents of coincidence, e.g., of internal logic of the statement of the verse of scripture at hand.

The proponents of comparative midrash in its present formulation argue quite reasonably that they too begin with a premise of shared traits. They compare what different people say about the same verse of scripture. So their generative category is the verse of scripture itself; that is what links exegesis to exegesis. That sounds reasonable, but it has yet to be demonstrated that the contents or form of a verse of scripture, independent of the documentary interests of the author of a midrash-exegesis or the compiler of midrash-exegeses into a midrash-compilation (document) uniformly governs the exegesis of said verse of scripture. In fact, the opposite is the case, as the most superficial comparison of Sifra, on the book of Leviticus, to Leviticus Rabbah ought to have shown decades ago. In New Testament terms: Matthew's reading of Isaiah is Matthew's reading of Isaiah and not Isaiah's immutable and enduring self-revelation, a position with which every Judaic exegete of Matthew's Isaiah-verses has concurred for nearly twenty centuries.

My view is that those who ignore documentary lines have selected the wrong traits and that therefore they do not describe the right things at all. They ordinarily describe and then compare the results of exegesis of a given verse in one document with the results of exegesis of that same verse in another place. By contrast I have argued that the correct thing to describe and compare first is the document that contains the results of the exegesis of diverse verses of scripture with another such document, so that comparison begins by comparing one whole document with another document, described in the way the first has been described. The present practitioners of comparative midrash produce information of this sort: on a given verse, X says this and Y says something else. That, sum and substance, is the result of their study of comparative midrash. What, then, defines that shared foundation that makes possible comparison and contrast? As I said, it is the object of midrash, namely, a verse of scripture.

Now to advance the argument another step. The proponents of comparative midrash invoke the continuity of scripture in defense of comparing and contrasting only the results of exegesis. They maintain that what one party says about a given verse of scripture surely is comparable with what another party says about that same verse of scripture. So they compare and contrast what two or more parties say about a given verse or story of scripture. That seems to me entirely correct and proper, but only in its appropriate setting. And what is that setting at which it is quite proper to undertake comparison of diverse results of exegesis and even modes of exegesis? It is when we know the setting in which people reached one conclusion and not some other. That is to say, when we know the issues exegetes addressed and the intellectual and political and theological setting in which they did their work, then the fact that they said one thing and not something else will illuminate what they said and may further explain their rejection of what they did not say. Since, moreover, we deal not with the gist of what people said but with a given version in one set of words rather than some other — a message captured in particular language governed by conventions of form — comparison of modes of expression and conventions of language and form proceeds apace. So comparing what people said demands that we notice also the different ways in which they may (or may not) have said the same thing (or the opposite things). Formal traits, involving use of language and highly formalized expression, define part of the task of interpreting what is like and what is unlike.

Everything we propose to examine finds its original place in some document rather than in some other (or in two or three documents and not in ten or twenty others). Have the framers or compilers of one document selected an item merely because that item pertains to a given verse of scripture? Or have they chosen that item because it says what they wish to say in regard to a verse of scripture they have identified as important? Have they framed matters in terms of their larger program of the formalization of language, syntax and rhetoric alike? Has their selection and formalization of the item particular relevance to the context in which they did their work, the purpose for which they composed their document, the larger message they planned to convey to those to whom they planned to speak? These questions demand answers, and the answers will tell us the "what else," that is, what is important about what people say in common or in contrast about the verse at hand. Without the answers provided by analysis of circumstance and context, plan and program, of the several documents one by one and then in comparison and contrast with one another, we know only what people said about the verse. But we do not know why they said it, what they meant by what they said, or what we learn from the fact that they said what they said about the verse in hand. The answers to these questions constitute that "what-else" that transforms catalogues of pointless facts into pointed and important propositions. The question about the precipitant of exegesis, namely, whether it is the literary and theological context, as I maintain, or principally the contents of what is said, as proponents of comparative midrash in its present formulation hold, brings us to the crux of the matter.

For our example of comparative midrash as presently carried out, I deal with Geza Vermes.[1] Vermes validates my insistence that the word "midrash" must relate to exegesis. He makes matters turn not on themes in general but on exegesis in particular. He further proves that when I point to the noncontextual comparisons accomplished in the name of comparative midrash, I do not argue with an absent enemy. There is a real position held and worked out by actual scholars in precisely the way in which I have maintained they do the work. Vermes does hold that the same interpretation of a scriptural story may occur in diverse documents. What is important in that fact he states explicitly. We therefore can investigate the time, circumstance, even determinant or precipitant of the change. Then when I point out that comparative midrash ignores the documentary context, treating all statements about the same verse without regard to the preferences and distinctive traits and viewpoints of the document in which they occur, I do not set up a straw man. This is a real view, carried on by scholars in their everyday work. And, as I have argued, it is wrong. Vermes makes explicit the grounds for joining the diverse occurrences of an exegetical program into a single composite: "The biblical text must afford the point of departure because it is the object of study, prayer, teaching, and preaching." I cannot imagine a more specific explanation of what is at issue. The studies that Vermes carries on then move in the directions dictated by his premise about the self-evident choice of the biblical text as the point of departure, by which he means, further, the point of differentiation, comparison, and analysis — the exegetical fulcrum. And that yields precisely that ahistorical formalism, that anticontextual cataloguing of uninterpreted coincidences, that for me yields mere facts,

---

1. Geza Vermes, *Scripture and Tradition in Judaism* (Leiden: E. J. Brill, 1961), 7–10. Later we deal with his *Jesus the Jew*, pointing out an entirely distinct set of flaws in his use of evidence.

but for him produces information on the topics he lists: "the structure and purpose of the re-writing of the Bible; the historical bond
between the Bible and its interpretation; the impact of theology on
exegesis, and vice versa." Once more, therefore, I point out that
my characterization of comparative midrash as presently practiced
constitutes no mere caricature but an accurate portrait of a field as
it is carried on. I find here ample justification for writing a whole
book to test the premises of the work and to show why they are
wrong.

Let me then ask two questions. Can it be that Vermes really
wishes us to ignore the documentary setting in which an exegesis
occurs? Does he propose paying attention only to the exegesis and
the date of the document in which it occurs, without further attention to what the compilers or authors of the document wished
to accomplish by making use of the saying or exegesis? Indeed so.
Here, too, I have not misrepresented his position that the sole fact
about the documentary context that matters is the date of the document. We have yet another statement in which Vermes underlines
what he regards as the validity of asking scripture itself to justify
simply collecting and comparing exegeses of scripture:[2]

> Interpreters of the Hebrew Bible cannot fail to benefit from the
> work of their predecessors in antiquity. Not only will they dis-
> cover which biblical texts were thought to demand particular
> interpretation: they will also notice that the midrashist's problems
> often coincide with their own, and may be surprised to see that
> "modern" solutions to scriptural difficulties are not infrequently
> foreshadowed in these ancient writings. But beyond any immediate
> exegetical assistance, midrash is by nature apt to provide the clos-
> est historical link with Old Testament tradition itself. Scholars not
> misled by the analytical tendency of the literary-critical school will
> fully appreciate the importance of primitive midrash to a proper
> understanding of the spirit in which scripture was compiled.
>
> The historian of the legal, social and religious ideas of post-
> biblical Judaism, seeking to make decisive progress towards a
> reconstruction of their complicated evolution, will in his turn find
> in Bible exegesis *that precious thread of Ariadne which will lead
> him safely through the literary labyrinth of Targum, midrash,
> Mishnah and Talmud. He will also discover there the unifying
> bond which ties biblical and post-biblical Judaism together.* (Italics
> added)

---

2. "Bible and Midrash: Early Old Testament Exegesis," in *Cambridge History
of the Bible,* vol. 1, ed. P. R. Ackroyd and C. F. Evans (Cambridge: University
Press, 1970), 228–31.

The words that I have italicized vindicate my insistence on what is at issue. But Vermes proceeds to state his larger theological program, and it turns out to derive from New Testament scholarship:

> There, too, lies the answer to a great many real problems confronting the New Testament scholar. Since the Christian kerygma was first formulated by Jews for Jews, using Jewish arguments and methods of exposition, it goes without saying that a thorough knowledge of contemporary Jewish exegesis is essential to the understanding (and not just a better understanding) of the message of the New Testament and, even more, of Jesus.

Comparative midrash indeed! In this statement Vermes reveals the underlying program that he, Bloch, and others attempted: a restatement of the theological situation of the foundation of Christianity, an insistence upon "the Judaism" of Christianity. That point of insistence, full of rich opportunities for contemporary religious reconciliation, bears no scholarly motive whatsoever: why, in descriptive terms, should anyone care? In fact comparative midrash in its present formulation forms a subdiscipline of irenics, now extended even to Judaism.

The premise of all that I have said is that scripture serves a diversity of purposes and therefore cannot establish a single definitive plane of meaning, the frame of reference against which all other things constitute variables. To state matters affirmatively, scripture constitutes the neutral background, not the principal and suggestive variable. The exegetes tell us what verses of scripture matter and what we should learn from those verses. Scripture dictates nothing but endures all things. What people tell us about the meaning of scripture represents the outcome of the work of exegetes and not the inexorable result of the character or contents of scripture. But our entry into the interpretation of the work of exegetes begins at the books that the exegetes wrote and handed on to us. Why so? Because all exegeses of verses of scripture come to us in the form of books or equivalent whole documents, and little if any work of exegesis of verses of scripture reaches us in discrete form, e.g., exegesis by exegesis (though, to be sure, some compilations of exegeses exist only in fragmentary form, but that is a different thing).

So to begin at the beginning, we must start with what we have in hand: the whole composite, not the individual compositions, let alone the matter of methods by which the compositions were worked out and the composites made possible. Not only so because, as I have already said, the exegesis of a verse of scripture contained in a composite of such exegeses may or may not have been selected and shaped to suit the purposes of the compilers of the composite of exegeses, not the ideas of the authors of the composition of exegesis. In the case of the documents I have studied at length, Sifra to Leviticus, Leviticus Rabbah, and Genesis Rabbah, that is an established fact. The state of the question elsewhere has not been systematically worked out, though a few have episodically commented on details.

Let me now frame the issue for debate as I think it should be argued:

1. Does scripture dictate the substance of exegesis?

2. Or do exegetes dictate the sense they wish to impart to (or locate in) scripture?

If the former, then the ground for comparison finds definition in a verse of scripture. What X said, without regard to circumstance or even documentary context, compared with what Y said, viewed also with slight attention to canonical context and concrete literary circumstance, matters.

If the latter, then canon and its components take pride of place, and what diverse persons said about a given verse of scripture defines only a coincidence unless proved on the basis of circumstance and context to constitute more than mere coincidence.

So I think the question must confront us. The answer to the question lies spread across the surface of the reading of scripture in the history of the scriptural religions of the West, the Judaisms and the Christianities in perpetual contention among and between themselves about which verses of scripture matter and what those that matter mean. That remarkably varied history tells the story of how diverse groups of believers selected diverse verses of the Hebrew scriptures as particularly important. They then subjected those verses, and not other verses, to particular exegetical inquiry. The meanings they found in those verses answer questions they found urgent. Scripture contributed much but dictated nothing; system — circumstance and context — dictated everything and selected what scripture might contribute in midrash. In this context, "midrash" means the whole extant repertoire of exegeses of verses of scripture we possess in various compilations of exegeses of scripture, made up of compositions of exegeses of verses of scripture, guided by diverse hermeneutical principles of interpretation of scripture. Since in midrash, as just now defined, system comes first, prior to exegeses of particular verses of scripture — all the more so prior to the hermeneutics that guides the work of exegesis — the documents that contain the system form the definitive initial classification for comparative midrash. System must be compared to system, not detail to detail, and therefore to begin with we compare compilation of exegeses to the counterpart, thus document to document. That is my whole case.

Comparative midrash as now carried on in total indifference to all documentary considerations ordinarily focuses on the classification defined by the verses on which people commented, ignoring the classification — the one of circumstance and context supplied by the document and the canon — intended to permit inquiry into why and how people chose one set of verses rather than some other. For comparison of the results of exegeses of a given verse of scripture ignores all questions of context and circumstance — that is, of system. But comparison of the repertoires of verses people chose and those they ignored yields the governing insight. Before we know the answers, we have to understand the questions people addressed to scripture. Why so? Because a group chose a repertoire of verses distinctive to itself, rarely commenting on, therefore confronting, verses important to other groups. When we deal with different groups talking about different things to different groups, what difference does it make to us that, adventitiously and not systematically, out of all systematic context, we discover that someone reached the same conclusion as did someone else of some other group? What else do we know if we discover such a coincidence? Parallel lines never meet, and parallel statements on the same verse may in context bear quite distinct meaning.

For instance, Pharisees appear to have found especially interesting verses in Leviticus and Numbers that failed to attract much attention from the evangelists. Evangelists found unusually weighty verses of scripture that the Pharisees and their heirs tended to ignore. Accordingly, scripture forms the neutral ground. It is the constant. Contending groups selected verses of scripture important to those larger programs that, to begin with, brought them to the reading and interpretation of particular verses of scripture. True, they may have reached the same conclusions about a given verse as did other groups. But so what? Do we therefore learn what that verse of scripture must mean? No one can imagine so. We learn little about scripture and still less about the diverse groups whose views on a given verse of scripture happened to coincide. What is neutral — the verse that is cited — conveys no insight; it only defines what is subject to contention.

That is why the choice of a given verse of scripture for sustained inquiry comes prior to inquiry into the meaning or message discovered in that verse of scripture. To conclude, scripture itself forms the undifferentiated background. It is the form, not the substance; the flesh, not the spirit. The fact that a single verse of scripture generates diverse comments by itself therefore forms a statement of a merely formal character. It is a sequence of facts that may or may not bear meaning. That statement hardly differs in logical status from the one that Australians are different from apples because all apples have stems and no Australians have stems. True enough, but so what? What else do we know when we know that apples and Australians, alike in some ways, differ in the specified way? The stress in comparative midrash, as presently done, on the (mere) formality that people are talking about the same thing (the same verse of scripture) and are saying the same thing or different things about that verse of scripture yields long catalogues of information about what different people say about the same thing. What is at stake in making these lists, what syllogism or proposition we prove by compiling information, rarely comes to expression. More often than not, the list is the thing. There is no "what else."

Let me now spell out the foundations of the view that the work of comparison should properly begin with the complete documents and only proceed to the components of two or more documents, set side by side for contrast and analysis through comparison. Why so? Because the work of analysis rests upon establishing first the genus and only then the species, and the comparison of one species of one genus with another species of a different genus proves parlous indeed. For when we do otherwise and deal with a species distinct from the genus that defines its traits and establishes the context of those traits, we do not really know what we have in hand. The context of a definitive trait not having been established, we cannot know the sense and meaning of a given detail, indeed, even whether the detail by itself defines and distinguishes the species of which it is a part. It is the genus that permits us to describe and analyze the species of that genus. When, therefore, we propose to undertake a work of comparison and contrast, we must begin at the level of the genus, and not at any lesser layer.

What that means is simple. The work of description, prior to analysis and to comparison and contrast, begins with the whole and only then works its way down to the parts. The work of analysis, resting on such a labor of description, proceeds once more, as I have proposed, from the whole, the genus, to the parts, the species. Why do I maintain that the document defines the genus — the document, and not the verse of scripture on which people comment? The reason is in part negative, namely, the miscellaneous character of the diverse exegetical traditions of Judaism and Christianity, as noted just now. But it is also positive, that is, the traits of the documents themselves decide the issue. They exhibit integrity so that their contents in detail testify to the plan and program of the compositors of the compilations of exegeses of scripture.

Let me turn to one specific document that, in an exemplary way, validates this judgment. In my study of Leviticus Rabbah, *The Integrity of Leviticus Rabbah: The Problem of the Autonomy of a Rabbinic Document,*[3] I proposed to demonstrate in the case of that compilation of exegeses of scripture that a rabbinic document constitutes a text, not merely a scrapbook or a random compilation of episodic materials. A text is a document with a purpose, one that exhibits the traits of the integrity of the parts to the whole and the fundamental autonomy of the whole from other texts. I showed that the document at hand therefore falls into the classification of a cogent composition, put together with purpose and intended as a whole and in the aggregate to bear a meaning and state a message.

I therefore disproved the claim, for the case before us, that a rabbinic document serves merely as an anthology or miscellany or is to be compared only to a scrapbook, made up of this and that. In that exemplary instance I pointed to the improbability that a document has been brought together merely to join discrete and ready-made bits and pieces of episodic discourse. A document in the canon of Judaism thus does not merely define a context for the aggregation of such already completed and mutually distinct materials. Rather, I proved that document constitutes a text. So at issue in my study of Leviticus Rabbah is what makes a text a text, that is, the textuality of a document. At stake is how we may know when a document constitutes a text and when it is merely an anthology or a scrapbook.

The importance of that issue for the correct method of comparison is clear. If we can show that a document is a miscellany, then traits of the document have no bearing on the contents of the document — things that just happen to be preserved there rather

---

3. Brown Judaic Studies (Chico, Calif.: Scholars Press, 1985).

than somewhere else. If, by contrast, the text possesses its own integrity, then everything in the text must first of all be interpreted
in the context of the text, and then in the context of the canon of
which the text forms a constituent. Hence my stress on the comparison of whole documents prior to the comparison of the results
of exegesis contained within those documents rests upon the result
of the study of Leviticus Rabbah. Two principal issues frame the
case. The first is what makes a text a text. The textuality of a text
concerns whether a given piece of writing hangs together and is to
be read on its own. The second is what makes a group of texts into
a canon, a cogent statement all together. At issue is the relationship
of two or more texts of a single, interrelated literature to the world
view and way of life of a religious tradition viewed whole.

Proponents of the comparison-of-midrash approach — who
compare the results of exegesis in various documents rather than
the nature of the documents that compile the exegeses — may claim
that the character of the documents supports their approach, not
mine. How so? They point to the fact that stories and exegeses
move from document to document. The travels of a given saying
or story or exegesis of scripture from one document to another validate comparing what travels quite apart from what stays home.
And that is precisely what comparing exegeses of the same verse
of scripture occurring in different settings does. The comparative
midrashists of the moment therefore maintain that traveling materials enjoy their own integrity, apart from the texts that quite adventitiously give them a temporary home. The problem of integrity
is whether or not a rabbinic document stands by itself or right at the
outset forms a scarcely differentiated segment of a larger and uniform canon, one made up of materials that travel everywhere and
take up residence indifferent to the traits of their temporary abode.

The reason one might suppose that, in the case of the formative
age of Judaism, a document does not exhibit integrity and is not
autonomous is simple. The several writings of the rabbinic canon
of late antiquity, formed from the Mishnah, ca. 200 C.E., through
the Talmud of Babylonia, ca. 600 C.E., with numerous items in between, do share materials — sayings, tales, protracted discussions.
Some of these shared materials derive from explicitly cited documents. For instance, passages of scripture or of the Mishnah or of
the Tosefta, cited verbatim, will find their way into the two Talmuds. But sayings, stories, and sizable compositions not identified
with a given earlier text and exhibiting that text's distinctive traits
will float from one document to the next.

That fact has so impressed students of the rabbinic canon as to produce a firm consensus of fifteen hundred years' standing. It is that one cannot legitimately study one document in isolation from others, describing its rhetorical, logical, literary, and conceptual traits and system all by themselves. To the contrary, all documents contribute to a common literature or, more accurately, religion — "the Torah," that is, Judaism. In the investigation of matters of rhetoric, logic, literature, and conception, whether of law or of theology, all writings join equally to give testimony to the whole. For the study of the formative history of Judaism, the issue transcends what appears to be the simple, merely literary question at hand: when is a text a text? In the larger context of that question we return to the issue of the peripatetic sayings, stories, and exegeses.

When I frame matters in terms of the problem of the rabbinic document, I ask what defines a document as such, the "textness," the textuality, of a text. How do we know that a given book in the canon of Judaism is something other than a scrapbook? The choices are clear. One theory is that a document serves solely as a convenient repository of prior sayings and stories, available materials that will have served equally well (or poorly) wherever they took up their final location. In accord with that theory, it is quite proper in ignorance of all questions of circumstance and documentary or canonical context to compare the exegesis of a verse of scripture in one document with the exegesis of that verse of scripture found in some other document. The other theory is that a composition exhibits a viewpoint, a purpose of authorship distinctive to its framers or collectors and arrangers. Such a characteristic literary purpose is so powerfully particular to one authorship that nearly everything at hand can be shown to have been shaped for the ultimate purpose of the authorship at hand, that is, collectors and arrangers who demand the title of authors. In accord with this other theory, context and circumstance form the prior condition of inquiry, the result, in exegetical terms, the contingent one. To resort again to a less than felicitous neologism, I thus ask what signifies or defines the "documentness" of a document and what makes a book a book. I therefore wonder whether there are specific texts in the canonical context of Judaism or whether all texts are merely contextual. In framing the question as I have, I of course lay forth the mode of answering it. We have to confront a single rabbinic composition and ask about its definitive traits and viewpoint.

But we have also to confront the issue of the traveling sayings, the sources upon which the redactors of a given document have drawn. By "sources" I mean simply passages in a given book that occur also in some other rabbinic book. Such sources — by definition prior to the books in which they appear — fall into the classification of materials general to two or more compositions and by definition not distinctive and particular to any one of them. The word "source" therefore serves as an analogy to convey the notion that two or more sets of authors have made use of a single, available item. About whether or not the shared item is prior to them both or borrowed by one from the other at this stage we cannot speculate. As I said, these shared items, transcending two or more documents and even two or more complete systems or groups, if paramount and preponderant, would surely justify the claim that we may compare exegeses of verses of scripture without attention to context. Why? Because there is no context defined by the limits of a given document and its characteristic plan and program. All the documents do is to collect and arrange available materials. The document does not define the context of its contents. If that can be shown, then comparative midrash may quite properly ignore the contextual dimension imparted to sayings, including exegeses of scripture, by their occurrence in one document rather than some other.

Let me now summarize this phase of the argument. We ask about the textuality of a document (is it a composition or a scrapbook?) so as to determine the appropriate foundations for comparison, the correct classifications for comparative study. We seek to determine the correct context of comparison, hence the appropriate classification. My claim is simple: once we know what is unique to a document, we can investigate the traits that characterize all the document's unique and definitive materials. We ask about whether the materials unique to a document cohere, or whether they prove merely miscellaneous. If they do cohere, we may conclude that the framers of the document have followed a single plan and a program. That would, in my view, justify the claim that the framers carried out a labor not only of conglomeration, arrangement, and selection, but also of genuine authorship or composition in the narrow and strict sense of the word. If so, the document emerges from authors, not merely arrangers and compositors.

For the same purpose, therefore, we also take up and analyze the items shared between that document and some other or among several documents. We ask about the traits of those items, one by one and all in the aggregate. In these stages we may solve for the case at hand the problem of the rabbinic document: do we deal with a scrapbook or a cogent composition? A text or merely a literary expression, random and essentially promiscuous, of a larger theological context? That is the choice at hand. Since we have reached a matter of fact, let me state the facts as they are. To begin with, I describe the relationships among the principal components of the literature with which we deal. The several documents that make up the canon of Judaism in late antiquity relate to one another in three important ways.

First, all of them refer to the same basic writing, the Hebrew scriptures. Many of them draw upon the Mishnah and quote it. So the components of the canon join at their foundations.

Second, as the documents reached closure in sequence, the later authorship can be shown to have drawn upon earlier, completed documents. So the writings of the rabbis of the talmudic corpus accumulate and build from layer to layer.

Third, as I have already hinted, among two or more documents some completed units of discourse and many brief, discrete sayings circulated as sentences or episodic homilies or fixed apothegms of various kinds. So in some measure, the several documents draw not only upon one another, as we can show, but also upon a common corpus of materials that might serve diverse editorial and redactional purposes.

The extent of this common corpus can never be fully known. We know only what we have, not what we do not have. So we cannot say what has been omitted or whether sayings that occur in only one document derive from materials available to the editors or compilers of some or all other documents. That is something we never can know. We can describe only what is in our hands and interpret only the data before us. Of indeterminates and endless speculative possibilities, we need take no account. In taking up documents one by one, do we not obscure their larger context and their points in common?

In fact, shared materials proved for Leviticus Rabbah not many and not definitive. They form an infinitesimal proportion of Genesis Rabbah, under 3 to 5 percent of the volume of the *parashiyyot* of Leviticus Rabbah for which I conducted probes. Materials that occur in both Leviticus Rabbah and some other document prove formally miscellany and share no single viewpoint or program; they are random and brief. What is unique to Leviticus Rabbah and exhibits that document's characteristic formal traits also predominates and bears the message of the whole. So much for the issue of the peripatetic exegesis. To date I have taken up the issue of homogeneity of "sources" in a limited and mainly formal setting for the matter of how sayings and stories travel episodically from one document to the next.[4] The real issue is not the traveling, but the unique materials: the documents, and not what is shared among them. The variable — what moves — is subject to analysis only against the constant: the document itself.

My point of insistence, therefore, is that the comparison of exegeses begins with the contrast and analysis of whole documents and their viewpoints. Why the resistance to what seems to me a rather obvious point? The reason is simple. To describe and analyze documents one by one violates the lines of order and system that have characterized all earlier studies of these same documents. Until now, just as people compared exegeses among different groups of a given verse of scripture without contrasting one circumstance to another, so they tended to treat all of the canonical texts as uniform in context, that is, as testimonies to a single system and structure, that is, to Judaism. What sort of testimonies texts provide varies according to the interest of those who study them. That is why, without regard to the source of the two expositions of the same verse, people would compare one midrash, meaning the interpretation of a given verse of scripture, with another midrash on the same verse of scripture. True enough, philologians look for meanings of words and phrases, better versions of a text. For them all canonical documents serve equally as a treasury of philological facts and variant readings. Theologians study all texts equally, looking for God's will and finding testimonies to God in each component of the Torah of Moses, our rabbi. Why so? Because all texts ordinarily are taken to form a common statement, "Torah" in the mythic setting, "Judaism" in the theological one.

But comparison cannot be carried out properly on such a basis. The hermeneutical issue dictated by the system overall defines the result of description, analysis, and interpretation. Let me give a single probative example. From the classical perspective of the theology of Judaism, the entire canon of Judaism — "the one whole Torah of Moses, our rabbi" — equally and at every point testifies to the entirety of Judaism. Why so? Because all documents in the

---

4. Jacob Neusner, *The Peripatetic Saying: The Problem of the Thrice-Told Tale in Talmudic Literature* (Chico, Calif.: Scholars Press, 1985).

end form components of a single system. Each makes its contribution to the whole. If, therefore, we wish to know what "Judaism" or, more accurately, "the Torah" teaches on any subject, we are able to draw freely on sayings relevant to that subject wherever they occur in the entire canon of Judaism. Guided only by the taste and judgment of the great sages of the Torah, as they have addressed the question at hand, we thereby describe "Judaism." And that same theological conviction explains why we may rip a passage out of its redactional context and compare it with another passage, also seized from its redactional setting. In the same way, comparative midrash as presently practiced moves freely across the boundaries of systems and documents alike. But the theological *apologia* for doing so has yet to reach expression; and there can be no other than a theological *apologia*. In logic I see none; epistemologically there never was one.

In fact, documents stand in three relationships to one another and to the system of which they form part, that is, to Judaism as a whole. The specification of these relationships constitutes the principal premise of this inquiry and validates the approach to comparative midrash I offer here.

1. Each document is to be seen all by itself, that is, as autonomous of all others.

2. Each document is to be examined for its relationships with other documents universally regarded as falling into the same classification as Torah.

3. Finally, in the theology of Judaism (or, in another context, of Christianity) each document is to be allowed to take its place as part of the undifferentiated aggregation of documents that all together constitute the canon of, in the case of Judaism, the "one whole Torah revealed by God to Moses at Mount Sinai."

Simple logic makes self-evident the proposition that, if a document comes down to us within its own framework as a complete book with a beginning, middle, and end, in preserving that book, the canon presents us with a document on its own and not solely as part of a larger composition or construct. So we see the document as it reaches us, that is, as autonomous. Accordingly, such a document demands description on its own.

If, second, a document contains materials shared verbatim or in substantial content with other documents of its classification, or if one document refers to the contents of other documents, then the several documents that clearly wish to engage in conversation with one another have to address one another. That is to say, we have to seek for the marks of connectedness, asking for the meaning of those connections. It is at this level of connectedness that we labor in comparative midrash. For the purpose of comparison is to tell us what is like something else, what is unlike something else. To begin with, we can declare something unlike something else only if we know that it is like that other thing. Otherwise the original judgment bears no sense whatsoever. So, once more, canon defines context, or, in descriptive language, the first classification for comparative study is the document brought into juxtaposition with, and contrast to, another document.

Finally, since the community of the faithful of Judaism, in all of the contemporary expressions of Judaism, concurs that documents held to be authoritative constitute one whole, seamless "Torah," that is, a complete and exhaustive statement of God's will for Israel and humanity, we take as a further appropriate task, if one not to be done here, the description of the whole out of the undifferentiated testimony of all of its parts. These components in the theological context are viewed as equally authoritative for the composition of the whole: one continuous system. In taking up such a question, we address a problem not of theology alone, though it is a correct theological conviction, but one of description, analysis, and interpretation of an entirely historical order.

In my view the various documents of the canon of Judaism produced in late antiquity demand a hermeneutic altogether different from the one of homogenization and harmonization, the ahistorical and anticontextual one definitive for comparative midrash as presently practiced. It is one that does not harmonize but that differentiates. It is a hermeneutic shaped to teach us how to read the compilations of exegeses first of all one by one and in a particular context, and second, in comparison with one another. How to begin this approach to comparison?

Let me answer by spelling out the method I applied to both Rabbah-compilations.[5] I have to prove that the document at hand rests upon clear-cut choices of formal and rhetorical preference, so that it is, from the viewpoint of form and mode of expression,

---

5. Reference is made to *The Integrity of Leviticus Rabbah,* cited above, and *Comparative Midrash: The Program and Plan of Genesis Rabbah and Leviticus Rabbah* (Atlanta: Scholars Press, 1985).

cogent. I have to demonstrate that these formal choices prove uniform and paramount. For both compilations I analyze three large *parashiyyot* (systematic and sustained compositions of exegeses) to show their recurrent structures. These I categorize. Then I proceed to survey all *parashiyyot* of each of the complete compilations and find out whether or not every *parashah* of the entire document finds within a single cogent taxonomic structure suitable classifications for its diverse units of discourse. If one taxonomy serves all and encompasses the bulk of the units of discourse at hand, I may fairly claim that Leviticus Rabbah or Genesis Rabbah does constitute a cogent formal structure, based upon patterns of rhetoric uniform and characteristic throughout.

My next step for both documents is to ask whether the framers of the document preserved a fixed order in arranging types of units of discourse, differentiated in accord with the forms I identified. In both documents I am able to show that, in ordering materials, the framers or redactors paid much attention to the formal traits of their units of discourse. They chose materials of one formal type for beginning their sustained exercises of argument or syllogism, then chose another formal type for the end of their sustained exercises of syllogistic exposition. This seems to me to show that the framers or redactors followed a set of rules that we are able to discern. Finally, in the case of both documents, I outline the program and show the main points of emphasis and interest presented in each. In this way I characterize the program as systematically as I described the plan. I also answer the question for the documents under study of whether or not we deal with a text, exhibiting traits of composition, deliberation, proportion, and so delivering a message on its own. Since we do, Leviticus Rabbah or Genesis Rabbah demands description, analysis, and interpretation first of all on its own as an autonomous statement. It then requires comparison and contrast with other compositions of its species of the rabbinic genus, that is to say, it demands to be brought into connection with, relationship to, other rabbinic compositions. The same is to be said of Genesis Rabbah. On that basis, comparison of the two compilations of exegeses — whole to whole — becomes possible.[6]

This leads me to one conclusion: redaction forms the centerpiece

---

6. The quite separate question of the use and meaning of scripture in Judaism is addressed in my *Judaism and Scripture: The Evidence of Leviticus Rabbah* (Chicago: University of Chicago Press, 1986).

in the formulation and selection of exegesis of scripture. The activity of scriptural exegesis constituted a cultural commonplace, a prevailing convention of thought, and therefore by itself cannot yield points of differentiation. Bases for analysis, comparison, and contrast derive from points of differentiation, not sameness. Comparing what unrelated groups said about the same matter tells us only facts, not their meaning. But the purpose of comparison is interpretation. We might as well attempt to differentiate within diverse ages and formulations of Israelite culture on the basis of so commonplace an activity as writing books or eating bread. True enough, diverse groups wrote diverse books and, we might imagine, also baked their bread in diverse ways, e.g., with or without yeast, with wheat, or barley, or rye. But so what? Only if we can show that people did these things as a mode of expressing ideas particular to themselves, their condition and context, can we answer the question, so what? That is why comparing merely what people said about the same thing, whether about the weather or the meaning of Gen. 49:10, without regard to the circumstance in which they said it — meaning in our case to begin with the particular book and canon in which what they said is now preserved — produces knowledge of a merely formal character.

We need not hunt at length for evidence of the work of collecting exercises in exegesis — of rewriting an old text in light of new considerations or values. Such a vast enterprise is handsomely exemplified by the book of Chronicles, which, instead of merely commenting on verses, actually rewrites the stories of Samuel and Kings. Anyone who without attention to the larger documentary context — the respective programs of the compilations as a whole — compares what the compilers of Samuel and Kings say about a given incident with what the compilers of Chronicles say about the same incident misses the point of the difference between the reading of the one and that of the other. For, as everyone now knows, the difference derives from the documentary context — there alone. So without our asking first of all about the plan and program of the documents, the formal comparison of contents produces facts, but no insight into their meaning. That, in my view, is the present situation of comparative midrash.

When people wished to deliver a powerful argument for a basic proposition, they did so by collecting and arranging exegeses of scripture — and, it goes without saying, also by producing appropriate exegeses of scripture for these compilations. Compilers also participated in the framing or rewriting of what they compiled, so that all we have is what they chose to give us in the language and form they selected. That is why I maintain study of comparative midrash must begin with the outermost point of contact, namely, the character of the compilation of exegeses. Comparing one compilation with another then defines the first stage of the comparison of exegeses: compilations, contents, principles of hermeneutics alike.

Turning to New Testament scholarship, I now wish to show how compilers and exegetes made their collections of exegeses in order to demonstrate propositions critical to their theological program. We detect here little that was wholly random in either proposition or proportion, selection and arrangement of exegeses, or propositions on the meaning of specific verses of scripture. All aspects — mode of exegesis, result of exegesis, purpose of compilation alike — address the point of the document as a whole, carrying out the established purpose. They demonstrate the unity of form and meaning, of purpose and proposition. The selection of exegeses, the creation of exegeses, the arrangement and compilation of exegeses, the use of a particular formal technique, and the larger polemic or theological proposition that motivated the compilers and exegetes — all of these together join in producing the document as we know it. Therefore we compare document to document, not uninterpreted detail ripped from one document to an equivalent detail seized from some other. We ask two questions.

We turn first to a passage of exegesis, the one of Hosea in the Essene library of Qumran. As presented by Geza Vermes,[7] the exegeses do form something we might call a collection, or at least a chapter, that is, a systematic treatment of a number of verses in sequence. Vermes's presentation is as follows:

Commentary on Hosea

In this interpretation, the unfaithful wife is the Jewish people, and her lovers are the Gentiles who have led the nation astray.

> [*She knew not that*] *it was I who gave her* [*the new wine and oil*], *who lavished* [*upon her silver*] *and gold which they* [*used for Baal*] (ii, 8).

Interpreted, this means that [they ate and] were filled, but they forgot God who . . . They cast His commandments behind them which He had sent [by the hand of] His servants the Prophets, and they listened to those who led them astray. They revered them, and in their blindness they feared them as though they were gods.

---

7. *The Dead Sea Scrolls in English* (Harmondsworth: Penguin, 1975), 230.

*Therefore I will take back my corn in its time and my wine [in its season]. I will take away my wool and my flax lest they cover [her nakedness]. I will uncover her shame before the eyes of [her] lovers [and] no man shall deliver her from out of my hand (ii, 9–10).*

Interpreted, this means that He smote them with hunger and nakedness that they might be shamed and disgraced in the sight of the nations on which they relied. They will not deliver them from their miseries.

*I will put an end to her rejoicing, [her feasts], her [new] moons, her Sabbaths, and all her festivals (ii, 11).*

Interpreted, this means that [they have rejected the ruling of the law, and have] followed the festivals of the nations. But [their rejoicing shall come to an end and] shall be changed into mourning.

*I will ravage [her vines and her fig trees], of which she said, 'They are my wage [which my lovers have given me'.] I will make of them a thicket and the [wild beasts] shall eat them. . . . (ii, 12).*

Treating the materials presented by Vermes as a document, we simply cannot categorize these several "units of discourse" within the framework of taxonomy suitable for a rabbinic midrash-compilation, e.g., Genesis Rabbah and Leviticus Rabbah. Why not? We do not have (1) a word-for-word or point-by-point reading in light of other verses of scripture of the verses that are cited, let alone (2) an expansion on the topics of the verses. The forms serving the two Rabbah-compilations obviously do not apply. What we have is an entirely different sort of exegesis, given in an entirely different form, namely, a reading of the verses of scripture in light of an available scheme of concrete events. The exegete wishes to place into relationship to scripture things that have happened in his own day. His form serves that goal.

If the generative principle of exegesis seems alien, the criterion of composition as a whole is entirely familiar. The compiler wishes to present amplifications of the meaning of a verse of scripture, not word-for-word or phrase-for-phrase interpretations. He also has not constructed a wide-ranging discussion of the theme of the verse such as we noted in the more philosophical taxon, let alone a mere anthology. Let me with appropriate emphasis state the main point. *The framer of the passage selected a mode of constructing his unit of discourse wholly congruent with the purpose for which, to begin with, he undertook the exegesis of the passage.*

He wished to read the verses of scripture in light of events. So he organized his unit of discourse around the sequence of verses of scripture under analysis. Had he wanted, he might have provided a sequential narrative of what happened, then inserting the verse he found pertinent. Thus: "X happened, and that is the meaning of (biblical verse) Y." (Such a mode of organizing exegeses served the school of Matthew, but not the framer of the text at hand. I do not know why.) In any event, the construction at hand is rather simple. The far more complex modes of constructing units of discourse in Genesis Rabbah and Leviticus Rabbah served a different purpose. They are made up, moreover, of different approaches to the exegesis of scripture. So we see that the purpose of exegesis makes a deep impact not only upon the substance of the exegesis, but also and especially upon the formal and redactional characteristics of the document, the mode of organizing the consequent collection of exegeses.

Obviously, there were diverse ways of undertaking scriptural exegesis and of organizing the collections of such exegeses. In the setting of examples of these other ways in which earlier Jews had responded to verses of scripture and then collected and organized their responses, we see that there was more than a single compelling way in which to do the work. It represented a distinctive choice among possibilities others in Israelite culture had explored. We may now argue that the rather episodic sets of exegeses presented to us by the Essene library of Qumran cannot be called documents and compared to the sustained and purposeful labor of both exegesis and composition revealed in the earliest rabbinic collections. Accordingly, in conclusion, let us turn for a second exercise of comparison to an exegetical passage exhibiting clear-cut and fixed forms of rhetoric, both of the exegetical passage itself and of the composition of several exegetical passages into a large-scale discourse — hence, units of discourse to be compared with units of discourse of Genesis Rabbah. We find in the literary composition of the school of Matthew a powerful effort to provide an interpretation of verses of scripture in line with a distinct program of interpretation. Furthermore, the selection and arrangement of these scriptural exegeses turn out to be governed by the large-scale purpose of the framers of the document as a whole.

To illustrate these two facts, I present four parallel passages in which we find a narrative culminating in the citation of a verse of scripture, hence a convention of formal presentation of ideas, style, and composition alike. In each case, the purpose of the narrative is not only fulfilled in itself, but also in a subscription linking the narrative to the cited verse and stating explicitly that the antecedent narrative serves to fulfill the prediction contained in the cited verse, hence a convention of theological substance. We deal with familiar materials. I cite only Matt. 1:18–23, but refer in addition to 2:1–6, 2:16–18, and 3:1–3 (I reproduce the Revised Standard Version).

MATT. 1:18–23

Now the birth of Jesus Christ took place in this way. When his mother Mary had been betrothed to Joseph, before they came together she was found to be with child of the Holy Spirit; and her husband Joseph, being a just man and unwilling to put her to shame, resolved to divorce her quietly. But as he considered this, behold, an angel of the Lord appeared to him in a dream, saying, "Joseph, son of David, do not fear to take Mary your wife, for that which is conceived in her is of the Holy Spirit; she will bear a son, and you shall call his name Jesus, for he will save his people from their sins." All this took place to fulfill what the Lord had spoken by the prophet: "Behold, a virgin shall conceive and bear a son, and his name shall be called Emmanuel" (which means, God with us).

The four passages, represented by the item at hand, show us a stunningly original mode of linking exegeses. The organizing principle derives from the sequence of events of a particular biography rather than the sequence of verses in a given book of scripture or of sentences of the Mishnah. The biography of the person under discussion serves as the architectonic of the composition of exegeses into a single statement of meaning. This mode of linking exegeses — that is, composing them into a large-scale collection such as we have at hand in the earliest rabbinic compilations — shows us another way than the way taken at Qumran, on the one side, and among the late fourth- and fifth-century compilers of rabbinic collections of exegeses, on the other.

The passages of Matthew, therefore, indicate a clear-cut, distinctive choice on how to compose a "unit of discourse" and to join several congruent units of discourse into a sustained statement, a document. The choice is dictated by the character and purpose of the composition at hand. Since the life of a particular person — as distinct from events of a particular character — forms the focus of discourse, telling a story connected with that life and following this with a citation of the biblical verse illustrated in the foregoing story constitutes the generative and organizing principle of the several units of discourse, all of them within a single taxon. The taxon is not only one-dimensional. It also is rather simple in both its literary traits and its organizing principle. We discern extremely tight narration of a tale, followed by a citation of a verse of scripture, interpreted only through the device of the explicit joining language: this is what that means. What we see so clearly in the work of the school of Matthew is a simple fact. The work of making up exegeses of scripture, selecting the appropriate ones and saying important things about them, and the labor of collecting and compiling these exegeses of scripture into a larger composite together express a single principle, make a single statement, carry out the purposes of a single polemic. Let me once more give proper emphasis to this simple result: *Three things go together: (1) the principles of exegesis, (2) the purposes of exegesis, and (3) the program of collecting and arranging exegeses into compilations.*

That is the fact of Matthew. It is true of Sifra, Genesis Rabbah, and Leviticus Rabbah and most, though not all, rabbinic midrash-compilations. What New Testament scholarship must know about rabbinic literature before appealing to rabbinic midrash-exegesis to clarify verses of the New Testament as these are supposed to have been read in the first century, in the Land of Israel, in Galilee, in Nazareth, is one governing fact. It is that these two considerations cohere: (1) what people wished to say about the meaning of a verse of scripture, and (2) why they then proposed to collect what they had said into cogent compositions. The point of analysis of a given midrash-exegesis is defined by the document in which it occurs. If we wish to maintain that how a late midrash-compilation reads a given verse of the Old Testament tells us how the verse was read in the first century, in the Land of Israel, and upward to the hills of Galilee, we have to show that the interpretation of that verse is independent of the interests of the midrash-compilation in which it occurs. It would also be nice to show that that midrash-exegesis belongs to the sage to whom it is attributed. But that is a separate story, to which we now turn.

# 3

# Sages Made Up
# Sayings and Stories

Ample evidence in virtually every document of rabbinic literature sustains the proposition that it was quite common for sages to make up sayings and stories and attribute the sayings to, or tell the stories about, other prior authorities. Considerations of historical fact did not impede the search for religious truth: the norms of belief and behavior. That is why, if all we want are historical facts, we cannot believe everything we read except as evidence of what was in the mind of the person who wrote up the passage: opinion held at the time of the closure of a document. That is the sole given, the datum we do not have to demonstrate. Using sayings and stories in rabbinic literature as though anyone in that time and place subjected himself to the disciplines of contemporary historical method is worse than anachronism; it is an accusation that "our sages of blessed memory" cared mostly about preserving and handing on information. That is not what their literature proposed to transmit; that is not what they wished to accomplish.

Historical questions accordingly take up a stance on the sidelines, being monumentally irrelevant to religious truth. That is the fact even though, to be sure, people who made up stories or sayings and assigned them to prior figures — whether to Abraham, Isaac, and Jacob, as in Genesis Rabbah, or to our lord Moses (*Moshe rabbenu*) in Mekhilta and Sifré to Deuteronomy, or to any and all of the prophets in the Talmud of Babylonia, or to Hillel, here, there, and everywhere. Such people certainly believed as truth everything they made up that morning. While a saying assigned to Hillel or Shammai resonates in the ears of some "historians" with "the ring of truth," one wonders why these same colleagues are deaf to the resonance of sayings assigned to Jeremiah or Moses. But some specialists in the Old Testament do not write lives of Jeremiah out of midrash-compilations, the way their colleagues in Talmud and "Jewish history in the period of the Mishnah and the Talmud" confidently report as historical fact what the same documents tell us about Hillel or Shammai.

In any event, these specialists give ample evidence that, to them, attributions were signals of a variety of things, the name of the original author being only one possible signal and not an important one. For as anyone who knows two or three pages of the Talmud of Babylonia will concur, it is easy to cite hundreds of passages in which, faced with a logical problem in a saying assigned to a prior authority, an exegete will rewrite the saying to conform to the requirements of logic. Not only so, but the Tosefta is rich in cases in which sayings assigned to first-century authorities are recast by sayings assigned to second-century ones. What is subject to dispute will be refined, and the range of debate will be redefined altogether. So we are not, to begin with, dealing with a literature that regards historical fact as probative or even recognizes a gap between the facts of history and the opinions of the moment.

A different criterion, that of rigorous logic, intervenes, and no one finds it an offense against truth to correct what is obviously a flawed version (not "tradition") of a saying or a story. On that basis, the innocent citation (as historical fact) of sayings and stories in the rabbinic literature to prove what was said or done by (other) Jews in the time of Jesus proves bizarre. Citing unexamined fables or versions of sayings as simple facts contradicts the norms of the rabbinic literature itself, which values other things than historical facts and never recognizes as consequential the issue of whether or not something really happened and, if it did, whether it happened in one way rather than in some other. On history, the rabbinic literature lays down a simple judgment: "what was, was" — and makes no difference. Other things make a great deal of difference.

Let us take as our case in point the evidence that people made up stories after the fact (if there ever was a fact to begin with). This we do through the comparison of stories as they occur in successive documents, a comparison that, for this literature, I invented. That is, I am the scholar who first in a systematic and comprehensive way undertook comparing parallel versions of the same saying or story, such as I accomplished in my *Development of a Legend, Rabbinic Traditions about the Pharisees, Eliezer ben Hyrcanus,*

and other books. Before me, the comparison and interpretation
of various versions of a single story, saying, or exegesis occurring in different compilations of rabbinic traditions had made little
progress; the method appeared episodically and anecdotally and
yielded only local results. The reason is that scholars, well aware
of variations of one sort or another, in general supposed that pericopes originally were transmitted by word of mouth until written
down many centuries after their formulation and introduction into
the processes of oral transmission.

That supposition was applied to the Mishnah, where it certainly
fit, and to the several compilations of midrashic traditions assembled from late talmudic times to the early modern period, where
it manifestly does not. But if people assumed that every version
represented a singular and authentic oral tradition, as valid a wit-
ness to the "original" formulation as any other, then they would
be unable to cope with, or even take seriously, the differences between one example of a story and the next. Since, moreover, a
pseudo-orthodox spirit of piety tends to prevail nearly everywhere,
it is difficult for scholars to raise searching questions, to call into
doubt the "historicity" of stories, sayings, and the attribution of
exegeses to particular masters of ancient times. Whether confess-
edly or otherwise, the larger number of students of talmudic and
midrashic literature take for granted that "chronological rules do
not pertain" applies to the oral Torah as much as to the written
one. Consequently they discern no sequence of development in a
given tradition for, as noted, each version is therefore uncommon,
except within fundamentalist, unhistorical presuppositions.

This brings us to the first of my two cases intended in a simple way to show how — over a sequence of documents, read in
the order of closure and completion — sages made up sayings and
stories, a case that is stimulated by a case familiar to New Testament scholarship. In *New Testament Apologetic,* Barnabas Lindars
shows that Mark 12:35–7 "is evidently derived from the exegesis preserved in Acts 2:34."[1] The pericope is seen as a product
of community-theology. Lindars says, "We conclude that the argument in Acts 2 preserves the original and fundamental use of Ps.
110:1, and that the Gospel passage about David's son represents
a slightly later stage, when the Davidic controversy has arisen. It
thus shows the use of this testimony in secondary and derivative
application." As in many other respects, New Testament scholars

---

1. London, 1961, pp. 46–47.

help students of the formation and development of rabbinic literature by indicating some of the possibilities of criticism. Here I shall
offer some examples of a similar development, from the exegesis of
a scripture to a story about a named master. I do not claim that the
procedures here followed reach the level of sophisticated analysis
manifest throughout Lindars's work.

The phenomenon to which I wish to call attention is relatively
obvious, and synoptic analysis will substantiate it. In a version of
a pericope appearing in an early collection, the exegesis of a scripture is given anonymously, then attributed to a master. In a version
appearing in a later stratum, the exegesis is turned into a story
*about* the master, concerning whom the original scripture then is
cited not infrequently. Having shown the existence of the phenomenon, I shall then suggest its implication for a pericope in which
we cannot demonstrate its presence.

Two examples suffice. The first is Hillel and the vain prayer.
The Mishnah states that if one is coming along the way and hears
an outcry and says, "May it be his will that this does not come
from my house," that is a false prayer. We then find the following
(Y. Ber. 9:3):

> He was coming from the way, what does he say? "I am sure that
> these are not in my house."
> Hillel the Elder says, "From a bad report he does not fear." (Ps.
> 112:7).

The next version is attributed to Tannaim, with (1) the redactional superscription: "Our rabbis taught" (*Teno rabbanan*), then
(2) a duplicated superscription, story about (Ma'aseh b). It follows
(B. Ber. 60a):

> Hillel the Elder was coming from a journey, and he heard the sound
> of an outcry in the city. He said, "I am sure this is not my house."
> And of him scripture says, "From a bad report he does not fear.
> His heart is steadfast, trusting in the Lord" (Ps. 112:7).

Hillel's "exegesis" of Ps. 112:7 thus has become a story, and the
verse of scripture earlier cited concerning Hillel is made to say
in the second story what anyone is supposed to say according
to the first. I take it for granted that the Bavli version comes
later than and is based upon the Palestinian Talmud's version. The
word-for-word correspondences make this virtually certain, and
the movement from an anonymous to a named teaching decisively
points to the dependence of the Babylonian upon the Palestinian
(prior) version.

But the fact that the latter — the earlier, Palestinian talmudic version — has no Tannaite attribution calls into question the notion that merely because a passage is introduced, "our rabbis have taught" or in a similar way, that means the passage "goes way back" to Tannaite times. To the contrary, those attributions serve a different purpose from a "historical" one. They assign to a passage Tannaite status, meaning, Tannaite authorities — professional memorizers of authoritative traditions — in the talmudic circles of Babylonia have repeated as authoritative the following story. That is a claim of hierarchization of stories or sayings, not a claim as to their historical origin. The upshot of course is the same: the saying or story is authoritative, but it is not because of its point of historical origin, rather because of its sponsorship, that is, its acceptance into Tannaite tradition. The hundreds and hundreds of cases in which Mishnah-repeaters are instructed by talmudic authorities, centuries after the closure of the Mishnah, to reword a Mishnah-passage to accord with the reasoning or logic of the academy that day shows the true facts of the matter. The scholars who adduce in evidence of first-century Judaism anything bearing the sign TN' err.

The second example concerns Hillel and the poor man. It is one of my favorite examples of how stories gain weight as they travel from document to document — something that will hardly surprise New Testament scholars. The tale starts with a completely anonymous exegesis. Then Hillel is introduced, in the same stratum, and to him is attributed the antecedent exegesis. The pericope begins with the law that one gives to a needy person according to his customary usage. If he normally requires a silver coin (M'H), they give it to him; if he is normally fed by hand, they feed him by hand, "As it is said, 'According to his need' (Deut. 15:8)" on which we have the anonymous gloss, "even a slave, even a horse." Then comes the rest of the verse. And there follows a Hillel story, introduced by Ma'aseh (T. Peah 4:10):

> Hillel the Elder purchased for one poor man, son of good parents, a horse that was to work for him and a slave that was to serve him.
>
> Further the story is told concerning the men of Galilee who would bring up for a certain elder a litre of meal in Sepphoris every day.

Clearly, the anonymous antecedent exegesis of Deut. 15:8 has now been developed into a Hillel story. All that is added to the extant exegesis itself are the qualifying words after "horse" and "slave." To this then is supplied the name of Hillel and his purchase for one poor man. The Galilean story is a good example of a story not shaped according to the exegesis of Deut. 15:8. It ignores it, in general and in detail, and serves merely as an illustration. Perhaps the adjectival clauses ("that was working...," etc.) are glosses.

Let us now see what happens to the story. It next occurs in Y. Peah 8:7, where it is cited without significant change. But then, in the Babylonian Talmud's stratum (B. Ket. 67b), we have the following:

> Hillel the elder bought for one certain poor man, son of good parents, a horse to ride upon and a slave to run before him.
> One time he did not find a slave to run before him, and he ran before him for three miles.

Two facts are remarkable. First, the scripture itself is dropped and with it the exegesis! The slave now runs before the man, rather than merely serving him. Second, this introduces an entirely new element: that Hillel could not find the slave, so he ran before the man for three miles. The Galilean story immediately follows, which proves that the original materials were before the person responsible for the Hillel pericope, and he made the changes we observed — presumably without referring to some independent "oral" tradition about what Hillel once upon a time did.

Now, if I may make up a source that we do not have (as we shall see later on New Testament scholars are happy to accomplish when they come to rabbinic literature!), I might imagine that some medieval compilation concerning Deut. 15:8 is going to add another, still more heroic gesture. This is what it will say (when we find it):

> One day he could not find a horse, so he carried him on his back instead — for ten miles.

Since we do not yet have that story, we return to reality. We have as fact only what the sources tell us. To be sure, I could always accuse doubters of lacking imagination. For example, not having sources does not prevent E. P. Sanders from criticizing me for not paying heed to nonexistent sources and what they "must" have contained. Sanders says, in so many words, "Neusner, in fact, has proposed that this was true of the early rabbis. This shows a lack of imagination and a failure to consider the accident of survival." What can anyone say, beyond, "What we cannot show, we do not know" — except to add, "and may not invent."

Clearly, even within a single pericope, we observe the development of an anonymous exegesis into a Hillel story. In later versions — that is, versions occurring in documents that reached closure later on — the exegesis will be dropped and the story embellished. In losing the exegesis, the embellishment can introduce new details prevented by the language of the exegesis itself. So, like Lindars, I claim that the exegesis comes before the story; the Hillel story is secondary, derivative, and invented. Yet it goes without saying, "historians" working in both rabbinic and New Testament materials cite stories about Hillel, including this one, to tell us what "the historical Hillel," supposedly the contemporary of Jesus, was like. And that they call critical history, which is supposed to tell us about the historical Jesus as against the Christ of faith. But all we have in Hillel stories is the Hillel of faith.

Readers will want more than one example. To provide another, I shall now offer the theory that one version of the Hillel and the *prozbul* tradition — Hillel invented the *prozbul,* which suspends the remission of debts in the seventh year, to make sure the poor can borrow money — consists of a similar development of exegeses of Deut. 15:3 and Deut. 15:9. Let us consider an earlier compilation of Hillel *prozbul* materials, the version of Sifré Deut. 113:

> "Whatever of yours that is with your brother your hand should release" (Deut. 15:3) — but not in the case of him who gives his mortgages into the safekeeping of the court [which is not subject to the remission of debts in the seventh year].
>
> > On this basis (MK'N) they said
> > Hillel ordained the *prozbul.*
> > On account of the order of the world.
>
> He saw the people, that they held back from lending to one another and transgressed what is written in the Torah.
> He arose and ordained the *prozbul.*
> And this is the formula of the *prozbul:* "I give to you, so-and-so and so-and-so the judges in such-and-such place, every debt which I have, that I may collect it whenever I like," and the judges seal below, or the witnesses.

What do we see here? We notice, first of all, an anonymous exegesis, which is then tied to Hillel's ordinance of the *prozbul.* The exegesis avers that debts in the hands of a court are not released in the seventh year. The rest of the pericope is supposed to depend upon that exegesis. In fact, the second part is unrelated to it. After telling us that Hillel ordained the *prozbul* on the basis of the exegesis of Deut. 15:3, the second and separate part of the peri-cope tells us he saw that the people held back from lending to one another and transgressed what is written in the Torah. He there-fore ordained the *prozbul*. We are not told what is written in the Torah! The second story is a play on the nominal and verbal forms of *tqn*: Hillel *ordained* (*htqyn*) the *prozbul* on account of the order (*tyqwn*) of the world.

An event is one time; a historical event really happened. The allegation that a historical event took place ("he saw...he or-dained...") on which the second explanation of the *prozbul* allegedly is based poses a problem. For the same conditions that in Hillel's time supposedly created a crisis and led to his enacting the *prozbul* surely pertained for many centuries before. How can one explain that "just this time" the people discovered the disadvan-tages of the sabbatical year? In fact, the "historical" version refers, without making it explicit, to the evil impulse described in Deut. 15:9–11, "Take heed lest there be a base thought in your heart and you say, 'The seventh year, the year of release is near,' and your eye be hostile to your poor brother and you give him nothing. You shall give to him freely... because for this the Lord your God will bless you.... For the poor will never cease out of the land." The absence of an explicit reference to this scripture is striking, for it is introduced in later versions. The story about people's not lend-ing before the year of release "at just the time of Hillel" takes the place of scripture's description of this same "event." So the story serves as an "exegesis" through a historical narrative, which is a paraphrase of Deut. 15:9–11. When other exegeses are turned into historical narratives about Hillel's deeds or events of his day, they normally are tied to the explicit citation of scripture, which we do not have here.

It remains to observe that the composite pericope ignores Hillel at the end; the formula of the *prozbul* is cited but not attributed to him. So what has happened is that two stories have been joined together. One is the citation and exegesis of Deut. 15:3; then, "On this basis, Hillel ordained the *prozbul,* and this is the formula," etc. The other is simply "Hillel ordained... on account of the re-pair of the world. He saw the people, that they held back.... He arose and ordained...."

If there are two versions, how can we account for them? That seems to be a necessary question, since part of our task as exegetes (not historians anymore) is to speculate on why a given version of an event or saying has been fabricated. In the Talmud we have ample occasions on which we are told in so many words precisely why a story is "revised" or made up fresh. Can we speculate on that matter for the two stories at hand?

The viewpoint of the first version is that Hillel's action was based upon sound exegesis of scripture. Hillel did not modify the law merely to accommodate the law to historical circumstances. The law always had been what Hillel now said. He recognized that fact and acted upon it. His greatness is in recovering the tradition, not in inventing new laws to meet the needs of the time. Then Hillel gives no aid and comfort to Reform Judaism (a conclusion that, as we shall see, Samuel Sandmel, a Reform theologian, never reached in his account of the historical Hillel). The second and contrary tendency ignores the exegesis of Deut. 15:3. Hillel indeed did change the law to meet social or historical needs. The decree that it was "for the good order of the world" has no exegetical basis. Therefore one spells out the specific problem. Likewise others who wish to issue *taqqanot* (reforms) are justified in doing so as circumstances require. The same question I have introduced in my reading of the two versions was raised in the names of second-century authorities with reference to Yohanan b. Zakkai's ordinances, but not with regard to Hillel's.

So the two stories circulated separately. Let us follow along part of their way. The first version occurs in *Midrash Tannaim*.[2] Here the exegesis is given anonymously, then explicitly attributed to Hillel:

> "Whatever of yours" — not he who gives.
> On this basis Hillel ordained the *prozbul:* And thus did Hillel expound, "Whatever of yours is with your brother" — he who gives his mortgages to the court.

The second part thus assigns the anonymous exegesis to Hillel, but this repeats the exegesis and then ignores the usage "on this basis," which is integral to the first part. Therefore the second looks like a gloss intended to make clear what is obvious. The next and most interesting instance is in Mishnah-tractate Shebiit 10:3:

> A loan secured by a *prozbul* is not released (by the advent of the Seventh Year).
> This is one of the things that Hillel the Elder ordained.
> For he saw that the people refrained from giving loans to one another (as the seventh year approached) and were transgressing

---

2. Ed. Hoffmann, p. 80.

what is written in the Torah, "Beware that there be not a base
thought in your heart" (Deut. 15:9).
    Hillel ordained the *prozbul.*

Now we have the version omitting the exegesis of Deut. 15.3 altogether. But instead the pericope provides both a citation of Deut.
15:9 and the historical reason! The two versions of Sifré Deut.
clearly circulated separately. As a separate pericope, the historical version has been given a new form. First, the exegesis of Deut.
15:3 is dropped — this is quite appropriate — and a new superscription is supplied in its place. Judah the Patriarch, to whom is
attributed the authorship of the Mishnah, then preferred for the
Mishnah the story that traces the *prozbul* to historical necessity.
It provided a precedent for two important propositions. First, Judah's ancestor — he supposedly claimed he was Hillel's descendant,
and that claim is confirmed in tractate Avot's chain of tradition
in a document that came to closure about fifty years after Judah's Mishnah was published — had exercised enormous power.
Second, the patriarch, or *nasi,* does not have to rely upon exegesis, but can do pretty much whatever he wants in response to
historical conditions. The *nasi,* whether Hillel or Judah, has the
power and authority to change the law on account of contemporary necessities and does not have to rely upon tradition, whether
explicit or formulated through exegetical means and validated by
the consensus of the schools. This conforms to Judah's tendency in
selecting materials of Yohanan b. Zakkai. He in general preferred
those materials that served as useful precedents in the conduct
of the patriarchate, and, in particular, he consistently portrayed
Yohanan's decrees of Yavneh as based upon historical necessity,
not on exegetical foundations. The Ushans, by contrast, just as
consistently supplied an exegetical basis and claimed Yohanan had
done nothing new.
    To complete our survey of the peregrinations of the exegesis/
law/tale: M. Git. 4:3 supplies merely the stock phrases, "Hillel ordained the *prozbul*" "on account of the order of the world." Then
the Palestinian Talmud, at Y. Sheb. 10:2, is based upon the historical version cited above. The rabbis therefore ask how could
Hillel have ordained an ordinance against the law of the Torah.
The absence of an explicit exegetical basis provokes the effort to
cite, then harmonize, the two separate and conflicting justifications
for the *prozbul* ordinance. The Babylonian Talmud, at B. Git. 36a,
has a similar discussion: "Is it possible that according to the Torah

the Seventh Year releases debts, yet Hillel ordained it should not
be so?" The pericope thus shows no knowledge of the exegesis of
Deut. 15:3. The exegetical foundations of the *prozbul* play no rule;
the rabbis of the discussion assume that it was only a response to
historical necessity. Then it would appear the exegetical element in
the Sifré Deut. 113 version was not known to the ones who wrote
up that discussion.

So what have we learned? Exegeses of Deut. 15:3, 8–10 are
turned into Hillel stories of one kind or another. The discussion
of the poor and what is to be done for them yields exegesis, law,
and fable, all having to do with Hillel. When, at Acts 2, we find
a reading of Ps. 110:1, which in Mark 12:35–37 is turned into a
story about Jesus, we deal with a comparable phenomenon: the
same thing in a variety of genres. In its own terms, this kind of result vastly enriches our understanding of what we are reading. In
historical terms, the same result marks as simply beside the point
all speculation on whether or not Hillel "really" did or said what
was attributed to him. No one in the writings at hand conceived
that that question should be asked. If pressed, I should claim two
reasons: first, because whoever told stories took for granted the
stories really did happen; second, because historicity defined an
issue no one addressed or even recognized. When we tell Hillel
fables as historical fact, we miss the point of those fables, which
is moral and religious. For when we have determined they are not
historical facts, we have said nothing interesting about them.

In the foregoing remarks, I dismissed as false the broadly held
conception that what bears the mark of Tannaite sponsorship is
earlier, and therefore more authentic, than what does not. From
the time of the editing of the Talmud and the earliest discussions
of its history, it has been an axiom that Babylonian talmudic *beraitot,* external traditions, marked by TNY', TNW RBNN, and
similar redactional elements, indeed derive from Tannaitic times,
along with the Mishnah and the Tosefta and the so-called Tannaite midrash-compilations — Mekhilta attributed to R. Ishmael,
Sifra, and the two Sifrés. It is now perfectly clear that the Tosefta
and the Tannaite midrash-compilations are post-mishnaic, since
they cite the Mishnah throughout, and that the Tannaite midrash-
compilations also are post-Tosefta, since they cite the Tosefta and
gloss that too. But what about the sayings and tales of the Talmuds
that bear the mark TNY and its parallels? It is time that we examined that "established fact," which has permitted historians of the
Jews to take for granted that TNY, or whatever is in the Tosefta,

or whatever is in the Tannaite midrashim, tell us about second- and even first-century opinion and history. The entirety of Moore's *Judaism*, as I said, rests upon that very premise.

That axiom has survived because of the reliance of literary critics upon the results of traditional historians and because of the uncritical reliance of those historians on the few "early" traditions that address historical questions. When, however, one examines the relationship between Babylonian talmudic *beraitot* and corresponding materials either clearly Amoraic or actually transmitted in the name of Palestinian sages, the picture changes. We shall here examine one of the many scores of pericopes in which a Babylonian talmudic *beraita* — that is, a passage not found in a Tannaite document such as the Mishnah but nonetheless bearing the marking of Tannaite origin and so assumed to belong to the first or second century — looks to be a development of an Amoraic lemma. Let us start with the Babylonian Talmud's story:

A. Our rabbis taught (TNW RBNN):

B. The story is told about (M'SH B) a certain man whose sons did not conduct themselves in a proper manner. He arose and wrote his estate over to Jonathan b. 'Uzziel.

C. What did Jonathan b. 'Uzziel do? He sold a third, consecrated a third, and returned a third to his sons [of the man].

D. Shammai came upon him with his staff and bag.

E. He said to him, "Shammai, if you can take back what I have sold and what I have consecrated, you can also take back what I have returned. But if not, neither can you take back what I have returned."

F. He exclaimed, "The son of 'Uzziel has confounded me, the son of 'Uzziel has confounded me."

—B. Baba Batra 133b–134a (trans. L. W. Slotki, p. 562)

The legal principles are of no great interest here. The story presents some odd points. Shammai appears from nowhere. He is planning to debate with Jonathan but cannot get a word in edgewise; Jonathan refutes what Shammai has never said; he is left to confess he has been confounded. The story serves the purpose of showing that one cannot transfer inheritances, even from bad sons to good ones. The story is contained in a set of fables on how great Jonathan b. 'Uzziel was; the above story is part of that little "tractate." The story seems to be a unity, but only if it depends on Y. Ned. 5, 6, below. Otherwise, part D–F is certainly separate, for we have no hint of Shammai's involvement in part A–C. Let us now see the version in the earlier of the two Talmuds:

A. R. Yosé b. R. Bun said, "This was a case: The father of Jonathan bar 'Uzziel prohibited by vow from deriving benefit from his property. He went and wrote them over to Shammai.

B. "What did Shammai do? He sold part, consecrated part, and gave (Jonathan) the rest as a gift.

C. "And he then said, 'Whoever comes and complains against this gift — let him get it back also from the possession of the purchaser and from the possession of the sanctuary, and then he can come and get it back from this one (Jonathan).'"

—Yerushalmi Nedarim 5:6

The Palestinian version of the Jonathan story is strikingly different from the Babylonian *beraita*. Here the gift is to Shammai, who acts in behalf of Jonathan by saving for him part of the father's property. Shammai's presence is now comprehensible. The classification is a story about Shammai; no new legal principle evidently is involved, though one is immediately inferred. The context, however, is identical to the Babylonian: the composite that tells how Hillel had eighty disciples, then Hillel's death scene, then R. Yohanan remarks, "This one is discerned to be a disciple of the sage." Then comes R. Yosé b. R. Bun as above. The story certainly is a unitary composition. No element comes as a surprise; nothing is intruded.

The comparison between the two stories yields a simple fact. One version completely reverses the account of the other. The first question is, Which comes first? It seems to me that the Palestinian version absolutely must precede the Babylonian *beraita,* and that the latter certainly had to have been shaped in complete dependency upon it The decisive fact is the intrusion of Shammai into the Babylonian version in D. The Babylonian *beraita* has translated the Palestinian Talmud's superscription into its own conventional superscription involving both Tannaite authority and *ma'aseb b.* It has supplied the reason for the disinheritance. In the Palestinian version we understand at the very outset why Jonathan was included — it was his own father. In the Babylonian, we are as mystified by the gift to Jonathan as by the intrusion of Shammai. The Babylonian concretizes his part to one-third, obvious but still an improvement. The action of Shammai in the Palestinian version is now copied by Jonathan in the other. Since Shammai is involved in the Palestinian one, the Babylonians have to invent a dramatic encounter to bring in Shammai. Now "whoever will come" is turned into "Shammai, if you can talk back...."

Since the Babylonian version is certainly later than the Palestinian one, we cannot avoid the conclusion that someone has intentionally changed Yosé b. R. Bun's story into an account hostile to Shammai and marked it as a *beraita*. That party must be a Babylonian of the fourth-century Pumbeditan school. Clearly the Babylonian account depends on important literary details in the Palestinian one so, as I said, we cannot readily imagine that the two versions circulated separately; we must rather suppose the Babylonian comes later than and represents a thoroughgoing revision of the Palestinian. Why would a fourth-century Babylonian have taken a story friendly to Shammai and turned it into a hostile account in which Shammai confesses his utter humiliation? I doubt that issues pertinent to the actual life and times of Shammai could still have aroused much vigorous interest in fourth-century Babylonia. Nor can anyone have wanted to make much of Jonathan b. 'Uzziel on the basis of Shammai's humiliation, except those responsible for the other materials on Jonathan in the same complex of pericopes in B. B. 134a. In that case, we must supply a fourth-century date to the whole set of Jonathan b. 'Uzziel pericopes.

It seems to me that such a circle would have been unfriendly to the Pumbeditan tradents who made use of Yohanan b. Zakkai as an example of how the true leadership of Israel devolved from Hillel not to Gamaliel, his son, but to Yohanan b. Zakkai, his best disciple. The obvious point was that the leadership of Israel now belongs not to the heir of Hillel/David, but to the sage. In that case the story humiliating Shammai would have released the opposition to sages who were denigrating heirs of Hillel, that is, David after the flesh — sages who served a master claiming to descend from David, therefore to be related to Hillel — the exilarch. The revision of Yosé b. R. Bun's story clearly served the polemical interests of such a circle. The humiliation of Shammai carried out the purposes of the circle friendly to the exilarch and hostile to the exilarch's critics, the circle that preserved stories of Yohanan b. Zakkai as Hillel's true heir.

So the revision of Hillel-Shammai materials relates to Babylonian politics, just as the citation of Yohanan b. Zakkai materials serves partisan purposes in the same place. As it stands, Yosé b. R.

Bun's story about Shammai is one of the few late stories in which Shammai appears as a genuine hero, a master of law and possessed of considerable virtue. We have no reason to imagine that that Yosé held any living traditions from the time of Shammai, nearly three centuries earlier. What motivated his fabrication of the story, however, is not clear to me. Why out of such a mishmash of fourth-century materials anyone should ask us to believe that we derive information on the first century B.C.E. — the time of Hillel and Shammai — I cannot say.

But, we shall now see, colleagues routinely present us with "history," "critical history," "the Jesus of history as opposed to the Christ of faith," their own fabrications based on precisely this kind of evidence. So from the true character of the rabbinic literature, let us turn to examine just how things are now being done by perfectly reputable scholars who present themselves as and are taken to be "critical" and "historical," as against Christian believers who (merely) take the Gospels as an account of the truth (as distinct from a set of historical facts) about Jesus Christ, God incarnate, who rose from the dead and sits with the Father in heaven (to use the language of Christianity). The historical Shammai, the historical Hillel, the historical Jesus — indeed!

# PART TWO

# HOW RABBINIC LITERATURE IS PRESENTLY USED FOR HISTORICAL PURPOSES

# 4

# If We Cannot Show It: Pseudo-orthodoxy and Pseudocriticism

Only when we have taken a detailed look at how people think the rabbinic literature serves for recovering the history of the Jews and Judaism in the first century will the strictures that I set forth in the prologue take on urgency. For my characterization of scholarship (people assume we know things about this literature that we cannot show and therefore do not know) will strike readers as implausible and extreme until they examine how people actually work today. When readers examine the character and premises of current academic writing, they will realize that my remarks are understated and moderate, in harsh emphasis wholly insufficient to the sad facts of the present condition of learning. My description of the uses of the rabbinic literature will appear to caricature the state of affairs until the actualities of what has been published on a single topic come under close inspection.

Accordingly, in this and the following chapters I show that, if anything, I understate matters. Ordinarily critical scholars abandon all pretense of criticism when they open rabbinic literature, ignoring its traits and history of documentary fabrication and imputing to it traits of historicity and facticity that literature does not exhibit or pretend to value. What I wish to show through this survey of opinion and the use of evidence in support of said opinion is simple. It is the striking contrast between the character of the evidence and the way in which scholars have made use of that evidence in presenting precisely how things were in the first century.

Enough has been said so far for readers to expect to observe a variety of unfounded presuppositions and undemonstrated propositions attached to these documents. But the entire dimensions of the abyss between the critical agendum of our century, as exposed in biblical scholarship in history and exegesis, and the uncritical reading and use of rabbinic literature for New Testament studies, can scarcely be imagined.

What we shall now see is evidence to support two propositions. (1) Nearly all New Testament scholars who have turned to rabbinic literature for studies on the Pharisees take for granted that they may use rabbinic writings in a way in which they never would imagine reading the New Testament counterparts. Where there is a critical dimension, it is episodic, therefore capricious and not systematic. (2) Their uncritical reading is abetted by nearly all scholars of Judaism (inclusive of the history of the Jews), for they read the same literature as though it were a collection of indisputable facts.

In both cases where the scholars claim to do "critical history" — on the Israeli side and in American rabbinical seminaries — it is within the premise: if you can't show it didn't happen, you have to believe it happened. More to the point, the kinds of questions they imagine they can answer to begin with impute to the rabbinic literature a standard of historical facticity — people really said what is attributed to them, people really did the things people claimed they did — that the same scholars allege they do not conceive the writings meet at all. At no point do most of the scholars of Judaism (whether of Jewish or gentile origin) introduce those critical considerations that are counterpart in historical study in general. Nearly all may be characterized as credulous and gullible when it comes to allegations as to fact made by rabbinic documents. The introduction of pseudocritical considerations ordinarily forms a symptom of pseudo-orthodoxy, as I shall explain.

I call the work we are about to examine "pseudocritical" in the context of "pseudo-orthodoxy," a word that derives from Morton Smith.[1] Smith defines pseudo-orthodoxy as "the attempt to reconcile the traditional beliefs about the OT with the undeniable results

---

1. "The Present State of Old Testament Studies," *Journal of Biblical Literature* 88 (1969): 19–35.

of scholarship." Of greatest interest here are Smith's remarks about higher criticism,

> which has always been the bête noire of the pseudo-orthodox. They were clever enough to see that its results had to be accepted. On the other hand, to attack higher criticism was the accepted way of vindicating pseudo-orthodoxy. Therefore higher criticism had to be both attacked and accepted. What could be done? The solution was: to concentrate the attack on the greatest and most famous representative of higher criticism, to announce to the public that his "system" had been destroyed, and to appropriate privately its elements.

Smith's pseudo-orthodox and our pseudocritical scholars have only the "pseudo" in common. The pseudocritical scholars claim to accept a critical approach. But in pretending that the sources are accurate historical records, and in failing to articulate and defend that notion, they reveal the fundamentalist convictions that they both hold and claim to transcend. They do not argue with the critical scholars. They either vilify or ignore them. Or the pseudocritical scholars will allege that they grant the presuppositions of the opposition and then completely bypass them, pretending nothing has changed. We shall therefore see here the opposite of Smith's pseudo-orthodox: pseudocritical scholars who announce to the public that they are "critical," but in reading the rabbinic literature for the study of New Testament history and exegesis they in fact appropriate nothing whatever of the literary and historical-critical advances of the past century and a half of biblical studies.

What commonly characterizes the pseudocritical school are some or all of these qualities:

1. the use of deductive reasoning;

2. the making of arbitrary and groundless judgments as to the historicity and the lack of historicity of various individual pericopes;

3. the failure to bring to bear a wide range of evidence external to the talmudic materials;

4. the assumption that whatever is alleged in any source is as well attested as what is alleged in any other;

5. the endless positing of untested and untestable possibilities;

6. the recurrent claim that a story "must have been supported by tradition";

7. the repeated argument that if a story were not true, no one would have told or preserved it;

8. the spinning out of large theories to take account of stories and sayings under some grand philosophical scheme (which is not much different from the next);

9. the invention of new definitions for old data;

10. the use of "presumably," "must" or "may have been," and "perhaps," a few sentences later magically converted into "was" and "certainly."

Every one of these ten no-nos is exposed in the writings we examine in Part Two of this book. The pseudocritical scholars claim to write history, but the historicity of their histories is superficial, not profound. They concentrate on the exegesis of discrete pericopes.

I take as a prime example the language and sources that are supposed to portray the historical Hillel in the writing of an otherwise entirely reputable, sedulously critical New Testament scholar, Helmut Koester:

Hillel. What would give to later rabbinic Judaism its characteristic mark was the practice of legal interpretation in the Babylonian synagogue. Hillel (who lived until about 20 CE) came from Babylon. He may have also studied in Jerusalem, but his exegetical principles, which together with his humaneness became determinative for rabbinic Judaism, reveal the diaspora situation, for which legislation related to the temple cult and to living conditions in an overwhelmingly Jewish country were of only academic interest. This perspective as well as his great gifts as a teacher made Hillel the father of rabbinic Judaism — much more so than his famous exegetical rules, like the conclusion *a minore ad maius* and the conclusion from analogy. In contrast, his often-quoted opponent Shammai represents a branch of Pharisaism which was closely related to the temple. Shammai is aristocratic, severe, and nationalistic. But Gamaliel I, Hillel's successor as the head of his school (probably a son of Hillel), had also become a member of the Jerusalem aristocracy. He was a member of the Jerusalem sanhedrin who became famous for his wisdom (and as such he appears in Acts 5:34–39), though he may have distanced himself sometimes from the prevailing opinion of that institution, as is indicated by the report of the Book of Acts. However, Gamaliel's son Simeon became the leader of the Pharisaic war party and was associated with the first government of the revolutionaries, although he later had to make room for a more radical leadership. This Pharisaic war party can be largely identified with the Shammaites with whom Simeon, grandson of Hillel, perished in the chaos of the Jewish war.[2]

Not analyzing a single source or even presenting the language for examination, Koester presents a pastiche of allusions to references to Hillel in a diverse body of writings, some of them separated from the time in which Hillel lived by only two hundred years, others by five hundred or even much longer.

On the same scale, a life of Jesus should incorporate our eclectic choices from not only the canonical but also the noncanonical gospels, not only first-century but fifth- and tenth-century "sources." For example, "Hillel the Babylonian" and merely "Hillel" do not occur side by side. Should we not ask whether overall "Hillel the Babylonian" references present a viewpoint about Hillel different from the merely "Hillel" sources? "His" (Hillel's) exegetical principles are assigned to him only in sources of the fourth century and beyond, four hundred years later. Remembering the opening chapter of this book, we have to ask ourselves: does Koester describe the life of Jesus on the basis of statements of fourth-century church fathers? I think not. The conclusion *a minore ad maius,* for example, is a commonplace in scripture and not Hillel's invention. I can direct him to chapter and verse, both in scripture and in the later rabbinic exegesis of scripture. More than a few passages in the canon of Judaism recognize that fact. He is copying what he read somewhere. He even favors us with the "gentle and humane Hillel" in the tradition of the stories, obviously partisan, that contrast the humane Hillel and the captious Shammai — stories that, in the main, circulated only in the latest parts of the canon. Then, with "But Gamaliel...," we jump into a different body of sources, now drawing on Josephus and Acts for the rest of the tale. So we mix up a rather diverse group of sources, some from the first century, some from the seventh, believing whatever we find in any one of them and forming the whole into a harmonious statement.

Koester has plenty of companions in his school. A well-known and, in his day, formidable Jewish scholar of New Testament, Samuel Sandmel, in his widely read book, *Judaism and Christian*

---

2. Helmut Koester, *Introduction to the New Testament*, vol. 1, *History, Culture, and Religion of the Hellenistic Age* (Philadelphia: Fortress Press, 1982), 406.

*Beginnings,*[3] provides an account of what he at the outset admits are "legends" about some of the holy men of the talmudic literature. But having called the legends legends, he turns them into history. That is to say, there is no difference in the language he uses to describe the historical Jesus and that for the historical Hillel, even though the sources for the former are read with astringent criticism and the latter believed with perfect faith. The rhetoric of a critical position masks what one might describe as a fundamentalist use of sources.

Now why do I insist that what Sandmel calls legends in one sentence he treats as historical facts in another? He tells these stories not in a book about the third- or fourth- or fifth-century development of holy men in Christianity and Judaism as mediators of the sacred, but rather in the context of his description of the state of Judaism in the formative century of Christianity. If it were not for his conviction that these fables told us facts about a real person who really lived at the time of Jesus, he would not have repeated them or paraphrased them; but his entire account is a mere paraphrase of fables. It is self-evident that he would not write about these particular men if he were discussing the Judaism of the third or fourth centuries — the centuries in which the stories he cites first are attested by the redaction (it is generally assumed) of the documents in which they occur. When, therefore, Sandmel chooses for contemporaries of Jesus, Hillel and Shammai, and tells stories about them to help us understand who Jesus was, he clearly wishes the reader to believe that he is telling about people who are contemporaries of Jesus. Sandmel's credulous narrative about Hillel shows that he has treated his "legends" as historical fact:

> Hillel loved his fellow man as deeply as he loved the Torah, and he loved all literature of wisdom as much as he loved the Torah, neglecting no field of study. He used many foreign tongues and all areas of learning in order to magnify the Torah and exalt it..., and so inducted his students.[4]

The voice of this paragraph is the historian; nothing is in quotation marks, and footnotes lead the reader directly to unanalyzed, unquoted sources. The language is thus not of analysis of fables or even (in the spirit of pseudo-orthodoxy) "traditions," but of pure, historical fact.

---

3. Samuel Sandmel, *Judaism and Christian Beginnings* (New York: Oxford University Press, 1978), 236–51.
4. Ibid., 237.

The cited paragraph, in fact, presents nothing but a paraphrase of materials found in rabbinic sources of a far later age than Hillel's own time. None of the sources emerging from the late second century (a mere two hundred years after Hillel is supposed to have lived) knows about Hillel's vast knowledge. Indeed, in an age in which the sources report conflict on whether or not Jews should study Greek and in which only a few highly placed individuals are allowed (in the mishnaic corpus) to do so, no one thought to refer to the "fact" of Hillel's having known many languages. The reason, I think, is that no one knew it until it was invented for purposes of storytellers in the age in which the story was told, whatever these purposes may have been.[5] It follows that to represent Hillel in this way is simply meretricious. If it is the Hillel of legend, then it is a legend that testifies to the state of mind of the storytellers hundreds of years after the time of Hillel (and Jesus).[6] The stories Sandmel tells us on the face of it record absolutely nothing about the age, let alone the person, of Hillel himself. In my judgment, this kind of historiography forms an act of deception.

When Sandmel claims to tell us about the time of Jesus and then arrays before us perfectly routine third-, fourth-, or fifth-century rabbinical hagiography, he is engaged in a restatement as history of what in fact are statements of the cultural aspirations and values of another age than Hillel's. It was one in which, in the present instance, some storytellers appear to have wanted people to ap-

---

5. I cannot point to a single study of why in third- and fourth-century writings, but not in earlier ones, the sages of the first and second centuries get biographies that they formerly had lacked. Yet this was the age of biographies in Greco-Roman life in general, and it also was the time that holy men came to prominence as mediators of the sacred. So the age of the documents that present the tales should make a difference...at least as a matter of hypothesis. But the people will not do the work. It is much easier, after all, to tell fairy tales and impress those Christians who want to hear them. They are not few.

6. It is commonplace to allege that there was a continuous process of oral tradition. But no one has proved in detail, not for all of the documents, not for all of the materials in them. It is a self-serving rationalization for the fundamentalism at hand, not a serious scholarly argument academically demonstrated through tests of falsification and validation. The argument from oral tradition, asserted but unproved, testifies to self-indulgence among people who in their own area know better. It is one thing to show that a given document indicates that it is formulated to be memorized, as I have proved for the Mishnah. It is another to allege on the basis of stories or sayings that all documents, or all traditions now contained in documents, were memorized. That allegation rests on the generalization of a few stories treated as absolute fact: about how God taught the Torah to Moses(!), and the like — fundamentalism at a new low. To this nonsense it suffices to respond: what we cannot show, we do not know; what we have not shown, we cannot adduce as fact.

preciate Torah-learning in a broad and humanizing context (if we may take a guess as to what is at hand in these particular allegations about Hillel). But if, for the turn of the first century, we have evidence that the ideal of Torah-study was not associated with the very movement of which Hillel is supposed to have been part, but of a quite different set of people entirely, then I am inclined to think Sandmel engages in serious misrepresentation of the character of the sources and of the kind of information they provide.

When New Testament scholarship comes to topics important to Judaism, such as the Pharisees, the astringent critical attitude brought to the Gospels in general gives way to perfect faith in whatever tales, whether in the Gospels or in rabbinic literature, the scholar wishes to accept as fact. Even though the New Testament scholar in the liberal Protestant tradition would not dream of writing a life of Jesus through paraphrase of the Gospels, such a scholar confidently paraphrases without a shred of historical criticism and as simple fact the kind of anti-Semitism that the New Testament contains. Here the "historical facts" about the Pharisees come to us in the "woe unto you, scribes, Pharisees, hypocrites" sayings, and the rest follows.

To take only one example among innumerable candidates, Protestant and Catholic alike, Reginald H. Fuller writes:

> The dominant concern of the Pharisaic movement was to preserve inviolate the Mosaic law and its way of life against the encroachments of alien cultures. Since that law had been given once for all through Moses there could be no new laws. Instead, the ancient laws, which had been intended for a more primitive society, had to be reapplied to later situations. In this reapplication there was no thought of introducing novelties: rather, the idea was to extract the real meaning of the law.[7]

Fuller seems not to have noticed the later rabbinic interpretations of the authority of ad hoc rulings made by sages (*taqqanot*). As the Jewish scholars repeatedly claim, considerable efforts were made to change the law, and not merely through reinterpretation or casuistry. In our examination of the *prozbul* attributed to Hillel and the discussions of its origins and authorities, we find in the later rabbinic literature ample evidence that Fuller is simply wrong; but

---

7. In G. Ernest Wright and Reginald H. Fuller, *The Book of the Acts of God: Contemporary Scholarship Interprets the Bible* (New York: Doubleday, 1957), 229–31.

it is not likely that he examined those sources when he set forth to characterize the Pharisees' "dominant concern." He simply caricatures it. Here Fuller shows that he has neither examined the evidence nor read the scholarly literature. Further, he reveals a theological bias:

> There was little attempt to search for an underlying principle behind the numerous commands and prohibitions. The two great commandments, love of God and love of the neighbor, were of course part of the law, but even in combination they were not accorded that central and unifying position which they were given in the New Testament. All this naturally led to legalism and scrupulosity, to a belief in the saving value of good works, and the consequent sense of pride which a doctrine of merit inevitably entailed.

Countless stories make precisely the point Fuller denies was central in the Pharisaic tradition. To Hillel, just as to Jesus, is given the saying that Lev. 19:18 was "the whole Torah," thus surely "central" and "unifying." To be sure, Hillel may never have said any such thing, but such critical considerations do not enter Fuller's argument. Fuller thus misrepresents the Pharisaic position, and one must ask why. The answer follows in his next sentence. The references to legalism and scrupulosity and the saving value of good works tells us that Fuller judges Pharisaic Judaism by the theology of classical Christianity. Legalism is a bad thing; belief in the saving value of good works obviously is inferior to "faith." The theological bias natural to a Christian theologian has prevented Fuller from carefully examining the Pharisaic literature and accurately representing what he finds there.

What is wrong with the Pharisees so far as the scholarship represented by Fuller is concerned simply is that they were not Christians. Therefore one may do with the evidence anything one likes. For example, Fuller writes, "Hellenistic Judaism became a missionary religion. The statement in Matthew 23:15: '...you traverse sea and land to make a single proselyte...' may be an exaggeration, as far as Palestine is concerned, but it was certainly true of the dispersion." Fuller carefully omits the opening part of the saying: "woe unto you, scribes and Pharisees." For Fuller the verse therefore testifies about "Hellenistic Judaism," of which it does not speak, and not about Pharisaic Judaism, to which it explicitly refers. This sort of "revision" of evidence may suit theological purposes, but hardly suggests that the canons of historical-critical inquiry come into play at all.

Fuller's account of the Pharisees is brief and plays no important role in his picture of early Christianity. I use it to exemplify traits that occur in grosser form in other works of the same origin. What it shows is that the large number of Christian scholars of Pharisaism, even in very recent times, (1) do not see differences between theology and history, and (2) do not take the trouble to examine the rabbinic evidences, either accepting or rejecting the whole without careful, thorough study. Of these faults, the second seems from a scholarly viewpoint the more damning, for it means scholars have not even bothered to do their homework. Fuller has merely repeated what he read in some books, decorating the picture with a few of his own embellishments.

Among the historiographical errors of pseudocritical scholars, three are so serious as to render their historical results virtually useless:

1. the failure carefully and critically to analyze the literary and historical traits of every pericope adduced as evidence;

2. the assumption that things happened exactly as the sources allege;

3. the use of anachronistic or inappropriate analogies and the introduction of irrelevant issues.

One or more of these three fundamental fallacies may account for every one of the specific faults listed above, as well as for many not specified. The historians might have learned the need for literary- and historical-critical analysis from classical and biblical scholarship of the past century and a half. Second, they might have proved less gullible and credulous had they taken seriously the historical and philosophical achievements of the Enlightenment, at least its skepticism. Finally, the study of the history of historical scholarship and of the sociology of knowledge ought to have suggested the dangers of anachronism, moralizing, and didacticism.

So much for the pseudocritical and the pseudo-orthodox. Next for the out-and-out believers: what you see is what there was; the sources tell us exactly how things were, depending on which sources you select as factual. That nonsensical mishmash will be shown to understate the results of two Jewish scholars who have told us precisely who Jesus was. To these we now turn.

# 5

# We Do Not Know It:
# Citing Sayings and Identifying
# *Ecce Homo*

If New Testament scholars abandon their critical principles when they approach the rabbinic literature, scholars of Judaism who propose to tell us precisely who Jesus was — *ecce homo* — appear never to have had critical principles to begin with. They read both the Gospels and the rabbinic literature as factual accounts of things really said and done by the people to whom sayings are attributed and about whom stories are told. So I do not exaggerate when I call attention to the hopelessly credulous character of the use of rabbinic literature for New Testament history and exegesis.

We now turn to the subfield of biography and ask how Jewish scholars have used the rabbinic literature to write up their lives of Jesus. We consider first how Harvey Falk proves Jesus was really a Pharisee, and then Geza Vermes's parallel effort to turn Jesus into a Galilean wonder-worker.

In Harvey Falk's *Jesus the Pharisee: A New Look at the Jewishness of Jesus*,[1] we find that Jesus was a Pharisee of the House of Hillel, and he was betrayed by the House of Shammai. While Falk thinks he is telling us things that happened in the first century, he actually discovered all these noteworthy facts in a letter published by Rabbi Jacob Emden to the Polish rabbinate concerning early Christianity. Emden published the letter in 1757. Falk has discovered Emden and proposes to resurrect Emden's thesis.

---

1. New York: Paulist Press, 1985.

In support of this thesis, however, Falk does not devote a single chapter of his book to Jesus. He does not deal with a single work of New Testament scholarship. He quotes his prooftexts from the New Testament without a shred of analysis. In point of fact, he does not commonly quote New Testament passages, but merely alludes to them. They, nonetheless, supply facts, just as the talmudic literature provides him with facts.

These are his chapter headings: "Rabbi Jacob Emden's Views on Christianity"; "Hillel's Convert Revisited, a Second Look"; "Talmud and Jewish Tradition on the Essenes"; "Relationship of the Essenes to Bet [House of] Hillel"; "The Arrest of Rabbi Eliezer and Its Relationship to the Beliefs of the Minim (Jewish Christians)"; "Hasidim of the Nations, Parallel Definitions"; "The Relationship of Rabbi Eliezer to the School of Shammai"; "The Roots of Christian Anti-Semitism: Bet Hillel vs. Bet Shammai"; "Understanding the Christian Bible through Bet Shammai and Bet Hillel." While the New Testament is cited, as are talmudic documents (chapter and verse), not a single passage is subjected to close analysis in a chapter or even in a paragraph. Falk seems to take at face value everything he finds everywhere. His list of modern scholars does not contain the name of a single New Testament scholar.

Let us turn directly to Falk's own words on pp. 30–31:

> Although Judaism never attempted to missionize for converts to its religion, the discussion of the Talmud (Sanhedrin 57a) and especially Maimonides (Melakhim, Chap. 8) would seem to indicate that Moses obligated the Jews to spread knowledge of the Noahide commandments to all mankind. It is surprising, then, that no historical record exists recording such an endeavor. Especially in ancient times, when the world was mired in pagan and barbaric beliefs, one would have expected such a movement.

For the uninitiated, Maimonides is not the same as the Talmud, but Falk routinely invokes medieval commentaries to testify about the state of affairs in the first century.

> I have previously presented Rabbi Jacob Emden's view (Sefer Shimmush and Appendix to Seder Olam) that the original intent of Jesus and Paul was to bring the seven Noahide commandments to the Gentiles, while the Jews should continue their adherence to Judaism. His view is generally unknown outside scholarly circles, although it is recorded in the three major Jewish encyclopedias (*Universal Jewish Encyclopedia* 3:190, *Jewish Encyclopedia* 5:623, and *Judaica* 3:198).

References to this "original intent" of both Jesus and Paul to bring the seven Noahide commandments to the gentiles do not include attention to the sources, only to secondary literature, faithfully cited, volume and page. How do we know what Jesus and Paul originally intended? What sources does Falk adduce in evidence? I see only references to three major Jewish encyclopaedias.

> It might be mentioned here that most scholars have rejected R. Emden's stance. Nor is it my intention here to discuss the pros and cons of his positive views on the founders of Christianity, as Jews are traditionally reticent to discuss other religions, and especially Christianity. But considering the extreme puzzles associated with the Dead Sea Scrolls, and specifically the evidence that Jesus and Paul were acquainted with the Qumran sect — as many phrases from the Christian Bible seem to have been borrowed from the older Scrolls — I would wonder whether R. Emden's thesis might not serve as a key to unravel the mystery.
>
> The majority of the scholarly community agrees that the Qumran sect were members of the Essenes (also known as Hasidim or Tze'nuim in talmudic literature). No doubt can be entertained that the Essenes were extremely observant of the halakha, and no evidence of basic Christological beliefs has been found in the Scrolls.

How does Falk know that the Essenes of Qumran are identical with the Hasidim and the like in talmudic literature? I find no footnote on the page at hand. It may be so, it may not be so. That is not at issue. What is at issue is how we know what we claim to have happened. While the Essenes had law, no one has succeeded in showing that their laws were the same as those of the rabbis, though there are points of intersection. On the contrary, the notions that there was a single halakhah, that at Qumran the halakhah now represented in the rabbinic literature prevailed, and equivalent views enjoy no proof whatever. Falk thinks them plausible or obvious, so they must be so.

> Wouldn't it therefore be quite logical to assume that the opening paragraph of the Manual of Discipline, giving the raison d'être of the sect as "to do what is good and upright...as He has commanded through Moses," would also include spreading the knowledge of the Noahide commandments to the Gentiles, as commanded by Moses? And when they further wrote "to love all the sons of light..." wouldn't that have included Gentiles who observed the Noahide laws? I am not, however, insinuating that Jesus or Paul acted directly in collaboration with the Essenes or any other body.

In his letter to the Council of the Four Lands, Rabbi Emden, in what might be construed as a prophetic statement by a German rabbi rather than a literary slip, urges Christians to help Jews observe the Torah as "commanded to you by your first teachers." He does not mention the names of Jesus and Paul here, but goes on to assure Christians that doing so will bring them reward and blessing. Could this rabbinic giant have sensed — two hundred years prior to the discovery of the Scrolls — that a group of pious Jews some two thousand years ago had sought to help their brethren observe the Torah during the coming exile by making Gentiles aware of its eternal binding character upon the Israelites?

The argument by the asking of questions speaks for itself. Let us, then, move on to another sustained passage so we may taste the full flavor of Falk's book. The following appears on pp. 49–51:

Talmud, Sukkah 28A: "Hillel the Elder had 80 disciples, 30 of whom were worthy of the Divine Spirit resting upon them...30 of whom were worthy that the sun should stand still for them.... The greatest of them was Jonathan ben 'Uzziel, the smallest of them was Johanan ben Zakkai...."

Jerusalem Talmud (Nedarim, end chap. 5): "Hillel the Elder had 80 pairs of disciples...."

Question: Why was R. Johanan ben Zakkai appointed Nasi — rather than one of the other 79, who were greater than he? And what became of the remaining 79?

Question: There seems to be a conflict here between the Babylonian and Jerusalem Talmuds as to whether Hillel had 80 or 160 disciples!

For a proper reply to these queries, I believe we must turn to Hagigah 16A, where the Mishnah speaks of the first dispute that arose among the sages of Israel: it deals with the issue of whether the laying on of hands (on the head of sacrifice) was permitted on a festival. Four succeeding pairs of Nasi (President of the Sanhedrin) and Av-Bet-Din (Vice-President of the Sanhedrin) disagreed, but Hillel and Menahem did not differ. Menahem went forth, Shammai entered (in his place). Hillel and Shammai then disagreed.

R. Jehiel Heilprin (Seder Ha-Dorot 2:271) identifies this Menahem, who first served with Hillel, as Menahem the Essene — whom Herod was fond of for having prophesied his rise to power. Such modern scholars as Kaufmann Kohler and Louis Ginzberg agreed with this identification.

The Talmud to this Mishnah asks what actually happened to Menahem. Abbaye and Rava — two Amoraim who lived during the fourth century C.E. — disagreed concerning this. Abbaye claimed that Menahem went forth into evil ways; Rava states he went forth to the King's service. The Talmud brings a baraita to support Rava's view, where it is stated that Menahem went forth to the King's service, along with 80 pairs of disciples dressed in silk.

This dispute among the later talmudic authorities over what happened to Menahem — probably about 20 B.C.E. — is also cited in the Jerusalem Talmud (Hagigah 2:2), albeit anonymously and with added detail. The first opinion describes Menahem as having left the Pharisees to join a conflicting religious group (the Essenes), which only reiterates Abbaye's negative stance toward Menahem — and the Essenes as well. To Rava's view is added a postscript explaining that Menahem was forced to leave because the Gentiles were coercing (or would soon coerce?) the Jews to abandon their religious beliefs, and he and the 80 pairs of disciples left to remedy this. Rava thus adopts a positive view of Menahem's departure, which according to R. David Fraenkel (Karban ha-Edah), was a mission to reconcile or appease "the nations." (It should be noted here that in scores of disputes between Rava and Abbaye in the Talmud, the view of the former is always — with six specific exceptions — accepted.)

We of course recognize that we are dealing here with an historic-philosophic dispute between Rava and Abbaye, and not one concerning a specific halakha. Also, Rava's statement concerning achieving a reconciliation with the Gentiles calls for further elucidation, as we do not recall mention of such a mission elsewhere.

Returning now to the Baraita of R. Phineas ben Jair mentioned at the beginning of this chapter, we recall that Hasidism was listed as a higher degree of spiritual attainment than Pharisaism; yet the sources would seem to indicate that most talmudic sages did not practice Hasidism — whether on an individual basis or in an organized state, such as the Essenes did. R. Moshe Hayyim Luzzatto, in his classic, Mesillat Yesharim (chap. 13), explains that both Pharisaism and Hasidism involve observance of the Torah beyond the letter of the law, and Pharisaism is also referred to as "Mishnah of the Hasidim," praised by the Prophet Elijah. However, while Pharisaism in the main denotes abstinence and "building fences," which is the first phase of Hasidism, Hasidism itself demands more positive action. We might also note here that Rava is mentioned several times by Luzzatto as one who practiced Hasidism.

Abbaye's negative outlook toward the Essenes and Hasidism might be understood in light of his remark (Berakhot 45A), "Go forth and see how the public are accustomed to act," in concert with Hillel's statement, "An ignorant man cannot be a Hasid" (Avot 2:5). In other words, some religious leaders feared that Hasidism might cause a schism between the laity and the scholarly community. But Luzzatto cites an even greater danger inherent in Hasidism (chap. 20) — namely, that an action in itself may seem worthy enough of performance, but the results might prove harmful. He cites two examples. Gedaliah ben Ahikam, appointed Governor of Judah by the Babylonians, who — because of his Hasidism — refused to accept Johanan ben Kareach's warning concerning Ishmael ben Nathaniah's treacherous intentions (Jeremiah 40). As a result, Gedaliah was killed, the Jews' last hopes for independence at the time were dashed, and Jeremiah considered Gedaliah personally responsible for those murdered by Ishmael. Luzzatto cites as another example the Talmud's condemnation of R. Zechariah ben Avkulot (Gittin 56A), whose act of Hasidism led to the Second Temple's destruction. This is surely why Abbaye and many others shunned (and deprecated) acts of Hasidism which might ultimately cause harm to the people.

And on and on. This, I submit, from the perspective of academic discourse is unintelligible. Why? Because someone who does not know all the sources will never understand what Falk wishes us to make of them.

If we take for granted that whatever is attributed to a rabbi really was said by him, we end up in a kind of fantasy world — a world in which if we ask a question, through what seems "logical" or self-evident, we answer it and so create a fact. No evidence, no analysis of sources, no differentiation among earlier, late, or medieval sources, no recognition that eighteenth-century rabbis were no more present in the first century than was George Washington — none of these simple and obvious traits of mind characterizes Falk's book. True, Harvey Falk is an Orthodox rabbi. But he claims to have an opinion we can subject to rational discourse. Otherwise why publish this book? And why should his Orthodoxy relieve him from the duty of constructing an intelligible argument? Since he writes for the twenty-first century, he has the obligation to speak in the language of the present, not to compose arguments consisting of rhetorical questions, on the one side, or medieval syllogisms (propositions proved by a peculiar deductive logic), on the other.

A distinguished scholar of the Dead Sea Scrolls and of comparative midrash, Geza Vermes, in his New Testament study drawing upon rabbinic literature, cannot of course be confused with Harvey Falk except in premise, presupposition, and method. In his *Jesus the Jew: A Historian's Reading of the Gospels,*[2] he too seems

---

2. New York: Macmillan, 1973.

to believe whatever he finds in the rabbinic literature (except what he chooses not to believe). That permits us to understand how he can adduce, as evidence for a "charismatic" context in which to interpret things Jesus said and did, the character of wonder-workers portrayed in rabbinic sources that reached closure long after the first century. Vermes never demonstrates why we should assume these stories portray a real person and the real things that person said or did. He simply proceeds as though he had in hand a set of facts. Let us consider, first of all, how he treats Honi, the circle-drawer.

> It is known that he was active in Jerusalem before being killed there, but since both the Mishnah and Josephus date the event close to the feast of Passover, he may as easily have been a pilgrim to the holy city as a citizen of the capital. Two of his grandsons, Hanan, his daughter's son, and Abba Hilkiah, his son's son, were also renowned for their powers as rain-makers. From the viewpoint of geographical connections it is of interest to note that in a parallel text Abba Hilkiah, instead of being mentioned by name, is referred to as "a Hasid from Kefar Imi," a village otherwise unknown but appearing in a Galilean context in the passage in question of the Palestinian Talmud. (p. 72)

The footnotes to this passage consist of references to sources; the sources are not themselves examined. If we may translate this farrago of faith into the facts that sustain the faith, this is the language we should have to use:

1. His "it is known" becomes "there is a story that places him in Jerusalem." Incidentally, we may forgive Vermes the lapse of telling us "he was active in Jerusalem before being killed there," even though quite how he could have been active afterward is left unexplained. I doubt that Vermes believes Honi was resurrected from the dead, but then neither does he portray a Jesus who was or could have been resurrected from the dead.

2. His "both the Mishnah and Josephus date the event" becomes "the Mishnah tells the story that...," and "Josephus tells the story that...."

3. His "he may as easily have been..." is simply filler. Vermes is making this up to suit the context. You could as well say "he may not have been" with the same evidence in hand. It appears that the rule is now: what you do not know, you do not have to show; just say it and it becomes so.

4. His "two of his grandsons...renowned" is in fact "about

two figures given names that would make them his grandsons, stories are told that...."

5. His "Abba Hilkiah, instead of being mentioned by name, is referred to as..." becomes "we have a story along the same lines about a Hasid from Kefar Imi," but whether the storyteller meant Abba Hilkiah or someone else about whom the same kind of stories are told, we cannot say. Vermes has not shown that the story parallel to the one told about Abba Hilkiah really refers to Abba Hilkiah ("instead of being mentioned by name"). What we cannot show, we do not know. So why say so?

This little exercise in translation from fable to fact — the literary fact — places Vermes into the camp of Falk. And that carries us to the key to Vermes's Jesus as a "charismatic wonder-worker," namely, the supposed "tradition" in Galilee of charismatic wonder-workers in which, naturally, Vermes locates Jesus as well. Precisely of what does this "tradition" consist? The answer is: stories about Hanina ben Dosa. So let us see how Vermes reads these sources and examine the process that leads him to maintain that the sources record events that really happened, persons that really lived, and the things that they really did. For at stake here is not the character of legends found in the rabbinic literature, but the biography of Jesus of Nazareth: who he really was and what he really did in the time and place in which he lived.

Here Vermes starts with the ritual obeisance to criticism: "The Galilean connections of his descendants, and even more those of Honi himself, remain purely conjectural." Why, then, tell us all about Honi? Vermes proceeds:

> Nevertheless, the hypothesis associating charismatic Judaism with Galilee acquires further support in the incontestably Galilean background of Hanina ben Dosa, one of the most important figures for the understanding of the charismatic stream in the first century AD. In a minor key, he offers remarkable similarities with Jesus, so much so that it is curious, to say the least, that traditions relating to him have been so little utilized in New Testament scholarship. (p. 72)

It is clear, I think, that I do not exaggerate when I insist that rabbinic literature is adduced in evidence of how things really were in the time and place of Jesus. Vermes maintains precisely that view. So let us consider how Vermes uses that evidence.

First, Vermes makes the bow to critical method: "Setting aside various secondary accretions according to which he was a wholesale wonder-worker, the primary rabbinic tradition represents

Hanina as a man of extraordinary devotion and miraculous healing talents." This is a puzzling sentence, since how we know what
are "secondary accretions" to a "primary" tradition is not explained. How we are to distinguish a "wholesale wonder-worker"
from "miraculous healing talents" — or why the distinction makes
a difference — Vermes does not explain. The very next paragraphs
have to be read to see what difference the foregoing "critical" prologue makes: none at all. We have carefully selected language —
"his name first appears..." and "an episode is chosen to illustrate..." — all fine critical initiatives, but then Vermes proceeds
happily to tell his tale as straight biography. I quote him at length,
because otherwise readers will doubt that so eminent a scholar
can have utilized rabbinic stories in such a remarkably uncritical
fashion.

> His name first appears in a chapter of the Mishnah where the early
> Hasid is depicted as spending a full hour on directing his heart
> toward his Father in heaven before starting his prayer proper, his
> rule of concentration being:
>
> > Though the king salute him, he shall not return his greeting.
> > Though a snake wind itself around his ankle, he shall not
> > interrupt his prayer.
>
> An episode in Hanina's life is chosen to illustrate this injunction.
>
> > When Rabbi Hanina ben Dosa prayed, a poisonous reptile
> > bit him, but he did not interrupt his prayer. They (the on-
> > lookers) departed and found the same "snake" dead at the
> > opening of its hole. "Woe to the man," they exclaimed, "bit-
> > ten by a snake, but woe to the snake which has bitten Rabbi
> > Hanina ben Dosa."
>
> As might be guessed, nothing untoward occurred to him, and when
> told later of the frightening event, he is reported to have declared:
>
> > May evil befall me if in the concentration of my heart I even
> > felt it.
>
> According to another version of the story, when Hanina was told
> of the presence of the snake, he asked to be led to its hole and
> deliberately put his foot on it. Whereupon he was bitten but re-
> mained unharmed. The snake, however, died immediately. At which
> Hanina proclaimed:
>
> > It is not the snake that kills, but sin.
>
> The present relevance of the message contained in this story,
> namely that total trust in God and communion with him render
> the holy man immune, is realized once it is understood that the
> ideal fulfilled by Hanina is not unlike that which Jesus set before
> his disciples.

Those who believe may take up/step on snakes...and nothing will harm them.

Hanina's intervention was principally sought in cases of sickness. His fame was such that the outstanding personalities of his own time are portrayed as requesting his help. Nevertheless, though later hailed as the saviour and benefactor of his generation, there are signs that he was in part resented by the leaders of contemporary Pharisaism and by representatives of the later rabbinic establishment.

When the son of his community chief, Yohanan ben Zakkai, fell ill, the father is described as having said to the young man:

"Hanina, my son, pray for him that he may live." He put his head between his knees and prayed; and he lived.

Although the actual cure is tacitly ascribed to God, Hanina's influence on Heaven is indirectly asserted in Yohanan's subsequent comment:

Though ben Zakkai had squeezed his head between his knees all day long, no attention would have been paid to him.

This humble admission of the superiority of the miracle-worker is, however, counterbalanced by a reassertion of Yohanan's momentarily lost dignity. To his jealous wife's question, whether Hanina was greater than he, Yohanan replies,

No, he is like a servant before the king and I am like a prince before the king.

The principal source of the renown won by this Galilean Hasid was his ability to heal from a distance and to announce from there an immediate cure. In this respect, the best story is that which tells of the cure of the son of the famous Gamaliel. The boy was suffering from a mortal fever. The head of the Jerusalem Pharisees therefore despatched two of his pupils to the far-away home of Hanina, who retired to an upper room and prayed, returning with the words:

Go home, for the fever has departed from him.

Incredulous and critical, the novice rabbis asked:

Are you a prophet?

He replied modestly:

I am no prophet, nor am I a prophet's son, but this is how I am favoured. If my prayer is fluent in my mouth, I know that he (the sick man) is favoured; if not, I know that it (the disease) is fatal.

Unimpressed by the explanation the envoys sat down and recorded the date and hour of the alleged cure, and reported the matter to Gamaliel, who happily and admiringly confirmed it.

> You have neither detracted from it, nor added to it, but this
> is how it happened. That was the hour that the fever left him
> and he asked us for water to drink.
>
> The cure from a distance of the centurion's servant (or the son
> of the royal official) belongs to the same category and illustrates
> what seems to have been a recognized charismatic pattern. It is of
> interest to note that both Hanina and Jesus are said to have sensed
> the efficacy of their cures, Hanina, by means of the fluency of his
> prayer, and Jesus, who normally came into bodily contact with the
> sick, by feeling that "power had gone out of him." (pp. 73–76)

The context — placing Jesus into the context of another "stream"
of Judaism of his own time and place, not merely surveying
rabbinic fables about wonder-workers — indicates that Vermes
maintains he is telling us about real people who did the things his
tales say they did at the time that Jesus lived. His entire contribution to the account consists in his paraphrase of his sources. But
paraphrasing tales does not yield critical history — except when
New Testament problems are supposed to be solved by reference
to rabbinic literature. Then we tell fables and declare history.

Readers may consult Vermes's book for more examples of the
same kind of gullibility when it comes to rabbinic fables. I see little
to be gained by further quotations from this narrative. Rabbinic
literature forms a source of labor-saving devices. Open a book and
you have a historical fact. Vermes finds some stories in rabbinic
literature that he thinks run parallel to stories told about Jesus.
He knows that these stories report actual events. He has as fact
that these stories took place in Galilee in the time of Jesus. That is
how — and the only means how — he can invent a Galilean charismatic tradition into which to place Jesus. Vermes has not shown
that these stories tell us about real people who lived at that time
in that place. All he has done is to paraphrase the stories. On that
basis he gives us the man himself: Jesus the Jew, part of a "charismatic Judaism" of Vermes's own making. He has not shown these
stories to provide facts about that time and place; therefore he does
not know there was a "charismatic Judaism" and, it must follow,
whatever Jesus really was or was not has yet to be defined. This
may or may not have been the man. On the basis of what Falk
and Vermes have to tell us, we know nothing more than that Falk
thinks Jesus was a Pharisee, and Vermes thinks he was a Galilean
wonder-worker, part of a supposed "tradition" or "Judaism" — or
"stream of Judaism" or what have you.

# 6

# The "Judaism" of E. P. Sanders

In his *Judaism: Practice and Belief 63 B.C.E.– 66 C.E.*,[1] Sanders
answers every question but the important one: if this was Judaism,
then how come Christianity? He tends to trivialize both, and to
come up with a "Judaism" that did not exist in the first or any
other century of antiquity. In essence, Sanders has given us the
history-of-religions equivalent to a harmony of the Gospels, calling upon sources of diverse origin and character to tell us about
one and the same "Judaism." The people who wrote the books
Sanders quotes, however, would not recognize his Judaism, because it never existed in any one time, place, or circumstance
except in the harmonizing and homogenizing work of Sanders
himself.

Sanders introduces his account of Judaism as "the book I always wanted to write," and he certainly has done a job far
superior to his predecessors. On the day of its publication, his
book replaced Jeremias's *Jerusalem in the Time of Jesus,* and in
many ways it excels other synthetic accounts known to me. That
makes all the more regrettable the errors of method that limit
the book's value. The following three important methods Sanders
employs mark the work as largely idiosyncratic.

First, having paid obeisance to the critical problem, Sanders
proceeds to cite whatever he wants to cite of the Mishnah for
evidence of what he calls "Judaism" as far back as 63 B.C.E. So
Sanders claims to know what is and what is not historical, but he
does not bother to tell the rest of us how he knows. He never ex-

---

1. London: SCM Press, 1992, and Philadelphia: Trinity Press International,
1992.

plains how he knows the difference between what he can use and what he cannot.

Second, he claims to know sources about this Judaism that no one else knows, so that he can tell us what, if we found said sources, they would say.

Third, he is the first scholar to imagine that all sources produced by Jews anywhere, any time, by any sort of person or group, equally tell us about one and the same Judaism. Schürer was far more critical nearly a century ago. The other major "Judaism" books — Bousset-Gressman's or Moore's, for instance — select a body of evidence and work on that, not assuming that everything everywhere tells us about one and the same Judaism.

Sanders's methods therefore call into question the reliability of his account of "Judaism as a functioning religion" with the "accent on the common people and their observances." That is not to suggest we must consign the book to the dustbin of academic curiosities. It is only to say that the work must be used with caution, until it is done again the right way. Sanders has an enormous amount of information in the book. But because he uses it to fabricate a single, unitary Judaism without ever telling us how he harmonizes all these conflicting sources, his *Judaism* is in the end unintelligible.

## I

In his methodological statement, Sanders explicitly tells us, "In this study, I shall sometimes cite second-century rabbinic passages in order to illustrate points; but when I wish to derive hard information about actual practice, I shall take a minimalist view of rabbinic evidence, making use only of material that can be confidently assigned to the early period" (p. 10). But whence this "confidence"? What Sanders does not tell us is the source of his confidence that he knows the difference. Let me give a single instance (p. 89) of how he uses a Mishnah-paragraph to tell us what really happened long before the closure of the Mishnah:

> There is one interesting rabbinic passage that indicates that the sale of birds was subject to the law of supply and demand (and therefore was not monopolistic).
>
> Once in Jerusalem a pair of doves cost a golden *denar* [=25 silver *denars*]. Rabban Simeon b. Gamaliel said: By this Temple! I will not suffer the night to pass by before they cost

but a [silver] *denar.* He went into the court and taught: If a woman suffered five miscarriages that were not in doubt or five issues that were not in doubt, she need bring but one offering, and she may then eat of the animal-offerings; and she is not bound to offer the other offerings. And the same day the price of a pair of doves stood at a quarter-*denar* each. (*Keritot* I.7)

The impurity under discussion is female "discharge" — blood that was not menstruation, of which the most frequent cause was miscarriage. The impurity required a sin offering (usually two birds). The anonymous mishnah (presupposed by the above discussion) states that for five cases that *were* in doubt, a woman need bring only one pair of birds, while for five cases that *were not* in doubt, she could bring one offering and then eat a share of sacrificial food, but she still owed the other four pair of birds, to be paid for later. Simeon b. Gamaliel wished to eliminate this future obligation. The result, we are told, is that the cost of birds fell to 1/100th of the previous value.

The details are at least exaggerated. Not many women, in any one year, had five "discharges" or miscarriages; eliminating four future offerings, thus cutting such women's total expenditure by 4/5th, could not have had such an effect on the overall price. Bird-sacrifices were required for many other purposes, and a fall of 80% in a minor category would not have been a catastrophe for dealers in pigeons. But apart from the details, the story is not unreasonable. People needed advice about what to sacrifice. They consulted experts, usually priests, but possibly non-priestly Pharisees. If their advisers told them that they need bring fewer sacrifices, they could do so with a clear conscience. The cost of sacrifices fluctuated with the market.

Sanders adduces this Mishnah-paragraph in support of the proposition that the sale of birds was subject to the law of supply and demand and therefore was not monopolistic. It seems to me that his "therefore" scarcely follows from the story, which says that it was subject to the monopoly of the temple, which was subject to rabbinical (Simeon b. Gamaliel's) authority. So the story does not prove what Sanders wants it to prove, but that is secondary, though perhaps more common in his use of rabbinic literature than we might wish. What he takes for granted is that Simeon b. Gamaliel could make such a rule and affect prices. But how does he know that fact? Does he then suppose that any reference to this Simeon b. Gamaliel tells us something that really happened: not only did he say it, but he could make it stick? Then why Simeon and not all the other rabbis? If only Simeon, then how have his practical and effective rulings survived, but no one else's? I do not know the answers to these questions, and I do not believe Sanders does either. It suffices, then, to repeat my mantra: if you cannot show it, you do not know it.

When we look at how Sanders wishes to use the passage at hand, we begin to wonder whether such use is legitimate. Let us repeat and closely examine the rationale he gives.

> The details are at least exaggerated. Not many women, in any one year, had five "discharges" or miscarriages; eliminating four future offerings, thus cutting such women's total expenditure by 4/5th, could not have had such an effect on the overall price. Bird-sacrifices were required for many other purposes, and a fall of 80% in a minor category would not have been a catastrophe for dealers in pigeons. But apart from the details, the story is not unreasonable. People needed advice about what to sacrifice. They consulted experts, usually priests, but possibly non-priestly Pharisees. If their advisers told them that they need bring fewer sacrifices, they could do so with a clear conscience. The cost of sacrifices fluctuated with the market.

These are the facts that Sanders knows without showing proof. First, "not many women...." How does he know that? Do we have a gynecological survey? Whence does he know that the "flow" derived from a miscarriage at all? Our sages of blessed memory had a clear knowledge of the difference between miscarriages and other sources of nonmenstrual blood, as a study of tractate Niddah would have told Sanders.

The very passage that Sanders cites makes the distinction between miscarriages and other causes of vaginal flow:

A. The woman who is subject to a doubt concerning [the appearance of] five fluxes,

B. or the one who is subject to a doubt concerning five miscarriages

C. brings a single offering.

D. And she [then is deemed clean so that she] eats animal sacrifices.

E. And the remainder [of the offerings, A, B] are not an obligation for her.

F. If she is subject to five confirmed miscarriages,

G. or five confirmed fluxes,

H. she brings a single offering.

I. And she eats animal sacrifices.

J. But the rest [of the offerings, the other four] remain as an obligation for her [to bring at some later time].

There follows the tale that Sanders cites. Now what is important is that we have a clear distinction between miscarriages and other "fluxes" (in my admittedly imperfect translation), and that distinction runs throughout. Sanders has in mind the demonstration of a critical attitude, so he announces as fact what, the sources make clear, contradicts the premise of the discussion! So the conclusion Sanders draws ignores the distinction that the text that he cites has made.

It is probably needless to ask more questions, e.g., "They consulted experts... but possibly non-priestly Pharisees...." How does Sanders know this, if not from his own suppositions? Since he maintains that the Pharisees were influential, he can add his "possibly." But "possibly" substitutes for proof only if we want it to and, I repeat, what we cannot show, we do not know. All of this is put forth for the purposes of the apologetic that is in fact hidden in parentheses ("and therefore was not monopolistic"). Without that intent, the entire passage could have been omitted with no loss to Sanders's argument in context.

The same kind of analysis occurs throughout the book, but let me give only a single example before moving on. Sanders's pan-Pharisaism persuades him that the slightest evidence proves what he wants it to prove. Thus on p. 226:

> Since this rule about the use of an 'otsar is found in rabbinic litera-ture, and since archaeology shows that someone followed it before 70, we may attribute it to the Pharisees. The revolutionaries who defended Matsada after the destruction of the temple also accepted it; they built miqveh + 'otsar complexes, despite having Herod's ca-pacious single miqva'ot to hand. The defenders of Matsada were Sicarii, and probably very few Pharisees were Sicarii. The infer-ence is that the Pharisaic rule was accepted by at least some other pietists (though not the Qumranians). The distribution of miqveh + 'otsar complexes in Jerusalem is interesting from this point of view: one such complex has been found in the aristocratic Upper City, a good number in the poorer Lower City. There is also one in a Hasmonean palace at Jericho. At least some of the Hasmoneans had accepted the (apparently) Pharisaic theory, as did some of the die-hard revolutionaries and some of the people in the Lower City.

Bypassing the details, let us focus on the "since" clause:

1. The rule is found in rabbinic literature.

2. Someone followed it before 70.

3. We may attribute it to the Pharisees.

Lest this appear to be a lapse, Sanders repeats the same reasoning:

1. The defenders of Matsada were Sicarii.

2. Few Pharisees were Sicarii (he really means: few Sicarii were Pharisees).

3. The inference is that the Pharisaic rule was accepted.

And, of course, what is argued three sentences earlier becomes a fact very quickly, which is, after all, an occupational hazard for us professors (all of us): "At least some of the Hasmoneans had accepted the (apparently) Pharisaic theory." The "apparently" changes nothing.

Let us start from the beginning. Somewhere in rabbinic literature we have a rule. We are not told the details, because they are not supposed to matter. Now, sometime before 70, somebody did something that the rule too says should be done. There is no "therefore" here. But the omitted "therefore" is, "he did it because he knew the rule that later on was written down, and he did it in conformity to that rule and to the authority behind the rule." Sanders does not articulate these connections between Nos. 1 and 2; he just takes for granted "we all make them." That is not my conception of showing what we know. And furthermore, he assumes that we all know that everything in rabbinic literature is Pharisaic in origin (except what is not), so "we may attribute it. . . . " And we may attribute it to anyone we wish. Do I claim he is wrong? Not at all. All I argue is: what we cannot show, we do not know.

For that reason I find the following somewhat confusing, weaving this way and that, aiming at a destination only Sanders knows for certain (p. 227):

> The socio-religious point is this: Herod and the Jerusalem aristocrats, many of whose houses have been excavated, had only single pools (with one exception). Some of the smaller houses of Jerusalem and Sepphoris also had single pools, but double ones are, with only the one exception, in smaller houses. The revolutionary defenders of Matsada also built double immersion pools. Thus I think it likely that *most people,* including the aristocrats, did not follow Pharisaic views about immersion pools, although other pietists

(such as the defenders at Matsada) may have shared the Pharisees' definition of valid water.

2. That some people added "drawn" water to their pools, and that the Pharisees and early rabbis objected, is proved by rabbinic passages. According to one, the Pharisees, down to the time of Shammai and Hillel, carried on a running dispute among themselves about how much drawn water could be added to a miqveh. They agreed that not much was allowed; proposals ranged from 0.9 to 10.8 litres in a pool that contained thousands of litres ('*Eduyyot* I.3). Presumably non-Pharisees would allow more.

3. The second passage is even more interesting. According to *Shabbat* 13b, the House of Shammai (one of the main wings of the Pharisaic party, obviously after the time of Shammai and Hillel themselves) "decreed" that people who immersed in drawn water, or who had drawn water poured on them, made heave offering unfit to eat. This seems to be directed against the practice of the aristocratic priests, who did not use the Pharisaic second pool, but probably added fresh "drawn" water to the miqveh, and who bathed afterwards by sitting in a tub while a servant poured warm water over them. The Shammaites ruled that they rendered their own food (heave offering) unfit and that they should not eat it. The aristocratic priests doubtless continued to do as they wished.

Whether or not I have correctly interpreted this passage, we see that, within general uniformity (miqva'ot in bedrock, seasonally filled with rain water) there were disagreements. Some people used water that other people considered invalid.

What Sanders seems to want to say is this: the Pharisees were influential, except where they were not influential. Rich houses had one kind of immersion pool (assuming that the holes in the ground qualify as immersion pools for the purposes of the present context!). Poor houses had another. So most people did not follow Pharisaic views about immersion pools. This "most people" should read, "we have X number of immersion pools, and of them, we have Y number of a given character or size." All the rest reads into archaeological data generalizations and rules and other considerations that the mute stones scarcely sustain or even announce.

I avoid discussions of matters of substance; I deal only with passages that seem to me to illustrate significant methodological problems. But it is worth noting that when Sanders takes for granted that everything in rabbinic literature derives from or represents the views of the Pharisees before 70 (except what Sanders knows does not stand for the Pharisees before 70), he solves a problem that the rest of the people who work on that subject find full of difficulties and not yet settled. I worked on that problem in particular. It was, in fact, the point of my *Eliezer ben Hyrcanus: The Tradition and the Man* I–II,[2] and I published some of the results in separate articles afterward, for example, " 'Pharisaic-Rabbinic' Judaism: A Clarification."[3] That book does not appear in Sanders's bibliography, and he apparently has failed in any way to address its results.[4]

In No. 2 in the above excerpt, Sanders has rabbinic passages "prove" his fact, since he "knows" that Shammai and Hillel really said what is attributed to them in the Mishnah-paragraph he cites. Does Sanders know that they really said everything else attributed to them? If he does, then why does he cite so little? If he does not, then how can he cite so much? The "presumably" adds only an obvious inference, that if the fathers of the houses took the positions they did, then outsiders took other positions, and presumably allowed more rather than less. Why the second "presumably" follows I cannot say; Sanders tells us nothing about these "non-Pharisees" or how he knows their attitudes, rules, and principles. Sanders's "more interesting" passage raises the same difficulties. Yet, I hasten to add, what Sanders wants to prove, which is, "there were disagreements," stands to reason. My only problem is that he has not proved his surmise; he has only illustrated it by citing or paraphrasing stories and sayings that yield the same surmise. The problem of how these stories and sayings tell us precisely how things were in the first centuries B.C.E. and C.E. is not solved, but simply finessed.

I hasten to add, in Sanders's defense, that wherever he wishes, he will pronounce a rabbinic tale a tale (p. 258). So what bothers

---

2. Leiden: E. J. Brill, 1972.

3. In *History of Religions* 12 (1973): 250–70, reprinted in my *Early Rabbinic Judaism* (Leiden: E. J. Brill, 1975), 50–73.

4. It suffices to say that Sanders's certainties rest not only on how he reads ancient sources, but also on how he avoids considering contemporary scholarship that does not strike his fancy. The absence from the bibliography of his *Judaism* of any book of mine published after 1981 shows that he just does not feel like keeping up; but his anecdotal criticism of my *Judaism: The Evidence of the Mishnah* in his *Jewish Law from Jesus to the Mishnah* imputes to me ideas and positions contradicted in so many words in work done before 1981, and in much work done after. Since he accuses me of arguments from silence, of a "lack of imagination," and of failure "to consider the accident of survival," I may say in my own defense that if he did his homework in my *œuvre* instead of just quoting — out of the context of a sustained and massive account of the sources and how they cohere — what he feels like quoting, he would find reason to rethink his conclusions about his subject and his judgments about my proposals.

me is not what he selects or what he rejects but how he knows the difference — for what we cannot systematically show, we also never really know:

> The best-known instance of the epigrammatic epitome occurs in a story told of Hillel, the great Pharisee who was Jesus' older contemporary:
>
>> On another occasion it happened that a certain heathen came before Shammai and said to him, "Make me a proselyte, on condition that you teach me the whole Torah while I stand on one foot." Thereupon he repulsed him with the builder's cubit which was in his hand. When he went before Hillel, he said to him, "What is hateful to you, do not to your neighbor: that is the whole Torah, while the rest is commentary thereof; go and learn it." (*Shabbat 3* I a)
>
> Since this appears for the first time in a late source, and since other sources attribute epigrammatic sayings to Hillel, but not this one (e.g., *Avot* 2.5–7), we cannot attribute it to him with confidence. Finally, we note that Paul twice summarized the law by quoting Lev. 19.18: Gal. 5.14; Rom. 13.8–10. In the second instance he also cited the commandments not to commit adultery, not to kill, not to steal and not to covet. Interestingly, he then explained that since "love does no wrong to a neighbor" it "is the fulfilling of the law" (Rom. 13.10). That is, Paul knew the negative form of the saying and found it useful.

But the story about Simeon b. Gamaliel before 70 also appears in a late source, namely, the Mishnah of about 200. Why the Mishnah is a less "late source" than the Talmud I do not know. How appearances of Hillel's sayings in "other sources," e.g., tractate Avot of C.E. 250, would have made them more authentic to the historical Hillel of the first century B.C.E. Sanders does not tell us.

What is Sanders's real point? If we cannot attribute this story to Hillel "with confidence," then why bother to cite it? And what is the purpose of juxtaposing something from the fifth or sixth century with something from Paul?

We seem to have three positions. First, Sanders quotes what he thinks authentic to the first century. Second, he does not quote what he does not think authentic. Third, he quotes what he does not think authentic to the first century when it suits his polemical purpose. In addition, the problem I find with Sanders's use of rabbinic evidence is that he is capricious in believing as historical fact what he wills, ignoring as historical fiction (as to the first centuries B.C.E. and C.E.) what he wants.

## II

In scholarship, salvation is never solely by faith, but invariably and only by evidence. Sanders, interestingly, accuses me of the sin of not believing enough. The faith that he seems to require is in his knowledge of sources that do not now exist at all.[5] Sanders expresses disappointment that I have not seen his particular vision of things; he suggests that I suffer from an absence of imagination, and he declares as worthless the part of my work he claims to know.

Here is Sanders in his own words (p. 414):

> We have seen that, for details, we must have recourse to rabbinic literature, especially to the passages that we can attribute to the earliest layer. Early rabbinic literature, however, is largely legal; one can derive from it general theological beliefs, such as that charity is important, but nothing like the rich substance that the Dead Sea Scrolls provide for the Essenes. If all we had from Qumran were the *Community Rule,* without its concluding hymn, the evidence would be analogous to what the Mishnah tells us about the Pharisees: the Dead Sea sect would look like a religion in which nothing mattered but rules. Neusner, in fact, has proposed that this was true of the early rabbis. This shows a lack of imagination and a failure to consider the accident of survival. If we had a collection of private Pharisaic prayers, we would find them as deeply devotional as are the hymns from Qumran. Since they did not survive, it will be important to reconsider the main themes of the Eighteen Benedictions, which probably show something of Pharisaic piety.
>
> The accident of survival poses a further problem. If the earliest rabbinic literature tells us too little about Pharisaic theology and piety, it tells us too much about their legal interpretation; that is, too much to be adequately covered in the present chapter. The required stratification is, in the first place, very difficult

---

5. In Hyam Maccoby's critique of my *Judaism: The Evidence of the Mishnah,* and in his contribution to the symposium on the book that is reprinted below, he makes the same point. Maccoby is quite honest that, historical critical considerations aside, he really is interested only in the consequences of scholarship for contemporary theology; he thinks my results reflect badly on Judaism. But the Judaism he defends is liberal and Reform, which has no greater regard for halakhah and commandment and covenant than does Sanders's liberal Protestantism, which deems "ritual" to be "unspiritual." The Judaism I believe and practice believes that the Torah records God's self-manifestation to Israel at Sinai, including the statement of what God commands Israel; and that statement encompasses the Sabbath, which is ritualistic, as much as honoring parents or refraining from adultery, thievery, and murder, which are matters of ethics.

to achieve. The earliest rabbinic document, the Mishnah, is usually dated c. 200–220 C.E. Much of the material is anonymous,
while other passages are attributed to named sages. Of the attributed material, the bulk is second century rather than first (even
assuming that all attributions are accurate). Separating the possibly first-century material from later passages in the Mishnah and
other rabbinic sources is slow, difficult work, and categorizing it
is almost equally hard. Neusner spent three volumes at the second
task, but he mis-categorized the passages, and the entire job needs
to be done again. I have attempted to do it for Purity (see n. 5), but
the analysis of rabbinic legal debates is not really my métier, and
I wanted to do just enough of it to see whether or not Neusner's
passages support his conclusions. They do not.

Sanders knows that if we had a collection of private Pharisaic
prayers, we would find them as deeply devotional as are the hymns
from Qumran. I have no imagination, because if I did, I would
know that fact that Sanders knows. I also have no confidence in
my capacity to make up evidence that does not exist, which accounts for my "failure to consider the accident of survival." So in
this sense, I plead guilty to Sanders's charges.

I do not know what that collection of private Pharisaic prayers
would say, and neither does Sanders, because at this time we have
no such collection. So while what he says "stands to reason," or
"is obvious," it is hardly very solid ground on which to base any
conclusions whatsoever: what we cannot show, we do not know.
Still, for not knowing what we cannot show, we should not accuse
our academic colleagues of a "lack of imagination." I am proud
to be accused of what I regard as a virtue: I do not make things
up as I go along. Sanders, on the other hand, knows what has not
survived, which is why "the accident of survival" is a considera-
tion. I simply describe what we have and draw conclusions based
on what we do know. I do not regard that characteristic of my
scholarship as a vice but as a virtue. Scholarship in general regards
certainty about what absent evidence says as odd, and conclusions
based on imagination as fiction.

But we cannot leave the matter there, for the polemic concerns
also the legalism of Judaism. Nearly all New Testament scholarship before George Foot Moore, and most of it afterward to
our own day, and virtually the entirety of the preaching clergy in
parishes and pulpits, describe the Judaism that Jesus reformed or
rejected as legalistic. Sanders wishes to show that this is not so.
In the paragraph just now cited, however, Sanders imputes to me

the view of Judaism as "a religion in which nothing mattered but rules." This is not by implication but stated in so many words: "Neusner, in fact, has proposed that this was true of the early rabbis." Sanders's evidence that this is my view is based on the following reference: "e.g., *Judaism: The Evidence of the Mishnah,* p. 86." The single example is regarded as probative, since he finds it necessary to give no other. I therefore determined to follow up and see how I could have given so egregious an account of my views — and so ignorant and wrong an account of the Judaism I was discussing in the Mishnah.

Since I have never said and obviously do not maintain that the Judaism of the rabbis of the Mishnah (or faithful Judaism today, in any of its systems) was (or is) one in which "only rules mattered," and since I have argued — quite to the contrary — that rules serve as a powerful medium of profound discourse, a way of making statements of principles about the social order and metaphysics alike, I looked up the reference. Where and how have I so badly composed sentences as to yield the wrong conclusion Sanders imputes to me? Or have I, unannounced and unknowing, changed my mind?

Here are the sentences of *Judaism: The Evidence of the Mishnah,* p. 86 (into p. 87) that may pertain (Sanders gives no hint as to which sentence or sentences he cites):

[In the context of the wording of prayers:] Overall, the tendency appears to have been not to attempt to standardize more than the principal outlines of worship. Not much value was placed upon a fixed wording or even structure....

There also was some work at defining appropriate blessings for various natural benefits....A fully articulated system of blessings after the meal is not attested for the present period. The rulings are episodic and not integrated.

Since it is not possible to suppose that there were no liturgies before the war [of 66], the probable reason for work on this topic at just this time has to be located in an intention not to create liturgy but to legislate about it. And even in the matter of legislation and thus standardization, it would appear that only the most basic issues came up, for instance, rules governing the saying of the Shema morning and night, for which, prior to the wars, we must assume there were established practices, as well as the saying of blessings for various gifts of nature. What is important in this part of the law is that matters were discussed which aforetimes people would have done in accord merely with local custom. But that same observation applies to the other matters — obeying the agricultural taboos, giving out the taxes to class and caste — which were subjected to substantial work of amplification and expansion at just this time.

My assumption here is that there were prayers that were long established; these were not written by the people under discussion ("rabbis," "Pharisees," whoever — not specified). After 70, some work was underway to standardize the outlines of worship (I refer here to *matbe'a shel tefilah*, the order of prayer). There was some further effort to make rules on liturgy, e.g., when the Shema was to be recited. Overall, that would seem to me to have been part of a larger effort to order local custom into a generally prevailing pattern. Absent the notion that if you make a rule, you think that all that matters is the rule — a classic non sequitur; I find no hint of a conception that "nothing mattered but rules." What I am saying is that to these sages, rules did matter. That is not the same thing as saying that to these sages, only rules mattered.

So much for what I say on p. 86. Now on to p. 87, where there may be better grounds for finding the view Sanders imputes to me:

> So what we see is that the method of the group which had taken shape before the war, which was to define itself through distinguishing and differentiating rules about eating and marrying, was carried forward. This same approach to confronting problems, namely, through making laws, now was taken over on a much larger scale, and for a broader range of purposes. Defining the way common practices were to be done then suggests that, in people's mind, was the intent to make even common practices into a mode of differentiation of an uncommon group. That at any rate is one possibility for interpreting both the continuation of an established mode of thought, namely, an obsession with rule making, and the expansion of the topics to which that mode of thought came to apply. . . .

Now what I think I am saying is this: (1) Before 70, the group responsible for some ideas that are carried forward and set out in the Mishnah two hundred years later distinguished itself by making rules that that group kept and others did not. (2) These rules covered what food members of the group would eat or not eat (outsiders being assumed to eat anything) and also what genealogical rules would govern whom they would marry or not marry (e.g., the laws of consanguineous taboos). (3) Defining themselves by setting forth rules that differentiated the group from outsiders (in Israel), the group after 70 carried forward its established mode of self-definition and self-differentiation.

Given the character of the Torah, with its chapters and chapters of rules, commencing with the Ten Commandments, I do not
think this group, one marked by an obsession with rule making,
vastly differed from the authors of J, E, P, and D, and Sanders's
"covenantal nomism" surely has already absolved the Torah of the
charge of maintaining that "only rules matter." Even the Priestly
Code in Leviticus joins right to rite, never imagining that all that
matters is a slavish obedience to rules.

# III

It seems to me that Sanders thinks that any and every source, whoever wrote it, without regard to its time or place or venue, tells us
about one and the same Judaism. Such a conflation of all sources
yields what I regard as a fabricated Judaism. The result of this Judaic equivalent of a "harmony of the Gospels" is, more often than
not, a dreary progression through pointless information.

The conflation of all the sources one thinks fit together and the
silent omission of all the sources one rejects is something Moore,
Schechter, and even Urbach never did. Nor can I point to any other
scholar of ancient Judaism working today who cites everything
from everywhere to tell us about one and the same Judaism. The
contrast between the intellectually rigorous attempt of James Dunn
to define "Judaism" in his *Partings of the Ways* and the work of
Sanders on the same problem is also worth noting.

This idea of a single Judaism is supposed to tell us something
that pertains equally to all: the Judaism that forms the basis for all
the sources, the common denominator among them all. If we know
a book or an artifact is "Jewish," then we are supposed automat-
ically to know various other facts about said book or artifact. But
the upshot is either too general to mean much (monotheism) or
too abstract to form an intelligible statement. Let me be specific.
How Philo will have understood the Dead Sea Scrolls, the authors
of apocalyptic writings, or those of the Mishnah-passages Sanders
admits to his account of Judaism from 63 B.C.E. to 66 C.E., we are
never told. Each of these distinctive documents gets to speak whenever Sanders wants it to; none is ever brought into relationship —
comparison and contrast — with any other. The homogenization
of Philo, the Mishnah, the Dead Sea Scrolls, Ben Sira, apocryphal
and pseudepigraphic writings, the results of archaeology, and on
and on and on turns out to yield generalizations about a religion

that none of those responsible for the evidence at hand will have recognized.

To understand what goes into Sanders's understanding of Judaism, let me provide a reasonable sample (pp. 103–4), representative of the whole, the opening paragraphs of his discussion, chapter 7, entitled "Sacrifices":

> The Bible does not offer a single, clearly presented list of sacrifices. The legal books (Exodus, Leviticus, Numbers and Deuteronomy), we know now, incorporate various sources from different periods, and priestly practice evidently varied from time to time. There are three principal sources of information about sacrifices in the first century: Josephus, Philo and the Mishnah. On most points they agree among themselves and with Leviticus and Numbers; consequently the main outline of sacrifices is not in dispute. Josephus, in my judgment, is the best source. He knew what the common practice of the priesthood of his day was: he had learned it in school, as a boy he had watched and assisted, and as an adult he had worked in the temple. It is important for evaluating his evidence to note that his description of the sacrifices sometimes disagrees with Leviticus or goes beyond it. This is not an instance in which he is simply summarizing what is written in the Bible: he is almost certainly depending on what he had learned as a priest.
>
> Though the Mishnah is often right with regard to pre-70 temple practice, many of the discussions are from the second century: the rabbis continued to debate rules of sacrifice long after living memory of how it had been done had vanished. Consequently, in reading the Mishnah one is sometimes reading second-century theory. Occasionally this can be seen clearly. For example, there is a debate about whether or not the priest who sacrificed an animal could keep its hide if for any reason the animal was made invalid (e.g., by touching something impure) after it was sacrificed but before it was flayed. The Mishnah on this topic opens with an anonymous opinion, according to which the priest did not get the hide. R. Hanina the Prefect of the Priests disagreed: "Never have I seen a hide taken out to the place of burning"; that is, the priests always kept the hides. R. Akiba (early second century) accepted this and was of the view that the priests could keep the hides of invalid sacrifices. "The Sages," however, ruled the other way (*Zevahim* 12.4). R. Hanina the Prefect of the Priests apparently worked in the temple before 70, but survived its destruction and became part of the rabbinic movement. Akiba died c. 135; "the sages" of this passage are probably his contemporaries or possibly the rabbis of the next generation. Here we see that second century rabbis were quite willing to vote against actual practice in discussing the be-

havior of the priests and the rules they followed. The problem with using the Mishnah is that there is very seldom this sort of reference to pre-70 practice that allows us to make critical distinctions: not only are we often reading second-century discussions, we may be learning only second-century theory.

Philo had visited the temple, and some of his statements about it (e.g., the guards) seem to be based on personal knowledge. But his discussion of the sacrifices is "bookish," and at some important points it reveals that he is passing on information derived from the Greek translation of the Hebrew Bible (the Septuagint), not from observation. The following description basically follows the Hebrew Bible and Josephus, but it sometimes incorporates details from other sources.

One may make the following distinctions among sacrifices:

> With regard to what was offered: meal, wine, birds (doves or pigeons) and quadrupeds (sheep, goats and cattle).

> With regard to who provided the sacrifice: the community or an individual.

> With regard to the purpose of the sacrifice: worship of and communion with God, glorification of him, thanksgiving, purification, atonement for sin, and feasting

> With regard to the disposition of the sacrifice: it was either burned or eaten. The priests got most of the food that sacrifices provided, though one of the categories of sacrifice provided food for the person who brought it and his family and friends. The Passover lambs were also eaten by the worshippers.

Sacrifices were conceived as meals, or, better, banquets. The full and ideal sacrificial offering consisted of meat, cereal, oil and wine (Num. 15.1–10, *Antiq.* 3.233f.; the menu was sometimes reduced: see below).

Now let us ask ourselves, what exactly does Sanders wish to tell his readers about the sacrifices in this account of *Judaism: Practice and Belief?* He starts in the middle of things. He assumes we know what he means by "sacrifices," why they are important, what they meant, so all we require is details. He will deal with Josephus, Philo, the Mishnah, and Leviticus and Numbers. Does he then tell us the distinctive viewpoint of each? Not at all. All he wants us to know is the facts common to them all. Hence his problem is not one of description, analysis, and interpretation of documents, but a conflation of the information contained in each that he deems usable. Since that is his principal concern, he discusses "sacrifice" by telling us why the Mishnah's information is useless, except when it is usable. But Sanders never suggests to his readers what the Mishnah's discussion of sacrifice wishes to find out, or how its ideas on the subject may prove religiously engaging. It is just a rule book, so it has no ideas on the subject. So Sanders; that is not my view. Philo is then set forth. Here, too, we are told why he tells us nothing, but not what he tells us. Then there follow the facts, the "with regard to" paragraphs.

Sanders did not have to tell us all about how Leviticus, Numbers, Philo, Josephus, and the Mishnah concur, and then about how we may ignore or must cite the several documents respectively, if his sole intent was to tell us the facts of the "with regard to" paragraphs. How he knows that "sacrifices were conceived," who conceived them in this way, and what sense the words made, "worship of and communion with God, glorification of him, thanksgiving, purification, atonement for sin, and feasting," and to whom they made sense, and how other Judaisms, besides the Judaism portrayed by Philo, Josephus, the Mishnah, and so on and so forth, viewed sacrifices, or the temple as it was — none of this is set forth. The conflation has its own purpose, which the following outline of the remainder of the chapter reveals: community sacrifices; individual sacrifices ("Neither Josephus, Philo, nor other first-century Jews thought that burnt offerings provided God with food … "), a family at the temple, an example; the daily temple routine. In this mass of information on a subject, one question is lost: what it all meant. Sanders really does suppose that he is telling us how things were, what people did, and, in his stress on common-denominator Judaism, he finds it entirely reasonable to bypass all questions of analysis and interpretation and so forgets to tell us what it all meant. His language, "worship of and communion with God, glorification of him, thanksgiving, purification, atonement for sin, and feasting" — that Protestant formulation begs every question and answers none.

But this common-denominator Judaism yields little that is more than simply banal, e.g., "The history of Israel in general, and of our period in particular, shows that Jews believed that the one God of the universe had given them his law and that they were to obey it" (p. 240). No one, obviously, can disagree, but what applies to everyone equally, in a nation so riven with division and rich in diversity, also cannot make much of a difference. That is to say, knowing that they all were monotheists or valued the Hebrew scriptures (but which passages he does not identify, how he reads them he does not say) does not tell us more than we knew about the religion of those diverse people than before. Sanders knows what people thought, because anything any Jew wrote tells us what "Jews" or most Jews or people in general thought. What makes Sanders's representation questionable is that he proceeds to cite, as evidence of what "Jews" thought, opinions of Philo and Josephus, the Dead Sea Scrolls, rabbinic literature, and so on and so forth. The generality of scholarship understands that the Dead Sea Scrolls represent their writers, Philo speaks for Philo, Josephus says what he thinks, and the Mishnah is whatever it is and is not whatever it is not. No one, to my knowledge, until Sanders has come to the facile judgment that anything any Jew thought has to have been in the mind of all the other Jews.

Finally, I quote two paragraphs from Sanders's book that strike me as condescending toward Judaism and the Pharisees:

> I rather like the Pharisees. They loved detail and precision. They wanted to get everything just right. I like that. They loved God, they thought he had blessed them, and they thought that he *wanted* them to get everything just right. I do not doubt that some of them were priggish. This is a common fault of the pious, one that is amply displayed in modern criticism of the Pharisees. The Pharisees, we know, intended to be humble before God, and they thought that intention mattered more than outward show. Those are worthy ideals. The other pietists strike me as being less attractive than the Pharisees. The surviving literature depicts them as not having much of a program for all Israel, and as being too ready to cultivate hatred of others: learn *our* secrets or God will destroy you. But probably they weren't all that bad, and we can give them credit for loving God and being honest.
>
> Mostly, I like the ordinary people. They worked at their jobs, they believed the Bible [sic! he means, the Old Testament, of course], they carried out the small routines and celebrations of the religion; they prayed every day, thanked God for his blessings, and on the sabbath went to the synagogue, asked teachers questions, and listened respectfully. What could be better? Every now and again they took their hard-earned second tithe money to Jerusalem, devoutly performed their sacrifices, carried the meat out of the temple to share with their family and friends, brought some wine and maybe even some spirits, and feasted the night away. Then it was back to the regular grind. This may not sound like much, but in their view, they were living as God wished. The history of the time shows how firmly they believed in God, who gave them the law [he means the Torah] and promised them deliverance.

Quite what is at stake here I cannot see; there is far less than meets the eye. Any objective person familiar with both this picture and also the Gospels is going to wonder what, in the Gospels, all the fuss is about. But that is beside the point in describing Judaism in the first centuries B.C.E. and C.E., since at issue is not history but theology. As I shall argue in the concluding chapter of this book, asking what really happened and how things really were — the quest for the historical Jesus — forms a narrowly theological venture in which what are called "historical facts" take the place of centuries of theological truths.

# 7

# What We Ask Exposes
# How We Conceive Our Sources

Let us now move from the answers formed out of an uncritical reading of rabbinic literature to the questions that people suppose we can answer on the basis of the rabbinic literature. We continue to focus on the use of rabbinic literature for the study of Judaism and the Jews in the first century, though we move from New Testament problems to those of Judaism itself. The principle I mean to advance remains the same: what we cannot show, we do not know. In this instance, I have selected Shaye J. D. Cohen, another of my critics, who addresses the history of Judaism. What I shall show is that Cohen's thesis takes up a question that he can have asked only with the assumption that answers of a historical order exist in the rabbinic literature he cites.[1]

In "The Significance of Yavneh: Pharisees, Rabbis, and the End of Jewish Sectarianism,"[2] Cohen presents an important thesis. In order to make certain he is represented accurately, I cite his own précis of his article, which is as follows:

> After the destruction of the second temple in 70 C.E. the rabbis gathered in Yavneh and launched the process which yielded the Mishnah approximately one hundred years later. Most modern scholars see these rabbis as Pharisees triumphant, who define "orthodoxy," expel Christians and other heretics, and purge the canon

---

1. I go over my critique of Cohen originally published in *Reading and Believing: Ancient Judaism and Contemporary Gullibility,* Brown Judaic Studies (Atlanta: Scholars Press, 1986). All of Cohen's work after 1986 repeats the same errors he made before I presented this discussion of his writing.

2. *Hebrew Union College Annual* 55 (1984): 27–53.

of "dangerous" books. The evidence for this reconstruction is inadequate. In all likelihood most of the rabbis were Pharisees, but there is no indication that the rabbis of the Yavnean period were motivated by a Pharisaic self-consciousness (contrast the Babylonian Talmud and the medieval polemics against the Karaites) or were dominated by an exclusivistic ethic. In contrast the major goal of the Yavnean rabbis seems to have been not the expulsion of those with whom they disagreed but the cessation of sectarianism and the creation of a society which tolerated, even encouraged, vigorous debate among members of the fold. The Mishnah is the first work of Jewish antiquity which ascribes conflicting legal opinions to named individuals who, in spite of their disagreements, belong to the same fraternity. This mutual tolerance is the enduring legacy of Yavneh.

What is important is not Cohen's theory, with which I do not undertake an argument, but whether or not to formulate and prove his theory he has exhibited that gullibility that seems to characterize pretty much everyone else.

Let us proceed to ask how Cohen uses the evidence, investigating the theory of the character of the sources that leads him to frame his questions in one way and not in some other. What we shall see, first of all, is that Cohen takes at face value the historical allegation of a source that a given rabbi made the statement attributed to him. On pp. 32–33, Cohen states:

> The text narrates a story about a Sadducee and a high priest, and concludes with the words of the wife of the Sadducee:
>
> A. "Although they [=we] are wives of Sadducees, they [=we] fear the Pharisees and show their [=our] menstrual blood to the sages."
>
> B. R. Yosé says, "We are more expert in them [Sadducean women] than anyone else. They show (menstrual) blood to the sages, except for one woman who was in our neighborhood, who did not show her (menstrual blood to the sages, and she died [immediately]" (Bab. Niddah 33b).

Cohen forthwith states, "In this text there is chronological tension between parts A and B. A clearly refers to a woman who lived during second temple times, while B has R. Yosé derive his expertise about Sadducean women from personal acquaintance." Why Cohen regards that "tension" as probative or even pertinent I cannot say. We may wonder whether Cohen believes Yosé really made the statement attributed him. We note that Cohen does not specify the point at which "the text" was redacted. The fact that the

Babylonian Talmud reached closure in the sixth or seventh century makes no difference. If the text refers to Yosé, then it testifies to the second century, not to the seventh.

We shall now hear Cohen treat the text as an accurate report of views held in the time of which it speaks. How does he know? Because the text says so: it refers to this, it refers to that. What we have is a newspaper reporter, writing down things really said and giving them over to the national archives for preservation until some later reporter chooses to add to the file. Here is Cohen again, in the same passage, starting with the pretense of a critical exercise of analysis:

> In this text there is chronological tension between parts A and B. A clearly refers to a woman who lived during second temple times, while B has R. Yosé derive his expertise about Sadducean women from personal acquaintance. He recalls a Sadducean woman who lived in his neighborhood and died prematurely because (R. Yosé said) she did not accept the authority of the sages to determine her menstrual status.

To this point Cohen simply paraphrases the text, and now he will verify the story. It seems to me that Cohen takes for granted Yosé really made the saying attributed to him and, moreover, that saying is not only Yosé's view of matters, but how matters really were. He says so in so many words: "This baraita clearly implies that R. Yosé is referring to contemporary Sadducean women. If this is correct, R. Yosé's statement shows that some Sadducees still existed in the mid-second century but that their power had declined to the extent that the rabbis could assume that most Sadducees follow rabbinic norms." It seems to me beyond doubt that Cohen takes for granted that what is attributed to Yosé really was said by him and, more interestingly, Yosé testifies to how things were not in one place but everywhere in the country. "If this is correct," Cohen concludes not that Yosé thought that there were still a few Sadducees around, but that there were still a few Sadducees around. There is a difference. Cohen does not tell us what conclusions he draws if this is not correct, because, in point of fact, he declines to explore that possibility.

Nonetheless, he wants to verify the story. How? By finding another text that tells the same story:

The version of the Tosefta is similar:

A. "Although we are Sadducean women, we all consult a sage."

B. R. Yosé says, "We are more expert in Sadducean women than anyone else: they all consult a sage except for one who was among them, and she died" (Tosefta Niddah 5:3).

The Tosefta does not identify Pharisees with sages, a point to which we shall return below, and omits the phrase "who was in our neighborhood." Otherwise, it is basically, the same as the Babylonian version.

The reader may rightly wonder whether perhaps Cohen intends something other than historical narrative about views Yosé held or opinions he taught. Maybe Cohen proposes to write a history of the tradition about a given matter. In that case simply citing this and that serves a valid purpose. I concur.

But Cohen leaves no doubt as to his intention. Let us listen as he tells us what really happened. Since Yosé made his statement, Yosé's statement tells us about the second century. Then Yosé's statement proves that there were Sadducees in the mid-second century, but they had no power. I find no evidence whatsoever that Cohen grasps the critical problem of evaluating the allegations of sources. He looks into a source and comes up with a fact. If he finds two versions of the same story, the fact is still more factual. And, if that were not enough, he gives us the "proof" of "according to rabbinic tradition." That tradition suffices: "They always failed, of course, but they resisted; by the second century they stopped resisting." Let us review those clear statements of his:

This baraita clearly implies that R. Yosé is referring to contemporary Sadducean women. If this is correct, R. Yosé's statement shows that some Sadducees still existed in the mid-second century but that their power had declined to the extent that the rabbis could assume that most Sadducees follow rabbinic norms. Contrast the Sadducees of the second temple period who, according to rabbinic tradition, tried to resist rabbinic hegemony (see below). They always failed, of course, but they resisted: by the second century they stopped resisting. This is the perspective of R. Yosé.

The "if this is correct" changes nothing. As soon as the "if" has been said, it is treated as a "then." "Then" it is correct, so Cohen here tells us the story of the Sadducees in the first and second centuries. In the first century they resisted "rabbinic norms," whatever they were, but in the second century, they gave up. This is Cohen's conclusion, based on his failure to ask how the Bavli and the Tosefta's compilers or the author of the story at hand knew the facts of the matter. The sole undisputed fact is that they represent the facts one way, rather than some other. But that does not suffice.

But let us give Cohen his due. Any fair-minded reader may claim that what we have is a mere lapse. Cohen may have made a minor lapse that we should forgive. So let us see how he analyzes sources. On p. 42 he says: "Rabbinic tradition is aware of opposition faced by Yohanan ben Zakkai at Yavneh but knows nothing of any expulsion of these opponents (Bab. Rosh Hashanah 2b). Yohanan ben Zakkai was even careful to avoid a confrontation with the priests (Mishnah 'Eduyyot 8:3)." Now what have we here? "Rabbinic tradition" indeed. What can that possibly mean? All rabbis at all times? A particular rabbi at a given time? Church historians these days rarely base their historical facts on "the tradition of the church." Would that we could write a life of Jesus based on the tradition of the church: how many problems we could solve. Cohen does not favor us with an exercise in differentiation among the sources. His is an undifferentiated harmony of the Jewish gospels. Indeed, to the opposite, he looks into "rabbinic tradition," undifferentiated, unanalyzed, and gives us a fact: Bab. Rosh Hashanah 2b. What can that be? It is a story about someone. What does the story tell us? Is it true? Why should we think so? Cohen does not ask these questions. He alludes to a page in the Talmud, and that constitutes his fact on which, it goes without saying, he proposes to build quite an edifice. So the Talmud is a kind of telephone book, giving us numbers through which we make our connections. In no way does he establish a critical method that tells us why he believes what he believes and disbelieves what he rejects.

But he does have a clear theory of matters. Cohen wants to prove that earlier there were disputes, and that later on disputes ended. Now some sources say that earlier there were no disputes, and that later on there were disputes. So Cohen rejects the historicity of the sources that say there were no disputes earlier and accepts that of the ones that say there were no disputes later. On p. 48 he cites T. Hagigah 2:9: "At first there was no dispute in Israel." He proceeds to point to an "irenic trend," Mishnah Yebamot 1:4 and 'Eduyyot 4:8, which alleges that while the Houses disputed various matters, they still intermarried and respected each other's conformity to the purity rules. Then Cohen:

> But this wishful thinking cannot disguise the truth. The two Talmudim find it almost impossible to understand this statement. The Houses could not marry or sup with each other. They were virtually sects — kitot the Palestinian Talmud calls them (Yer. Hagigah 2:2). At Yavneh sectarian exclusiveness was replaced by rabbinic pluralism, collective authority was replaced by individual authority.

What Cohen has done is to reject the statements in earlier sources — Mishnah, Tosefta — and adopt those in later ones (the Palestinian Talmud). He has done so simply by fiat. He cites what they say, and then he calls it wishful thinking. The truth, he discovers, is in the judgment of the Palestinian Talmud.

I find this strange, for two reasons. First, it is odd to reject the testimony of the earlier source, closer to the situation under discussion, in favor of the later. Second, it is not entirely clear why and how Cohen knows that the Mishnah's and Tosefta's statements represent wishful thinking at all. Had he cited the talmudic discussions of the passage, readers would have found that the problem confronting the later exegetes is not quite what Cohen says it was. The Talmuds do not say that the parties were "virtually sects." That statement, it is true, occurs where Cohen says it does — but that is not on the passage of M. Yebamot 1:4 etc. that Cohen is discussing. It is on another passage entirely. The talmudic discussion on the Mishnah-passage and its Tosefta-parallel is a legal one; the sages are troubled by the statement that people who disagree on laws of marriage and of purity can ignore those laws. The talmudic discussion in no way sustains Cohen's statement. If we reread the sequence of sentences, we find an interesting juxtaposition:

1. The two Talmudim find it almost impossible to understand this statement.

2. The Houses could not marry or sup with each other. They were virtually sects — *kitot*, the Palestinian Talmud calls them.

3. At Yavneh sectarian exclusiveness was replaced by rabbinic pluralism, and collective authority was replaced by individual authority.

Sentence 3 does not follow from sentence 2, unless sentence 2 has had something to do with "sectarian exclusiveness" replaced by "rabbinic pluralism." But the passage cited by Cohen does not say that; it has no bearing on that proposition. Cohen writes as though the evidence supports his thesis when, in fact, the evidence has no bearing on that thesis. The sentences in fact do not follow from one another. No. 1 is factually inaccurate. No. 2 makes the valid point that the Yerushalmi calls the sects *kitot*. That is an undisputed fact. It, however, bears no consequences for the statements fore or aft. And No. 3 is parachuted down — Cohen's own judgment. So, to repeat, Cohen believes what he wishes to believe (the later sources' allegations), disbelieves what he does not wish to believe (the earlier sources' statements), and finds in a source not related to anything a statement he wishes to believe, cites that, then repeats — as though it had been proved — the fundamental thesis of his paper.

It follows that Cohen's reading of the source begins with a generous view of the a priori accuracy of his own convictions about what the source is saying. Yohanan's "care" in avoiding a confrontation is Cohen's allegation, for the source does not quite say that. It says, in point of fact, not that he avoided confrontation, but that he did not think he could force the priests to do what they refused to do. That is the exact language of the source though, as we see, Cohen is indifferent to detail in his effort to prove his point. The statement imputed to Yohanan ben Zakkai may mean he was careful about avoiding confrontation. It may also mean he did not feel like wasting his time on lost causes. It may mean a great many other things. Cohen does not know. He simply cites the tractate and its chapter and paragraph number, and lo, another fact, another proof.

I shall now show that Cohen can tell us the truth, because he knows which source is giving us facts and which source is giving us fancies. That explains why what gets a question mark "(at Yavneh?)" half a dozen lines later loses the question mark and becomes a fact: "At Yavneh sectarian exclusiveness was replaced by rabbinic pluralism." On what basis? Let us hear. For this purpose we review the materials just now set forth. On pp. 48–49, Cohen says:

> Some of the rabbis were aware that their ideology of pluralism did not exist before 70. "At first there was no dispute (mahloqet) in Israel" (Tos. Hagigah 2:9 and Sanhedrin 7:1). How did disputes begin? According to one view in the Tosefta, disputes were avoided by the adjudication of the great court which sat in the temple precincts and determined either by vote or by tradition the status of all doubtful matters. In this view, when the great court was destroyed in 70, disputes could no longer be resolved in an orderly way and mahloqot proliferated. According to another view, "once the disciples of Hillel and Shammai became numerous who did not serve [their masters] adequately, they multiplied disputes in Israel and became as two Torahs." In this view Jewish (i.e., rabbinic) unanimity was upset by the malfeasance of the disciples of Hillel and Shammai, a confession which would later be exploited by the Karaites. What happened to the disputes between the Houses? They ceased at Yavneh, how we do not know. Amoraic tradition (Yer.

Yebamot 1:6 [3b] and parallels) tells of a heavenly voice which declared at Yavneh, "Both these [House of Hillel] and these [House
of Shammai] are the words of the living God, but the halakha
always follows the House of Hillel." As part of this irenic trend
someone (at Yavneh?) even asserted that the disputes between the
Houses did not prevent them from intermarrying or from respecting each other's purities (Mishnah Yebamot 1:4 and 'Eduyyot 4:8;
Tos. Yebamot 1:10–12) but this wishful thinking cannot disguise
the truth. The two Talmudim find it almost impossible to understand this statement. The Houses could not marry or sup with
each other. They were virtually sects — *kitot* the Palestinian Talmud
calls them (Yer. Hagigah 2:2 [77d]). At Yavneh sectarian exclusiveness was replaced by rabbinic pluralism, collective authority was
replaced by individual authority. The new ideal was the sage who
was ready not to insist upon the rectitude of ("stand upon") his
opinions. The creation of the Mishnah could now begin.

This repeated reading of Cohen's statements allows us to avoid the
charge of quoting him out of context or only in part. I believe I
have quoted him accurately, verbatim, and in context. So let us
review the substance of the case.

When Cohen says, "were aware," he treats the thesis of his
article as the fact of the matter. Who were these rabbis? How
do we know of what they were or were not aware? Did they
live at Yavneh, in 70? Or did they live in the early third century when the Mishnah had reached closure, or did they live a
hundred years later when the Tosefta was coming to conclusion?
Cohen does not tell us. But he clearly thinks that their awareness
is evidence of historical fact. Now these in the aggregate constitute
historical statements, e.g., "the Houses were virtually sects." That
Cohen prizes Y. Hag. 2:2 — a late source — and dismisses the evidence of the Mishnah and Tosefta surprises me. In fact, he has set
out to prove at the end of his paragraph the very point he takes
for granted at the outset of his paragraph. Some might call that
"begging the question."

Cohen's review of the stories makes a feint toward criticism. He
cites diverse views, balancing one view against another. But in the
end, we do not have a history of people's opinions from Cohen, we
have facts. "What happened to the disputes between the Houses?
They ceased at Yavneh, how we do not know." Here Cohen tells
us that Neusner has shown that some of "the House disputes were
later scholarly constructs, but these are not our concern." I do not
know why it is not our concern. The Mishnah contains substantial

evidence that the names of the Houses served to identify positions held by later disputants, of the mid-second century it would appear. Materials deriving from the period after the Bar Kokhba War are particularly rich in allusions to Houses' disputes that take up moot principles otherwise debated entirely in the age beyond Bar Kokhba's war. We clearly have mid-second-century literary conventions.

I do not mean to suggest that the names of the Houses served as more than literary conventions; I demonstrated that they served at least as literary conventions. Why? Were there "Houses of Shammai and Houses of Hillel" in the time of Yosé, in the mid-second century? Is that why so many sayings about the relationships among the Houses are assigned, in fact, to mid-second-century authorities? But the assignments of those sayings occur in documents edited only in the third century, at which point (some stories have it) the patriarch Judah discovered that he descended from Hillel. So perhaps the disputes of the Houses served a polemical purpose of the patriarchate, since the ancestor of the patriarchate — everyone knew — kept winning the disputes. These are only possibilities. In answering the question as Cohen phrases it, all we have are possibilities, few of them subject to tests of falsification or validation.

It seems that Cohen knows facts, while the rest of us know only possibilities. But why in particular, much more than half a century beyond the point at which Cohen knows the Houses went out of business, "They ceased at Yavneh, how we do not know"? Just what ceased at Yavneh, if the names of the Houses persisted as literary conventions and points of polemic for a hundred years and more? It must follow that Cohen's claim of knowledge of an "irenic trend" rests on nothing more than two things: (1) the source's claim of such a trend, and (2) Cohen's opinion as to the facts. This is proved by the stories cited from M. Yeb. 1:4 and M. Ed. 4:8 and so on. Let us review in sequence Cohen's statements:

1. But this wishful thinking cannot disguise the truth.

2. At Yavneh sectarian exclusiveness was replaced by rabbinic pluralism, collective authority was replaced by individual authority.

3. The new ideal was the sage who was ready not to insist upon the rectitude of his opinions.

4. The creation of the Mishnah could now begin.

All of these statements may well be true. But in the paragraph I have cited, in which these statements occur, not a single source, not a single piece of evidence, proves any such thing. I cite No. 1 to prove that Cohen claims to make a historical statement. No. 2 then tells us he sees a movement from sect to church (though he does not appear to have read Max Weber, who saw much the same movement). Cohen has not proved that the "new ideal" of the sage antedates the Mishnah, in which it is said that that is the ideal. But he has ignored the fact that the Mishnah imputes that irenic position to none other than the House of Hillel — who lived long before "Yavneh." And what does all this have to do with "the creation of the Mishnah"? If a passage in the Mishnah refers to the time of the Houses, but Cohen thinks that the fact does not apply to the time of the Houses, he ignores the allegation of the Mishnah's passage. If a passage in the Yerushalmi, two hundred years later, refers to the earlier period and says what Cohen thinks was the fact, then that later passage is true while the earlier one is not.

Let us not forget where we started. Does Cohen believe that if the source says someone said something, then that person really said it? Yes, on the one side, Cohen does believe it when the source says something he thinks the source should have said the person said, as in the case of Yosé. But no, on the other side, Cohen does not believe it when the source says something he thinks the source should not have said the person (or group) said, as in the case of the Houses when they are represented in an irenic mode. Let us also not miss the simple point that his thesis, to begin with, rests on the conviction that the sources as we have them present us with the facts we require to test and prove. That framing of the question is terribly important. Because Cohen assumes the rabbinic literature answers the questions he has in mind, he asks those questions. With a different theory of the literature (such as I have given in Part One of this book), we have to form different questions altogether. That fact, Cohen's essay shows, he does not understand.

# PART THREE

# DIFFERENCES OF OPINION ON HOW RABBINIC LITERATURE SHOULD BE USED FOR HISTORICAL PURPOSES

# 8

# The Mishnah and the Smudgepots

When my *Judaism: The Evidence of the Mishnah* appeared, it received a remarkable response. Entire articles on the book were published in periodicals of Judaism or Jewish politics, *Conservative Judaism* and *Midstream* being the principal ones, and Shaye J. D. Cohen and Hyam Maccoby made names for themselves by their attacks on the book and its author. Since — as I have explained in chapter 2 — the reading of the Mishnah ran parallel to routine efforts in New Testament studies to read the various Gospels, each in its own terms, the basic premise of the book — that a document's system could be described in its own terms and not only as part of a much larger "Judaism" — fully accorded with the methods and presuppositions of scholarship then and now.

The issues in scholarship in Judaism being theological, not merely academic in any sense, it is easy for us to understand why in Judaic Studies book reviewing should be a blood sport. But the enormous controversy surrounding so ordinary a work as *Judaism: The Evidence of the Mishnah* — the context of which is fully described in chapter 1 of this book — is difficult to explain. In what follows, I spell out the controversy and deal with the issues raised by Cohen and Maccoby. *Midstream* subsequently printed a symposium on the book, and I reproduce that as well.

The heated debates surrounding the character and meaning of the Mishnah, ca. 200 C.E., the first document of Judaism after the Hebrew scripture, present a puzzle. Why, one wonders, should people get so excited about a law code seventeen hundred years old, most of whose laws no one observes in their original form? Yet, in the recent past, two librarians on either side of the Atlantic heaped fire and brimstone on the head of someone whose views on the Mishnah they reject.[1] The rhetoric seems out of proportion to the scholarly, even arcane, character of the issues. The smoke of ad hominem attacks on competence frequently obscures such flame of truth as may yet burn. And, in point of fact, some may wish to conclude that, as in Joe McCarthy's time, where there's smoke, there's a smudgepot.

If we wish to interpret the debate and its issues, we do well, first, to ask whether it is only in our day that the Mishnah has defined the focus for such rancor, so acrimonious a version of scholarly discussion. We seek perspective on the remarkably heated character of discourse, on the sounds and fury of a war about what are, in point of fact, trivialities, facts of a long-gone age and their interpretation. Christian onlookers to the brawl propose that, anyhow, that's how Jews argue, another example of that "Jewish excess of emotions" that our gentile neighbors deplore. But if we concede that Jewish scholars treat scholarly issues as a blood sport, we still must wonder why in other areas of Jewish learning, cool, near-gentile restraint prevails. We should look in vain for personal imprecations to fill up articles on such topics as the definition of midrash, the interpretation of Maimonides' doctrine of the messiah, or even the history of Qabbalah in Spain. And if people propose that, because the Mishnah constitutes the first document of the oral Torah, debates about the history and character of the Mishnah gain their intensity and their sour spirit from the presence of theological poison, two facts intervene. First, an equivalent spirit does not characterize Jewish discourse on biblical problems. Second, parties to the present debate to begin with are not Orthodox but Reform and Conservative. So on the face of it, no fiercely defended doctrinal issue can account for the fury of the fray. In point of fact, at the very beginnings of modern Jewish scholarship a century and a quarter ago, people conducted their disputes about the history and character of the Mishnah exactly as they do today.

I

I refer, in particular, to one of the founding documents of modern Jewish scholarship, Zechariah Frankel's *Darkhe Hammishna*

---

1. Hyam Maccoby, "Jacob Neusner's Mishnah," *Midstream* 30 (1984): 24–32. Also Shaye J. D. Cohen, "Jacob Neusner, Mishnah, and Counter-Rabbinics," *Conservative Judaism* 37 (1983): 48–63.

*(The Ways of the Mishnah)*, originally published in Leipzig in Hebrew in 1859 and republished as recently as 1959 in Tel Aviv in
Hebrew. Frankel, who was born in 1801 in Prague and died in
Breslau in 1875, served as a rabbi, mainly in Dresden, then in Breslau as founding director of the Jewish Theological Seminary. He
enjoys credit as the founder of what is called "positive-historical
Judaism," to which present-day Conservative Judaism traces its
lineage. What this meant in practice, in synagogue life, was in-
troducing a choir, organ, and German-language sermons. But he
rejected the Reform rabbis' changes, which he held arbitrary. His
earlier scholarly work, proving that a Jew's oath can be trusted
(1846) and demonstrating the antiquity of Jewish law, somewhat
later, excited no great animosity. *Darkhe Hammishnah* did.

Nothing in the outline of the work or on the surface explains
why anyone should get excited about the book. Frankel proposed
to define the Mishnah and explain the nature of its contents,
treat the halakhah in relationship to the Torah, and explain why
halakhah changes. He reviewed the lives of authorities on the
Mishnah in a long sequence of thumbnail sketches, made up of
compilations of tales about the several principal figures. This biographical (in context: historical) exercise covers a third of the
whole. Then Frankel treats the history of the formation of the
Mishnah, its text, literary character, and structure. His special interest in all this was to prove the antiquity of the oral Torah. This
he does by demonstrating that, in content, the oral Torah — that
is, the Mishnah — dates back to a very early period. In the words
of Joel Gereboff, "By citing examples...Frankel asserts that the
development of the Mishnah was a conservative process. Nothing
from the past was changed.... Later generations worked systematically to build on what they had received."[2] So much for the
character of the book and its argument: deeply conservative, if
anything an attack on Reform Judaism, entirely consistent with the
author's earlier interests and publications.

The response to the book was enormous. Samson Raphael
Hirsch, for the Orthodox opposition, and Shelomo Rappoport, for
the defense, engaged in vigorous and heated debate. About what?
Hirsch focused on the critical issue: was the Mishnah the work
of man or God? Again Gereboff: "The discussion centered about
three points: the origin of the halakhah, divine or in the Great

---

2. Joel Gereboff, "The Pioneer: Zecharias Frankel," in J. Neusner, ed., *The
Modern Study of the Mishnah* (Leiden, 1974), 59–75.

Assembly? The origin of the hermeneutical principles, divine or human? The meaning of 'a law revealed to Moses from Sinai,' a divine or very old or self-evident law?" What had gone wrong was simple. Frankel had treated the Mishnah as the work of men. He even interpreted matters in a way other than is found in the Babylonian Talmud, turning instead to the Palestinian one.

In fact, Frankel presented too small a target. The seminary he headed bore the brunt of attacks. One of his critics stands for them all: "There has arisen in the land a new group of people who do not trust in the truth of faith, but have followed the desires of their hearts. They have vented their disgusting spirit upon the Torah, which they have not accepted as Mosaic and now will do the same to the Talmud." So Shelomo Klein. When this kind of splenetic outburst takes the place of serious criticism, it is for one reason only. The critic, terribly angry to begin with, cannot either join the issue as framed by the author or find some other. But the critic here was right — not about Frankel's "disgusting spirit" but about the issue at hand. Frankel really had done what the critics said. He had treated the Mishnah as the work of men. Why the violence?

What happened between the time of Frankel's earlier work, beginning in the 1840s, and the publication of his book on the Mishnah? The question seems pertinent, for the violent reception of the ideas in the later book presents a puzzle in light of the irenic response to the essentially congruent premises revealed in the earlier work. In the words of Bernhard Brilling, "The first modern Jewish theological seminary, the Juedisch-Theologisches Seminar, was established in Breslau by Zechariah Frankel in 1854. With its celebrated library it became a center of Jewish scholarship.... It also published the first comprehensive Jewish learned journal, *Monatschrift für Geschichte und Wissenschaft des Judentums.*"[3] So what Frankel had done in the years just before publishing his great work was to establish two things: (1) a new kind of institution for Judaic learning, and (2) a new type of medium for public discourse in Judaic learning. In these two ways, Frankel had defined a new social setting for Judaic studies, different from the established one in important and obvious ways.

The new school was not individual but ongoing; it conducted an organized curriculum; it pursued subjects (whether of Jewish interest or not) earlier ignored; it represented a viewpoint deriving from a source other than the established yeshiva world view of the same

---

3. See his article, "Breslau," *Encyclopaedia Judaica* 4:1355.

time and region. The new journal, in German, accorded with the standards of public discourse not of that same yeshiva world but of the university world of Germany. It was meant, for one thing, to be judicious, civil, and restrained, virtues lacking in the home circumstances of the yeshiva world. Frankel's reply to his critics is a case in point: "People should read the book [*The Ways of the Mishnah*] without presuppositions. It is a book on the development of the halakhah and the Mishnah and not on theology. Attacks should be made against the book and not against its author or his seminary."

## II

If we may generalize from a single case, what I think we see is a shift in the social and institutional foundations of a field of study as much as a change in the modes of thought or the paradigms of learning. It was one thing for Frankel to cite the Talmud of the Land of Israel (the "Palestinian Talmud") instead of the Babylonian one. People could even swallow his interest in the Septuagint, the Greek translation of scripture, and other studies outside of the range of the rabbinic writings of antiquity. But when he asked a set of questions formerly not raised about the historical and therefore human origins of the Mishnah, and when he raised those questions in the sanctuary of an institution beyond the power of the yeshiva world and in the context of a journal not controlled by that world's values, that was another matter. In publishing his book on the Mishnah, the critical document of the faith, the first constituent of that oral Torah that defined Judaism, Frankel threw down the gauntlet.

The heat of debate, the uninhibited personal attacks — these expressed not power but pathetic weakness. The other side could not argue with Frankel nor, still worse, could the critics get to him. He could not be dismissed or ignored or merely boycotted or humiliated. These modes of public pressure lacking, the enemy on the right, the Orthodox, had to resort to saying what they really thought. It did no good. Frankel's work defined the program of scholarship for the next century. His critics could do nothing about it, because they could not persuade the people who received Frankel's work — his colleagues, his students, and those that carried on from them. The enemies crept back into the protected domain of their own institutions, their own social setting, their own media of public discourse. They had no choice. Scholarship continued on its way without them. Today there are Orthodox Jewish scholars who defend Frankel as Orthodox.

## III

This long detour through events of a century and a quarter ago places into perspective accusations that someone holds the views he does, and expresses them, so that he can get a job in a university. Why make one's place of employment an issue, let alone a mode of explaining scholarly views one is constrained, after all, to refute? And what sort of scholarly refutation takes the form of pointing to the source of an opponent's paycheck? In other words, you have to wonder why someone would bother to construct such a puzzling argument.

In this context, I am reminded of yet another mode of refutation, one that consists of listing misprints in a book, on the one side, or catalogues of trivial errors, on the other — always joined by cries of "worthless" and "comic."[4] After all, errors are there to be corrected, but the work goes on. It is not as if by reason of a misprint or a trivial error, one that scarcely affects the meaning of a paragraph, let alone a page, someone went out and committed murder or adultery or even ate pork! At issue in scholarship is only learning, that is, a labor of trying to grasp and make sense of the text and of the world.

Yet that, of course, vastly misrepresents matters. At issue in scholarship, when it comes to Judaism, are many things, and least

---

4. See Saul Lieberman, "A Tragedy or a Comedy?" *Journal of the American Oriental Society* 104 (1984): 315–19. Nothing about that review (the review was handwritten and found in Lieberman's *Nachlass,* the author's intentions for which we will never know), its treatment, and its reception, accorded with the established norms of scholarly ethics. For example, the responsible editor of JAOS claimed that I had declined to answer, when, in fact, I made an altogether different statement, which he did not accurately report. In this context, I take note that Lieberman's posthumous review was circulated prior to publication by the book editor of the JAOS for about a year. Hearing about it, on April 19, 1983, I wrote to him, "It seems to me out of the question to reply at all to a dead man; I cannot imagine how it could be done with dignity and decency. If you choose to print the review and if you wish a comment from me, it is as follows: 'People do not reply to a lion after [his] death,' Y. Git. 9:1." Lieberman's corrections are valuable and appreciated, in line with Prov. 9:8–9. I list them in an appendix to my *Talmud,* vol. 23, the first available volume. The rest is covered by my statement of April 19, 1983. This reply was not printed by JAOS; they printed that I had declined to reply, which of course was incorrect. I had replied. Then I had in mind to discuss the matter further in some later issue, but JAOS refused to print any further reply at all.

among them, it often seems, is the pursuit of natural curiosity about why things were or are the way they seem rather than some other way. It is for good reason that the Mishnah forms the centerpiece of debate again and again. Why so? Because it indeed is the first document of Judaism beyond the Hebrew scriptures. Everything we know about the world from the end of the Hebrew Bible to the formation of the first writings of Judaism, beginning in ca. 200 C.E., derives, to begin with, from the Mishnah and from the writings that flow from the Mishnah.

So when paradigms shift, as they have, and the social foundations of learning change, as they have, we return to the original arena of Judaic discourse, the Mishnah. Scholarly debates today take the place of theological ones in medieval times; at issue in a misprint or a mistranslation is not correcting secular error but demonstrating sin and heresy.

## IV

Then why the furor just now, just here? Since Frankel's work came under attack only as part of a full-scale assault against his seminary, we have to ask what institutional difference defines today's disputes and accounts for the heat and rancor. Phrased in this way, the question answers itself. Just as Frankel's approach to learning, his interest in questions of history, accorded with the character and requirements of the new institution he had founded, so the new approaches to the problem of the Mishnah come to full expression in a new setting for Judaic studies, secular universities.

It is no accident, in my view, that when people ask new questions, they do so in a new setting, for new types of students, and in a new medium of discourse. People in the Conservative and Reform Judaic seminaries take deep offense not only at what is said but, as their rhetoric tells us, also at who says it, to whom, and where he or she prints it.

It is in a university. It is to a neutral audience, made up not only of insiders, such as rabbis. It is in a book published not by a rabbinical press or a Jewish publisher but by a university press of premier standing. And, the important point for last: the issues also are new ones. And they derive from the secular humanities of today's university discourse. Let me explain.

In *Judaism: The Evidence of the Mishnah*, I analyze a single document, essentially out of all relationship to the other documents of the larger canon of authoritative and holy books of Judaism. I read that document on its own. This is just as scholars of the history of the American Constitution read the Constitution not only in light of all of the court decisions of the past two hundred years but also in its own setting and context. Why does that decision, to read a book all by itself (with the clear plan of reading other books of the same canon one by one), make so much trouble?

When we take up a single document in the canon of Judaism and propose to describe, analyze, and interpret that text in particular, we violate the lines of order and system that have characterized earlier studies of these same documents. Until now people have tended to treat all of the canonical texts as testimonies to a single system and structure, that is, to "Judaism." What sort of testimonies texts provide varies according to the interest of the scholars, students, and saints who study them. Scholars look for meanings of words and phrases, better versions of a text. For them all canonical documents equally serve as a treasury of philological facts and variant readings. Students also look for the sense of words and phrases and follow a given phrase hither and yon, as their teachers direct them on their treasure hunt. Saints study all texts equally, looking for God's will and finding testimonies to God in each component of the Torah of Moses, our rabbi.

Among none of these circles — Orthodox, Reform, Conservative, Israeli alike — will the discrete description, analysis, and interpretation of a single text make sense. Why not? Because all texts ordinarily are taken to form a common statement, "Torah" in the mythic setting, "Judaism" in the theological one. From the accepted perspective the entire canon of Judaism — "the one whole Torah of Moses, our rabbi" — equally and at every point testifies to the entirety of Judaism. Why so? Because all documents in the end form components of a single system. Each makes its contribution to the whole. If, therefore, we wish to know what "Judaism" or, more accurately, "the Torah" teaches on any subject, we are able to draw freely on sayings relevant to that subject wherever they occur in the entire canon of Judaism. Guided only by the taste and judgment of the great sages of the Torah, as they have addressed the question at hand, we thereby describe "Judaism."

Accordingly, as Judaism comes to informed expression in the Judaic pulpit, in the Judaic classroom, and above all in the lives and hearts and minds of Jews loyal to Judaism, all parts of the canon of Judaism speak equally authoritatively. All parts, all together, present us with one harmonious world view and homogeneous way of life, one Torah ("Judaism") for all Israel. That view of "the Torah," that is to say, of the canon of Judaism, characterizes every organized movement within Judaism as we now know it, whether Reform or Orthodox, whether Reconstructionist or Conservative, whether in the exile (diaspora) or in the State of Israel. How so? Among circles of Judaism indifferent to considerations of time and place, anachronism and context, every document, whenever brought to closure, testifies equally to that single system. For those circles Judaism emerges at a single moment ("Sinai"), but comes to expression in diverse times and places, so that any composition that falls into the category of Torah serves, without further differentiation, to tell us about the substance of Judaism, its theology and law.

# V

For a person such as myself, by contrast, engaged in such an inquiry into the historical formation of Judaism studied through the analysis of the unfolding literary evidence of the canon, documents stand in three relationships to one another and to the system of which they form part, that is, to "Judaism," as a whole. They are relationships of autonomy, connection, and continuity.

1. Each document is to be seen all by itself, that is, as autonomous of all others.

2. Each document, again as a matter of theory, is to be examined for its relationships, as connected, with other documents universally regarded as falling into the same classification as Torah.

3. And, finally, each document is to be allowed to take its place as part of the undifferentiated aggregate of documents that, all together, constitute the canon of Judaism, that is to say, "Torah." It is shown to form part of a continuity.

Simple logic makes self-evident the proposition that, if a document comes down to us within its own framework and as a complete book with a beginning, middle, and end, in preserving that book the canon presents us with a document on its own and not solely as part of a larger composition or construct. So we, too, see the document as it reaches us, that is, as autonomous.

If, second, a document contains materials shared verbatim or in substantial content with other documents of its classification, or if one document refers to the contents of other documents, then the several documents that clearly wish to engage in conversation with one another have to address one another. That is to say, we have to seek for the marks of connectedness, asking for the meaning of those connections.

Finally, since, as I said at the outset, the community of the faithful of Judaism, in all of the contemporary expressions of Judaism, concur that documents held to be authoritative constitute one whole, seamless "Torah," that is, a complete and exhaustive statement of God's will for Israel and humanity, we take as our further task the description of the whole out of the undifferentiated testimony of all of its parts. These components in the theological context are viewed, as is clear, as equally authoritative for the composition of the whole: one, continuous system. In taking up such a question, we address a problem not of theology alone, though it is a correct theological conviction, but one of description, analysis, and interpretation of an entirely historical order.

In my view the various documents of the canon of Judaism produced in late antiquity demand a hermeneutic altogether different from the one of homogenization and harmonization, the ahistorical and anticontextual one I have rejected. It is one that does not harmonize but that differentiates. It is a hermeneutic shaped to teach us how to read the texts at hand one by one and in a particular context, exactly in the way in which we read any other text bearing cultural and social insight. The texts stand not as self-evidently important but only as examples, sources of insight for a quite neutral inquiry. Let me spell out what I think is at issue between the established hermeneutic and the one I propose. Why in universities and not in seminaries do I find my audience?

# VI

The three key words of the inherited hermeneutic are "continuity," "uniqueness," and "survival." Scholars who view the texts as continuous with one another seek what is unique in the system formed by the texts as a whole. With the answer to what is unique, they propose to explain the survival of Israel, the Jewish people. Hence: continuity, uniqueness, survival.

The words to encapsulate the hermeneutic I espouse are these: "description," "analysis," and "interpretation." I am trying to learn how to *describe* the constituents of the canon, viewed individually, each in its distinctive context. I wish to discover appropriate *analytical* tools, questions to lead me from description of one text to comparison and contrast between two or more texts of the canon. Only at the end do I address the question of *interpretation:* how do all of the texts of the canon at hand flow together into a single continuous statement, a "Judaism."

Within the inherited hermeneutic of continuity, survival, and uniqueness, the existence of the group defines the principal concern, an inner-facing one, hence the emphasis on uniqueness in quest, in continuities, for the explanation of survival. Within the proposed hermeneutic of description, analysis, and interpretation, by contrast, the continued survival of a "unique" group does not frame the issue. For my purposes, it is taken for granted, for the group is not the main thing at all. That is an insider's question. The problematic emerges from without. What I want to know is not how and why the group survived so as to help it survive some more. It is how to describe the society and culture contained within, taken as a given, how to interpret an enduring world view and way of life, expressed by the artifacts in hand. How did, and does, the group work? That is an issue of benign curiosity.

So I claim that the results of the literary inquiry will prove illuminating for the study of society and culture. I have now to explain why I think so. The answer lies in our will and capacity to generalize out of details, a judgment on a broad issue of culture, as it is exemplified in the small problem at hand. The issue here is secular.

True, I also ask how the components of the canon as a whole form a continuity. I wonder why this document in particular survived to speak for the whole. But for me the answers to these questions generate theories and promise insight for the study of other canonical religions. So far as I shall succeed, it will be because I can learn from these other canonical religions. I have tried to learn from and also teach something to those who study the history, the thought, the social reality, of religions that, like Judaism, form lasting monuments to the power of humanity to endure and to prevail so far. Judaism presents a mere example of a truth beyond itself, a truth of humanistic interest.

## VII

Let us turn to the substance of the debate and see whether we can sort out what matters from what is merely personal or mostly incoherent. What bothers the critics most of all? It is the very definition of the work and, to the critics' credit, they do pick out the main innovation. What I have done is to ask a very simple question. If we read the Mishnah all by itself, without reference to any other corpus of writing, what sort of system, if any, do we find in the document?

To show, first of all, that this is the critical issue, I point to the substantive and entirely relevant argument. One critic takes the view that one cannot look at a single document in isolation. Why not? All of the rabbinic literature constitutes a single mass, each element present among all others (thus: continuity). Another critic takes umbrage that someone has read the Mishnah out of phase with the Babylonian Talmud (as though Maimonides did not do the same thing in his Mishnah commentary nearly eight hundred years ago!) Why is that wrong? Because, again, we should not read the Mishnah by itself but only as it has been read through the eyes of the authors of documents that received the Mishnah and, particularly, the Babylonian Talmud, completed four hundred years after the closure of the Mishnah.

Finally, we are told that since the documents of the rabbinic canon intersect and overlap, as they do, we must "always" read them "synoptically," meaning in light of one another. If these criticisms prove valid, then the very notion of asking about the system, the "Judaism" of the Mishnah, in particular, rests upon a totally wrong premise. One need not read a book about "Judaism: the evidence of the Mishnah," because the Mishnah by itself cannot testify to any system, any "Judaism," by itself.

When we turn to the Mishnah itself, the document does exhibit traits we associate with autonomous documents. That is to say, if you study the Mishnah from outside to inside, seeing it whole and not merely as a scrapbook or collection of bits and pieces, the document turns out to follow a cogent program and to make a coherent set of statements. We know that fact on the basis of two traits of the Mishnah, its formal character and its substantial message.

The language of the Mishnah follows patterns. These patterns repeat themselves, often in groups of three or five examples of a single pattern. The substance of a set of three or five such examples is cogent. How so? Each of the five makes the same point that the others do. If you take up a sizable piece of the document, then, and trace the units of thought — that is, the groups of examples of the same point — you discover an interesting thing. Sets of three or five examples of one basic notion resort to a single distinctive pattern of language. Then, when a new point is made by a new set of examples, it will come to expression in a pattern different from the one before. This is a roundabout way of explaining that in the Mishnah when the subject changes, so does the rhetorical pattern.

Now that trait of speech, the matching of rhetoric and topic, is so pervasive in the Mishnah that we must wonder whether the document stands by itself, or whether the Mishnah is simply another instance in which rabbis, wherever and whenever they lived, expressed their ideas. If that striking trait proves commonplace in many writings, then, on merely formal grounds, we cannot treat the Mishnah as special and ask about its ideas, its system in particular. In point of fact, however, only the Mishnah is so formulated. Its closest companion, the Tosefta, a collection of supplementary teachings concerning the topics and rules found in the Mishnah, is not. And no other rabbinic writing, from the Mishnah through the Bavli four centuries later, exhibits those distinctive traits of formalization that the Mishnah does. (Many documents produce other traits of careful formulation, but not the Mishnah's.)

One may well argue that the mere fact that a document is written in a special way does not prove the writing is special. That is indeed so. A second, well-known fact does make us suppose that the Mishnah follows its own program not only in form but also in meaning. It is the simple datum that, after the Mishnah, no other sustained piece of writing takes up exactly the program of topics that the Mishnah's authors treat. The Mishnah is composed of six divisions on six principal topics: agriculture, the calendar, women and the family, civil law, the cult, and purity. The heirs of the Mishnah in the Talmud of the Land of Israel (ca. 400 C.E.) ignored the fifth and sixth divisions. The heirs of the Mishnah in the Talmud of Babylonia (ca. 600 C.E.) skipped the first and the sixth. Only two important heirs to the Mishnah follow the Mishnah's program, the authors of the Tosefta and Maimonides a thousand years later.

## VIII

These rather obvious and simple considerations justify asking what the Mishnah, when read whole and complete, appears to say as a cogent message. But what of the repeated criticism, that it is improper to read the Mishnah by itself simply because the Mishnah forms part of a larger whole? A classic statement of this view, not with reference to the Mishnah in particular, comes from Lawrence H. Schiffman: "This system, composed of interlocking and re-interlocking parts possessed of an organic connection one to another, is never really divisible."[5] If that were so, then I have sinned grievously in taking up not only one of the parts, but the principal one, distinguishing it from all others and reading it on its own.

But do all the parts turn out to be indivisible and indistinguishable from one another? That remains to be demonstrated. The critics assuredly stand on firm ground, so a superficial glance would suggest, in seeing as intersecting the rabbinic documents of late antiquity. From the Mishnah to the Tosefta, the Talmud of the Land of Israel, the Talmud of Babylonia, the Mekhilta, Sifra, two Sifres, Genesis Rabbah, Leviticus Rabbah, Pesiqta de R. Kahana, and on and on, sayings and stories do circulate hither and yon. The meaning of the fact that a saying may make its way from one document to the next awaits systematic investigation.

We have, for example, to ask how much of a document must be shared with some other(s) before that document loses all integrity and melts into an undifferentiated mass? If the bulk of a document is shared with others, then we may see the book at hand as a mere container, lacking all power to shape the traits or change the taste of what is poured into it. A text is then merely a context, a place for storing things, so to speak.

We must also demonstrate, to the contrary, that when a document makes use of a saying or a story, it is for a purpose, part of a larger program, distinctive to the document at hand. In that case, a text possesses integrity and enjoys autonomy even though, at some points, it is concentric with some other text(s).

---

5. Lawrence H. Schiffman, *Sectarian Law in the Dead Sea Scrolls: Courts, Testimony, and the Penal Code* (Chico, Calif.: Scholars Press, 1983), 3.

# IX

Obviously, the issues before us demand detailed sifting and sorting out. Generalizations prove premature, when each of the texts has not been analyzed in detail, both by itself and in relationship to others. I have conducted such analysis of integrity in a systematic way on three texts: the Mishnah, the Tosefta, and Leviticus Rabbah. Each exhibits its own quite distinctive traits. The Mishnah's authors cite nothing but scripture, and then only occasionally. The Tosefta's authors depend heavily upon the Mishnah, which they cite verbatim and upon which they depend for the order and organization of their ideas. Leviticus Rabbah only rarely goes over materials found in any text prior to its own day (though the later composition, Pesiqta de R. Kahana, borrows heavily from Leviticus Rabbah). On that basis, we surely cannot generalize that "every" document must "always" be read in the light of every other document.

When, at the end, critics ask why I do not read the Mishnah in light of everything said by everybody from the publication of the Mishnah to the day before yesterday, my answer is simple. Why should I? Does anybody in philosophy read Plato only through the eyes of the neo-Platonists? And who, any more, insists that the Hebrew Bible be read as Rashi dictates we should read it — except to understand Rashi? The history of the exegetical tradition of the Mishnah yields the intellectual history of the legal tradition of Judaism from the time of the Mishnah onward, an extraordinarily interesting story.

I know, because in my commentary,[6] I followed the whole of the exegetical tradition of the Mishnah and of the Tosefta for the Division of Purities and published twenty-two volumes on that division, dealing with the important received exegeses of each passage in sequence. I should be the last to claim that I grasped it all in all its depths. No person of conscience would ever make such

---

6. Cf. my *History of the Mishnaic Law of Purities* (Leiden, 1974–77), I–XXII. I covered the remainder of the Mishnah, the second through the fifth divisions, in another twenty-one volumes, and my former students completed the work for Mishnah and Tosefta Zeraim, the first division, in a sequence of monographs and dissertations. On the basis of this labor of infinite care about detail, I am declared by a scholar whose work we have noted as notoriously self-indulgent to be "notoriously indifferent to detail." On the basis of a few, very occasional mistakes, then, work of genuine care, accurate over the vast majority of its details, is found "sloppy." No one can accuse these critics of an excessive concern to be meticulously fair.

a claim. But I did work my way through the bulk of the received exegesis.

I found most of the commentaries prolix and absorbed by debate on exegesis, not by the sense of the passage at hand. Much of the commentary, moreover, concerns legal issues vivid only long after the Mishnah was published, so, as classicists have known since the Renaissance and Bible scholars since the time of Spinoza, to read an ancient text in light of its later exegesis is to commit anachronism.

True, no one proposes to ignore what other, earlier commentators have said about a given text. But it seems only in the subject at hand do we not only err but *sin* if we ask the text to form its own first, best commentary, as I did in my Mishnah commentary.

# X

Readers who have come this far will wonder, as I still wonder, why the heat, the nasty and the mean rhetoric, when all I want to know is what a text is and means. But the issues really do matter. I do not blame the other side for its anger. It proves they care. I care too, but about something else.

I perceive the classical literature of Judaism as a great work of humanity. (As a religious Jew, I hasten to add, it is humanity responding to God's revelation.) We have in the writings of the ancient rabbis an amazing intellectual achievement. What, in sum, the rabbis did was to search out the most profound layers of logic and order concealed in the superficial levels of triviality and nonsense. They took up much the same philosophical program as occupied other philosophers of their time, asking, for example, about the relationship between the potential and the actual, the acorn and the oak. They inquired about the power of human will to change the facts of life. They speculated about the nature of mixtures, just as did the Stoic physicists and in exactly the same logical classifications and categories. But our sages of blessed memory delivered their judgments not in engaging and accessible dialogues, as did Plato, nor even in response to the immediately accessible essays on virtue, the good life, and the ideal state — essays we read today with pleasure, such as Aristotle wrote.

Our sages spoke of things people really knew and could feel and touch — sweat and excrement, menstrual blood and the excretions of the sexual organs. They asked about mixtures of gravy and meat, of wool and linen. They taught theory only through example, and they drew example from commonplace and workaday realities. Out of all this they produced with extraordinary art a book of great poetry, the Mishnah, which also, when properly read, turns out to be a book of great philosophy: an orderly and disciplined statement of the order and rule of life.

## A Symposium on
## *The Mishnah and the Smudgepots*[7]

*Meir Bar-Ilan, Shaye J. D. Cohen, William Scott Green, Samson Levey, Hyam Maccoby, and a Response*

### *Meir Bar-Ilan:*

Suppose an outsider offered to bring an ancient culture to the consciousness of modern man, would he find any takers? Would anybody be interested in buying merchandise two thousand years old, dusty pots, some of them broken?

In view of the unlikelihood of a positive response, Jacob Neusner's efforts ("The Mishnah and the Smudgepots," June/July 1985) deserve our sincere appreciation. The aim of dozens of his books and translations, apparently, is to make the impossible possible and offer the ancient Mishnah as an attractive and meaningful field for modern scholarship. However, while acknowledging the virtues of Neusner's studies, and his resounding publications, I must admit that if he were the advocate of the Mishnah in any court, the Mishnah would be found guilty. He doesn't make much of an effort to beautify the Mishnah by describing it in rosy colors, perhaps because he does not have the responsibility of a pulpit; nor does he aspire to be the Mishnah's advocate but rather its critical researcher. His function is not to represent many years of tradition but rather to describe and analyze the text, and later on present his prolific findings to the student of Judaism.

From one point of view, at least, the Jewish people should be grateful to Neusner as the salesman the Mishnah has had for many years. No one else can claim to have aroused so much interest in cultivating the garden of the study of the Mishnah; no

---

7. Originally: *Midstream* 33 (1986): 38–42.

one has raised so many students — and questions — as Neusner. Not only that, he has succeeded in getting many people involved in what is happening in that garden and has incidentally added to the prestige of all the workers in it, at least in North American universities. So, if Neusner were only a "salesman," we might be satisfied, but Neusner is not, and the products of his research, presented in his conclusions, portray fresh insights, not just sales promotion. It doesn't matter whether or not there is general agreement with his observations on the Mishnah. It can be claimed that some of his descriptions and his methods are not convincing, but this claim should be dealt with in the world of study and not by denunciations outside of academe.

There is a personal issue I think should be mentioned here: Neusner is the first Mishnah scholar whose studies didn't begin in the traditional Beth Midrash. Like Rabbi Akivah in his time, Neusner came to the oral Torah at a relatively advanced age, without having the Mishnah imprinted on his heart during childhood and early manhood. It is a truism that the outsider can often see more clearly than the insiders.

It seems that in "The Mishnah and the Smudgepots" Neusner deliberately changes an academic matter into a theological one. He is not being crucified by the religious establishment, nor is he accused of a religious offense, God forbid! (though he prefers to say he has "sinned" rather than "failed" or "erred"). The main subject under discussion remains in the area of research: Is he correct in his claims and conclusions? Should we accept his findings as founded?

I see in this article more than a little pride; it is misleading when Neusner writes: "In none of these circles, Orthodox, Reform, Conservative, Israeli alike, will the discrete description, analysis, and interpretation of a single text make sense." Why are religious and geographic circles mixed? Not only that, but one gets the impression that he is the first scholar to use the "right" method; all the other research in the field is useless. His claims that everybody is against him seem to be mainly rooted in his own mind, though it is true he is different from the others. Nevertheless, despite his subjective feeling, Neusner's studies and claims deserve to be studied carefully.

Sadly, that traditional controversy, more than a thousand years old, seems to be returning with a vengeance. One hopes Jewish studies will not be harmed by this ugly fray, and may even be strengthened.

*Shaye J. D. Cohen:*

In responding to his critics Jacob Neusner attacks my review of his *Judaism: The Evidence of the Mishnah.*[8] Neusner's critics are a diverse lot, each with his own things to say, but Neusner lumps them all together and treats them collectively as sons of darkness. The result is that his response does not do justice to any of them, much as a scholar who interprets every document of rabbinic Judaism in the light of every other will not be able to interpret any one of them correctly. I do not wish to defend my fellow critics here; I wish only to correct the errors and misleading statements that apply to me.

In the opening paragraph of his response Neusner states that I "heap fire and brimstone" on his head, that I use "rhetoric out of all proportion to the scholarly...character of the issues," and that my review is full of "the smoke of ad hominem attacks." At the conclusion of his response Neusner writes that my review contains "nasty and mean rhetoric." All of this is false. I challenge Neusner to quote a single sentence from my review that will substantiate these statements. The opening paragraph of my review ends with the sentence "The publication of this work...is an event in the modern study of rabbinics." The last sentence of my review reads, "...this is a brilliant and imaginative book of the first rank, an important and stimulating contribution to the modern study of rabbinics." I would like to think that my review is trenchant, substantive, and hard-hitting, but it contains no "fury" and does not engage in "blood-sport."

The crucial question before us is how we should interpret the Mishnah. Neusner argues that the Mishnah can and must be read as "a single document, out of all relationship to the other documents of the larger canon of authoritative and holy books of Judaism." In principle I agree, and I regard this point as one of Neusner's major contributions. However, the Mishnah's connections with some of the other rabbinic documents is so intimate that we cannot understand what the Mishnah is saying without considering these other documents as well — one illumines the other. Neusner deduces from my argument that I am one of those who believe that every document of rabbinic Judaism must be read in the light of every other, as a seamless oral Torah delivered to Moses at Mount Sinai. This is false. In my review I reject this

---

8. *Conservative Judaism* 37 (Fall 1983): 48–63.

approach; my disagreement centers on the technical question how best to interpret the Mishnah "on its own terms."

Even if this question were settled, we still have other questions before us. In my review I argue that Neusner is primarily an allegorist who reads into the Mishnah the humanistic message he wants it to convey, that he is a Holocaust theologian eager to find in the Mishnah a message for contemporary American Jewry, and that his unending emphasis on the crucial importance of the destruction of the temple is a theological judgment not advanced by the Mishnah itself. I regret that Neusner chose not to address any of these questions in his response.

I encourage the readers of this journal to read the reviews to which Neusner is responding and to decide the merits of each case. In order to facilitate this exercise, I shall be happy to send a copy of my review to anyone who sends me a self-addressed stamped envelope (business-size).

### William Scott Green:

Strong criticism of others' work is an academic commonplace. It is the principal form of public intellectual engagement — the way scholars transact their business — and is supposed to promote the understanding of ideas, the assessment of theories, and the advancement of knowledge. When criticism degenerates into mere condemnation and overt insult, the dispute is political or personal, not academic and professional. When criticism aims simply to discredit rather than to discern, the conflicting positions are irreconcilable, perhaps incommensurable.

The harsh reactions to Jacob Neusner's *Judaism: The Evidence of the Mishnah* reveal a sharp disagreement within Jewish Studies about the proper way to study ancient rabbinic writings. The dispute ostensibly is academic and its central issue allegedly epistemological, but the tone and character of the criticisms suggest otherwise. "The Mishnah and the Smudgepots" points to two kinds of Jewish Studies, one ethnic, the other disciplinary.

From the perspective of ethnic Jewish Studies, materials are deemed interesting because they are Jewish. This school of thought is marked by a fundamentally romantic view of all things it defines as Jewish. Ethnic scholarship tends to be avenging and celebratory. Ethnic education, at whatever level, makes learning into a ritual of attachment to the heroic people. Ethnic intellectual discourse tends to be restricted, often in Hebrew, and directed primarily to those within the ethnic group or those who share its romantic suppositions.

In short, ethnic Jewish Studies is a self-validating enterprise designed to preserve Jewish distinctiveness. Ethnic Jewish scholarship serves a powerful communal purpose and therefore is highly charged. It aims to teach the Jews about themselves and thereby to create a usable Jewish past, a workable Jewish present, and a viable Jewish future. Within this framework, reasoned intellectual dissent is all too often ignored or censored, or discounted and dismissed, as a form of disloyalty and disrespect.

Disciplinary Jewish Studies share none of these aims and suppositions. They apply to Jewish sources and materials the standardized inquiries, analytical criteria, and Cartesian skepticism of university studies in the humanities and social sciences. These disciplines attempt to address common questions to various texts, cultures, and societies and thus deny special privilege to any of them. They reject in principle private, self-validating worlds of experience whose meaning is pertinent, and can be transmitted, only to initiates. Within a disciplinary framework, the study of discrete Jewish materials is shaped by general questions about human imagination and behavior, questions extrinsic to particular Jewish needs, concerns, and preoccupations.

These descriptions are caricatures, Weberian "pure types," and no one in Jewish Studies conforms fully to either. But more deliberately than any other, Jacob Neusner has appropriated the disciplinary agenda and applied it relentlessly and methodically to the classics of Judaism. His work has subverted nearly every supposition of ethnic scholarship on the Talmud and cognate writings and has ended the academic political domination of their study by a few seminary and Israeli professors. The results and reactions have been chronicled in the pages of this magazine.

There is a surrealism to the entire dispute. Ethnic and disciplinary Jewish Studies operate in incongruous worlds, have incompatible motivations, and address disparate constituencies. The dispute between them is bitter because it is pointless. Not enough is shared between them to allow the possibility of communication, much less persuasion.

The diversion within Jewish Studies need not be regretted. It is the natural result of Jewish life in a free society. Ethnic Jewish Studies, which serve communal political needs and have communal support, will continue. But disciplinary Jewish Studies have taken firm root in American universities, and they will endure there. No amount of ethnic resentment, hostility, or anger can change that.

*Samson H. Levey:*

The tantalizing Tannaitic text, the core of which is the Mishnah, is an exciting challenge to creative rabbinic scholarship. The giants who interpreted rabbinic lore in the light of *Wissenschaft,* did so with a sense of scholarly dignity. Even in the case of Zechariah Frankel, the argument was regarded as a *mahloqet l'shem sha-mayim* (debate for the sake of Heaven). The vast majority of Jewish scholars since then, and in our own day, have maintained high standards of ethics in expounding their respective points of view, while respecting one another's right to differ.

However, when pedantic tyrants dominated the scene, woe unto those who would dare to trespass upon their sacred precincts by suggesting a new idea, or a different approach or method or interpretation. With ferocious impudence and arrogant authoritarianism they engaged in *mahloqet l'shame,* and disgrace, and left an ugly stain on the superb quality and exemplary ethic of higher Jewish learning and scholarship.

A personal case in point demonstrates the difference between scholars. In 1972 I ventured my Ben Zoma hypothesis, which was but a shade different from the views of the leading authorities of the past hundred years. Robert Gordis, who disagreed with me, nonetheless printed the article in *Judaism* ("The Best Kept Secret of the Rabbinic Tradition," Fall 1972), and in a following issue included the correspondence my article evoked and my rejoinder.

The editor of the *Jewish Quarterly Review,* on the other hand, used his lead article[9] in an ugly effort to discredit my scholarship and to impugn my right to interpret the rabbinic sources, heaping denigration and calumny upon all American-trained scholars. I sent him a response and was assured by him that it would be printed. Years dragged on, but my response never appeared. Until now I did not divulge these facts publicly, but the scholarly world deserves to know the truth.

Jacob Neusner, John Bowker, and other capable rabbinic scholars have also been subject to unwarranted attack. Jacob Neusner's unforgivable sin lies in being the most prolific and one of the most

---

9. "The Plague of Pseudo-Rabbinic Scholarship," Winter 1973.

gifted rabbinic scholars of this century, creative, innovative, systematic, pioneer of the form-critical approach to Mishnah. That he took refuge in a secular university is to his credit. His example has helped expand rabbinic learning throughout this country, in the secular colleges and universities, where it is free and unshackled, and removed from theological-political pressure. He has fulfilled the dictum of Avot 1:1, raising up many disciples, and what is even more important, helping them get established in academia.

Neusner needs neither defense nor apologia. His work is ample testimony to his greatness. To be sure, he is not infallible; but then, who is, other than the Sauls and the Solomons who were anointed to rule by divine right? And as for the Yerushalmi, its difficult Aramaic text is frequently flawed and often obtuse, and there is ample room for honest misunderstanding, which does not call for outbursts of wrath.

Withal, the stature of Jacob Neusner looms more gigantic. He has conducted himself with amazing restraint and admirable dignity, and when he is in error he readily admits it. And who but a Jacob Neusner would a dedicate a volume (*In the Margins of the Yerushalmi,* 1983) to the memory of his detractors who hated him without cause?

## Hyam Maccoby:

Jacob Neusner's remarks in reply to my essay "Jacob Neusner's Mishnah" (May 1984) are very much off the point. I did *not* object to his treating the Mishnah on its own terms, in isolation from later commentaries on the Mishnah (i.e, the Talmudim and their medieval exegesis). This obviously needs to be done, and Maimonides gave a good example of how to do it. My objection was that Neusner was attempting to interpret the Mishnah in isolation from the aggadah (non-legal material found in all rabbinic literature, including the Mishnah itself).

Neusner argues that since the Mishnah has its own style and program, nothing outside it is relevant to explaining it. This is an obvious fallacy. The Mishnah, as a digest, in the main, of the legal (Halakhic) aspect of rabbinic Judaism, necessarily has its own style and program. But to treat it as something intended to be a comprehensive compendium of the oral Torah is simply to beg the question. Neusner does not answer the point, put to him by E. P. Sanders and myself, that the liturgy, being presupposed by the Mishnah, is surely relevant to the Mishnah's exegesis. Nor does he answer the charge that he ignores the aggadic material within the Mishnah itself, e.g., Avot; or explain why the copious aggadic material found in roughly contemporaneous works should be regarded as irrelevant. Instead, he insists that he is right to carry out the highly artificial project of deliberately closing his eyes to all aggadic material and trying to explain the Mishnah without it.

This leads to absurdities, such as saying that the Mishnah is not much concerned with justice, or with repentance, or with the Messiah. It also leads to Neusner's endorsement of nineteenth-century German anti-Jewish scholarship, the aim of which was to substantiate the New Testament charge against the Pharisees, "You pay tithes of mint and dill and cummin; but you have overlooked the weightier demands of the Law, justice, mercy and good faith" (Matthew 23:23). Neusner attempts to obfuscate the issue by expressing great admiration for the Mishnah, and this will no doubt impress people who accept his protestations at their face value. But he admires the Mishnah for the very things that the New Testament alleges *against* the Pharisees: for formalism, attention to petty legalistic detail, and for a structuralist patterning of reality in terms of "holiness" rather than of morality, justice, and love of neighbor.

The work of Schürer, Ferdinand Weber, and Billerbeck, representing rabbinic theology as an anxious, obsessional ritualism, was countered by George Foot Moore, James Parkes, and E. P. Sanders. However, the work of these fair-minded Christian scholars has been dismissed with scorn and abuse by Neusner, whose writings are already being quoted in support of a return to the position of German anti-Jewish scholarship that "the Pharisees were interested mainly in ritual purity." This is not merely a recondite dispute among scholars. Neusner's professed wonder that anyone should take the matter so seriously is disingenuous. If, as seemed likely until quite recently, Neusner's work were to be accepted at his own valuation as the only objective and scientific approach to rabbinic studies, this would represent a major defeat for Judaism — not in any fundamentalist sense, but in the sense that the Christian claim that the New Testament is the true heir and continuation of prophetic concepts of justice and mercy, rather than Pharisaism and rabbinic Judaism, would be vindicated.

Neusner attempts to make light of the blunders that have been found in his work. These, however, are not mere slips, but serious lapses of scholarship that throw doubt on his pretensions to authority as a scholar. It was not for nothing that Saul Lieberman wrote that he was "stunned" by Neusner's "ignorance of rabbinic Hebrew, of Aramaic grammar, and above all of the subject matter with which he deals," a judgment endorsed by Morton Smith, Neusner's own teacher. This was in connection with Neusner's attempted translation of the Palestinian Talmud, of which Lieberman wrote, "The right place for [this] translation is the waste basket."

Finally, I did not accuse Neusner of holding his views "so that he can get a job in a university." I merely suggested (at the end of a long article about the substantive issues) that a university environment is not as free from pressures as Neusner naively supposes, and that his repeated slur against the objectivity of scholars working in "seminaries" may thus be open to a similar retort.

## *Jacob Neusner:*

1. *Meir Bar-Ilan:* I concur that religious issues do not generate fires. Still, the reading of texts one by one and on their own terms does represent a fresh approach.

2. *Shaye J. D. Cohen:* Cohen now concurs in my view that rabbinic documents should be read, to begin with, one by one. But in his review he states, "Synoptic texts must always be studied synoptically, even if one text is 'later' than another." That statement self-evidently contradicts the position outlined here. I believe I grasped Cohen's original point (as I demonstrate in my extensive treatment of an article of his in my *Ancient Judaism and Contemporary Gullibility,*[10] and I am glad that he now retracts it.

As to Cohen's denying that any statement of his falls into the category of "nasty," he reviews the author, not the book. I point to his gratuitous personal attacks on me and my students, for instance the following: "he is raising a generation of graduate students many of whom have minimal expertise in 'the traditional' aspects of the study of rabbinics." That in fact — he is calling all my doctoral students *am haratzim* — is false, since most of my doctoral alumni graduated from Jewish Theological Seminary, Yeshiva University, or Hebrew Union College, and all have studied, in addition, at the Hebrew University. Also: "His inattention to matters of detail is notorious and disgraceful." Find a dozen errors in a hundred thousand possibilities and forthwith: "notorious inattention to details." I found proofreading errors all over Cohen's book,

---

10. Atlanta: Scholars Press, 1986.

but did not allude to them in my review in *American Historical Review*. And: "As is well known, whatever Neusner considers worthy of publication is published at least twice." Very far from the truth. These and many similar remarks are not only beside the point, they also are *ad hominem* and so very nasty. However, I take at face value Cohen's present claim that he did not mean to engage in character assassination of myself and my students.

As to the critical importance of the destruction of the temple and the later calamity of Bar Kokhba's war, I believe that in my position I state the consensus of all Jewish historians, and Cohen takes up a rather idiosyncratic and indeed bizarre opinion, which he has announced but has yet to demonstrate through sustained research. When he prints his book, we shall all read it.

3. *William Scott Green:* I concur with the distinction between ethnic and disciplinary Jewish studies, and, with him, I wonder whether anything of an academic character is at stake in the debate at hand, of which more when we reach the end.

4. *Samson H. Levey:* This great man suffered far more than I ever have in the campaigns of character assassination that plague Jewish studies of the ethnic camp. His generosity of spirit illuminates Jewish learning, wherever it takes place, and he proves that even in a theological seminary learning of an analytical character goes forward.

5. *Hyam Maccoby:* Just now I had the genuine pleasure of reading Maccoby's work on medieval disputations. I found it by far the best treatment of the subject, informed, balanced, beautifully argued, and, in all, a monument to intelligence joined to critical learning. That helped me to understand Maccoby's difficulty in approaching the subject at hand. Where he knows the texts well and also grasps the scholarly problems of dealing with them, he sets a high critical standard and does not practice anachronism. Where he does not, in total ignorance of the problems of critical reading of the sources at hand and the issues of learning that dictate work in one way rather than some other, he blunders. And that is especially so where considerations of doctrine intervene and prevent scholarly discourse. Maccoby on that account does not grasp the methodological, particularly epistemological, issues before us, shown, for instance, by his rather primitive reading of the Gospels he uses to make up his life of Jesus. Necessities of disputation with contemporary anti-Semitic Christians have distorted his grasp of both the sources and the critical traditions of reading them.

As to his specific, and interesting, point on the premises and presuppositions of texts, I take the view that what we cannot show we do not know. But I have completed my work on texts read as autonomous statements, and am beginning to study the connections between and among them. So in due course I shall offer a statement of both method and result on the issue Maccoby raises.

As to Maccoby's illusion to Saul Lieberman's posthumous review, I refer him to my reply, which he has evidently not seen. There are two sides to every argument. But since the *Journal of the American Oriental Society* (like Zeitlin's *JQR*) refused (sight unseen) to print my reply, I had to place it in media Maccoby may not regularly see. The editor of that periodical would not even reply to my letter asking him to print a reply, showing the true character, as to collegiality and authentic academic decency, of the American Oriental Society. Other, very numerous, and rather more positive reviews of my translation likewise seem to have escaped Maccoby's attention. He did not want to see them; he made up his mind to believe whatever he wished to believe. Lieberman listed not quite a score of rather trivial items, none of them affecting the sense of the context of a given passage, all of them readily corrected. He took his best shot and missed by a mile. Perhaps because he himself never translated a rabbinic text, he did not understand the issues. Nor did he believe in the enterprise, printing most of his scholarship in Hebrew. Given the problems of translating a document lacking a critical text, authoritative commentary, and even a decent dictionary, I take great pride in the result. I believe that upward of 90 percent of the whole will stand the test of time, and nothing in Lieberman's review remotely suggested otherwise.

I read with genuine sympathy Maccoby's anguish that some of my conclusions concur with conclusions reached for entirely adventitious reasons by anti-Semites, whom he and I abhor. I care as much as he does about the good name of Jewry, and I have done my share to contribute to that good name. Maccoby may not know these efforts. But his argument — which I call the "argument from Hitler's dog" — against my scholarly results on grounds that bad people have produced comparable results falls into the category of the one that would prohibit all of us from eating sauerkraut and loving our dogs, because Hitler ate the one and loved the other. Well, I do not like sauerkraut. But that does not make me a better Jew. And, also, I love my dog and I am not a Nazi on that account.

*Note:* Maccoby's further criticism should be noted as well, "Neusner and the Red Cow," *Journal for the Study of Judaism* 20 (1990): 59ff. Maccoby states his basic objection to my treatment of that subject—and, by extension, of pretty much everything else—in the following statement:

> His general thesis . . . is that the Mishnah expresses, through the details of ritual, a philosophy of holiness that is, in significant respects, different from that of the Bible, being a response to the historical circumstances of Jewish political helplessness after the destruction of the temple. It may be objected, however, that this schema is flawed by considerable special pleading and inaccuracy [sic!] on Neusner's part. Details of rabbinic law which Neusner wishes to attribute to innovative rabbinic philosophy turn out, time after time, to be mere responses to the biblical text. The 'myth' which Neusner wishes to extract from alleged rabbinic ritual innovations is constructed out of non-existent materials; while the myth to which the rabbis really subscribed is that of the Bible itself, with its major themes of Exodus, Revelation, Desert, and Promised Land—a myth powerful enough to induce submission to the text of scripture and faith in its ability to provide answers to all possible difficulties. Neusner's offered paradigm case of the Mishnah's treatment of the Red Cow rite may serve to illustrate the above criticisms.

There is no reason to quibble at great length with the vague, inaccurate, and misleading précis of my ideas that Maccoby seems to have fabricated for himself. The Mishnah took shape after the Bar Kokhba War, not "after the destruction of the temple." It is represented by me as a response not to "Jewish political helplessness," which vastly understates Judah the Patriarch's power, but to the religious crisis represented by the failure of the scriptural paradigm set forth by Deuteronomy and Jeremiah and Isaiah, destruction, three generations, return and renewal. It is not the destruction of the temple in 70 that precipitated a crisis, but the debacle of Bar Kokhba's effort to replicate the rebuilding in the time of the Second Isaiah, that I think accounts for the distinctive emphases of the Mishnah upon the enduring sanctification of the Land and of the people, Israel. Maccoby's inaccurate reading of both sources and scholarship is legendary, and he has yet to persuade a scholar in the area of his own concentration, which is the study of Jesus and Paul, that he has mastered either the sources or the secondary literature. His ignorance of the former and distortion of the latter as a matter of fact have denied him all hearing in reputable scholarship. That is why a protracted response to his "criticism" has not been found productive by any of the many scholars with whom he has tried to pick his fights. In the present context, a brief reply therefore is more than sufficient. On the face of it, this is a claim that the rabbinic system merely restated what the written Torah (Maccoby's "Bible," but of course he cannot mean that the rabbis drew also upon the New Testament, which is one half of the Bible). That hoary apologetic hardly serves the authentic Judaism of the dual Torah, which alleges that the oral part of the Torah complements and completes the written part, but also is free-standing. Since numerous Mishnah-tractates take up subjects of which the written Torah knows nothing, Maccoby's basic allegation is simply ignorant and inaccurate. But — despite his obvious program of theological apologetics for his particular Judaism to accord him a fair hearing — if I understand Maccoby, what he wishes to claim is that "details...turn out...to be mere responses to the biblical text." I gather that his argument is that since the framers of tractate Parah found support for some of their propositions in verses of scripture, therefore any claim that they did more than state the plain meaning of scripture must be rejected. If that is what he wishes to say, then his criticism is simply charming for its naiveté. Every writer from Ezra's closure of the Pentateuch in 450 found in scripture whatever he wanted, whether Bar Kokhba, Philo, Jesus, or the Teacher of Righteousness, the School of Matthew, or the authorship of a tractate of the Mishnah. Mentioning those six who can well have claimed merely to say what the written Torah had said ("not to destroy but to fulfil") underlines that people could find not only what they wanted, but also the opposite of what they wanted. So at stake in explaining a piece of writing is not whether verses of scripture can have been adduced in support of what an authorship wished to say, for they always can and were found, ready at hand, when wanted. At issue, rather, is why someone who went looking for proof chose a given subject to begin with. Maccoby begs the question, of course, unless he can explain why a particular verse of scripture to begin with attracted attention. Maccoby does not seem to take seriously that the school of Matthew as much as the authorship of Mishnah-tractate Parah found ample support in scripture for whatever they wished to say. Precisely what he says about the authorship of Mishnah-tractate Parah can and should be said about Mark, Luke, Matthew, and John (among many!). Then are we to dismiss the School of Matthew or the authorship of Mishnah-tractate Parah as mere epigones of scripture? Not very likely. To the contrary, when we wish to understand a document, the first question (in this context) must be, why this particular topic, as against a vast range of other scriptural topics that are neglected? If the Red Cow, then why not the flight to Egypt? I should be interested in Maccoby's evidence for his allegation that "the rabbis" (I assume in this context he means the authors of the tractate under discussion) have found in "Exodus, Revelation, Desert, and Promised Land" anything pertinent to their Red Cow. I should be curious to know just where, in the tractate under discussion, Maccoby finds his grand themes of "Exodus...," etc. While Sanders is a scholar (though in writing about the law of Judaism, he pretends to an expert knowledge that as we have seen he simply does not have), Maccoby persistently exhibits the deplorable tendency to make things up as he goes along. The widespread realization that his writings on Jesus and Paul are simply bigoted joins with the broad recognition that he is scarcely a master of the sources. Whenever I have had occasion to test an allegation on which Maccoby displays his marvelous certainty, I have found not the evidence in support of that allegation, but rather, evidence of Maccoby's incomprehension of the sources and also of the considerations that have led scholars to the conclusions that they have reached. So if I ignore his treatment of the Mishnah, as much as Sanders's, it is because I find it ignorant, and as a matter of fact riddled with inaccuracy. Accordingly, there seems to me no reason to pay much attention to Maccoby any further, and, as I said, I have the impression that colleagues in New Testament scholarship have reached that conclusion as well. In any event the most decisive refutation of Maccoby is given in *Jewish Law* by Sanders himself: "The idea of human intention, greatly and correctly emphasized by Neusner, is original to the Pharisees so far as we know. Thus even when they are only defining or clarifying biblical law, they are operating with some post-biblical categories" (p. 187). What is said in this small context applies throughout, and with that we may dismiss Maccoby as not merely uninformed but, alas, simply uncomprehending. Sanders is a far more formidable figure and demands a sustained and serious hearing for all of his ideas.

# PART FOUR

# WHAT WE CAN SHOW AND WHAT WE WANT TO KNOW

# 9

# Who Needs "the Historical Jesus"?

*With special reference to:*

Morton Smith, *The Secret Gospel: The Discovery and Interpretation of the Secret Gospel according to Mark.* New York: Harper & Row, 1975.

John P. Meier, *A Marginal Jew: Rethinking the Historical Jesus.* New York: Doubleday, 1992.

John Dominic Crossan, *The Historical Jesus: The Life of a Mediterranean Jewish Peasant.* San Francisco: Harper, 1992.

Historical facts do not emerge in abundance from the rabbinic literature, because that literature concerns itself with other issues altogether. Rabbinic literature portrays part of the Torah: God's self-manifestation in the form of the covenant between God and Israel. Rabbinic literature conveys the manifestation of God through intellect: words that convey norms of law and lore, belief and behavior for the holy people Israel. These are, in secular language, religious writings about religious topics.

Any other characterization of these sources misses their point and purpose. No one wrote to tell what really happened on some one day, which is to say, to describe the kind of event of which history is constructed. People wrote to tell the truth about what happens every day, which is to say, the Torah and what it tells about what God is and what humanity should strive to become: "in our image, after our likeness," as portrayed in the Torah, written and oral, of Sinai. That is what the rabbinic literature proposes to accomplish and, for the faithful, does achieve. Those writings concern (in modern academic categories) Judaism, and not the history of the Jews as an ethnic group, which figures marginally and rarely and unimportantly, except as evidence, also for God's self-manifestation, then and now.

In my view, the narrowly historical reasons that compel New Testament scholars to take an interest in the rabbinic literature to begin with distort not only the character of that literature but also the task of New Testament study itself. The error that asking the historical question of religious writing commits is simple: it is to dismiss what the sources wish to discuss in favor of that about which they are, at best, indifferent. The basis for the error is the confusion of historical study with the study of two entirely valid, free-standing disciplines: history of religion and theology. To neither of those disciplines is historical fact relevant.

From the beginnings of the quest for the historical Jesus, before the middle of the last century, to the present day, intense historical study has addressed to the Gospels a secular agendum grounded in three premises. These have been (1) historical facts, unmediated by tradition, themselves bear theological consequence, the gift of the Reformation (show me as fact in the sources, e.g., scripture); (2) historical facts must undergo a rigorous test of skepticism, the donation of the Enlightenment (how could a whale swallow Jonah, and what else did he have for lunch that day?); and (3) historical facts cannot comprise supernatural events, the present of nineteenth-century German historical learning (exactly how things were cannot include rising from the dead).

These premises set a standard of historicity that religious writings such as the Gospels cannot and should not attempt to meet. For, after all, all three dismiss what to the evangelists is critical: these things happened in the way the church has preserved them (also) in the Gospels, tradition also being a valid source, to which evangelists appeal; these things really did happen as the narrative says (would the Gospels lie?); and Jesus Christ assuredly performed miracles in his lifetime and rose from the dead (ours is the story of the unique man, God among us). The quest for the historical Jesus commences with the denial of the facticity of the Gospels in favor of their (sometime, somewhere) historicity. So beginning with the quest of the historical Jesus — from the "Lives of Jesus" movement in the middle of the nineteenth century forward — theological issues were laid before the tribunal of secular history, and theologians thought to sort out historical facts to settle theological questions.

Advocates of such a theological enterprise, conducted in accord with the rules of another secular field of knowledge altogether, set forth extravagant claims in behalf of their results, which (in the Reformation tradition) serve as a medium for the reform of the faith (as Catholic scholars before us explicitly state, as we shall see). But, in point of fact, the historical objectivity and rationality to which those who go off in quest of the facts behind the faith lay claim even at the outset come under question. The reason is that while in historical studies it is rare for the nationality or religion of a scholar to find a legitimate place in the evaluation of results, in this field whether a scholar is Catholic, Orthodox, Protestant, Jewish, Muslim, or secular invariably plays a role. Anyone who speaks of a "Jewish physicist" is a curiosity; but even Meier, who, as we shall see, has given us the definitive account of the quest and a judicious picture of its results, starts by inventing a meeting of a Catholic, Protestant, Jewish, and secular scholar, required to come up with a consensus on who Jesus really was — that is, the historical Jesus.

That simple datum of biblical studies calls into question the premise of objectivity and, at the threshold of study, invokes the very opposite: faith, conviction, commitment. Then why insist that there is a kind of knowledge about Jesus that not only conforms to the kind of knowledge we have about George Washington but also distinguishes between the epiphenomena of piety and the hard facts of faith? "Who he really was" also means "who he really was not." I cannot point to another religion besides Christianity that has entertained in the intellectual centers of the faith a systematic exercise in learning commencing with unfaith; certainly not Islam, as Salman Rushdie's awful fate has shown, and certainly not Judaism, where the issues of theological learning — Talmud study and scripture study, for example — do not confuse secular history with the pattern of religious truth or ask Moses to submit to the mordant wit of Voltaire.

Nor can anyone claim that out of the quest for the historical Jesus has come determinative truth, vastly enriching the intellectual resources of the faith. Clearly, we understand the Gospels differently from the way they were understood before the enterprise got underway in nineteenth-century evangelical Lutheran Germany.

But whether or not we know Jesus better than we did before because we now know who he really was and what he really did — as distinct from what the faithful have known all along — remains open to doubt. As a matter of historical fact, the results of the quest have produced nothing short of chaos — along with the first-rate scholarship that both Meier and Crossan, of whom more below, have given us. As many as are the scholars who have written lives of Jesus, so many are the Jesuses whom we know now but did not know before the quest began. In general, a review of the upshot of the quest for the historical Jesus yields the simple observation, which every history of the quest for the historical Jesus has yielded and which Crossan's book has provoked even now, that each generation gets the Jesus that it wants; pretty much every scholar comes up with the historical Jesus that suits his or her taste and judgment.

Indeed, the Gospels scholar Luke Timothy Johnson concludes his reading of the books before us with the observation that, once more, we have a Jesus for our times: "Does not Crossan's picture of a peasant cynic preaching inclusiveness and equality fit perfectly the idealized ethos of the late twentieth-century academic? Is not both authors' hope for a historical foil to theology or faith still fundamentally a theological, rather than a historical project?"[1] Discouraged, some ask, "What is left to believe in Jesus after the scholars have done with him?"[2] And, invariably the answer, as in the case at hand, proves less incisive than the question — and revealing of not precisely what the questioner had in mind at all. For the quest for the historical Jesus conventionally portrays the questioner, and Meier says so in so many words, even as Crossan shows that fact with surpassing eloquence.

Yet the diversity of the results does not take first place in the indictment of two hundred years of theological learning, not even the paucity. Rather, the character of the results does. People can make a great name for themselves by saying whatever they want to about "the historical Jesus," making the front page of the *New York Times* if what they say is sufficiently shocking, therefore newsworthy. Announce that Jesus was precisely what the Gospels say he was — and still is — and even in churches some will yawn. But suggest to the world that he may have been a homosexual magician, as the late Morton Smith did, and your day is made. In no other field of study, whether claiming historical objectivity or glorying in utter subjectivity (as in current literary criticism), can solecism

---

1. Luke Timothy Johnson, "A Marginal Mediterranean Jewish Peasant," *Commonweal* (April 24, 1992): 26.

2. Philip L. Culbertson, *Journal of Ecumenical Studies* 28 (1991): 1ff. His question is better than his answer. He has "a Pharisaic context for the historical Jesus," but exactly what he means by "Pharisaic" he does not tell us, and he is alarmingly ignorant of nearly all of the scholarship on that subject done in the past twenty years.

pass for scholarship, and out-and-out fiction win a hearing as a new fact.

Morton Smith's "historical" results, of course, depended upon a selective believing in what he thought was historical.[3] Even at the time, some of us told Smith to his face that he was an upside-down fundamentalist, believing anything bad anybody said about Jesus, but nothing good. His quest for the historical Jesus, of course, produced a scandal, not only because of the results. As a matter of fact, Smith's presentation of the evidence for his understanding of Jesus, a Clement fragment he claims to have discovered in a library in Sinai in 1958, ranks as one of the most amateur presentations of an allegedly important document in recent memory, leaving open the possibility of forgery. Smith himself was an expert on such matters, having devoted scholarly essays to great forgeries in antiquity. Reviewing Smith's results, the New Testament scholar Quentin Quesnell ended his questioning of the evidence with the simple colloquy: "Is there a reasonable possibility of forgery? The answer, working only with the evidence Smith presents, seems to be clearly, yes."[4]

Quesnell pointed out that Smith presents photographs, but not the manuscript itself, and the photographs are unsatisfactory: "He made them himself...with a handheld camera." So, in fact, no one has ever seen the document but Smith himself. Smith claims that various experts said the text was genuine, but Quesnell says, "Unfortunately...Smith does not include the text of the answers which the experts gave." Smith wants the primary test of authenticity to be the wording. Quesnell: "The primary test of authenticity is examination of the manuscript." That leads Quesnell to wonder whether someone might have forged the document. When the Dead Sea Scrolls came to light, entire academic careers were devoted to precisely the issues of validation of the manuscript itself: the ink, the medium of writing, orthography, a variety of types of physical evidence. Solomon Zeitlin, now forgotten but then a mighty figure, called into question the early dating of the scrolls and maintained they were medieval forgeries — that in the

---

3. Morton Smith, *Jesus the Magician,* a popularization of his findings in his *Clement of Alexandria and a Secret Gospel of Mark* (Cambridge: Harvard University Press, 1973) and *The Secret Gospel: The Discovery and Interpretation of the Secret Gospel according to Mark* (New York: Harper and Row, 1975).

4. "The Mar Saba Clementine: A Question of Evidence," *Catholic Biblical Quarterly* 37 (1975): 48–67; note Smith's reply, *CBQ* 38 (1976): 196–99, and Quesnell, *CBQ* 38 (1976): 200–203.

face of the most rigorous testing of the physical evidence. Imagine the donnybrook that Smith's explanation of the "disappearance" of the "original documents" would have precipitated had a Zeitlin still been around. Indeed, we have to imagine it, since, in the case of the historical Jesus, too little evidently was at stake to maintain rigorous standards of verification even of physical evidence.

Smith makes much of the correctness of the fragment's vocabulary. Quesnell points out that if a Morton Smith can check the correctness of the letters' vocabulary and phrase construction against the 1936 critical edition of the works of Clement, any other forger can have done the same: "So could a mystifier have checked every word and phrase with the same index and successfully eliminated them [errors] from the first draft of a mystification whatever was not characteristic of Clement." He notes, "There is no physical evidence to compel admitting a date earlier than 1936." Quesnell states matters very simply: "What Smith is able to 'authenticate,' the 'mystifier' would have been able to imitate."

Smith argued on the basis of mistakes a forger would have been stupid to make. But Quesnell responds: "If Smith can construct arguments for genuineness from his insights into what a forger would not have done . . . there seems to be no reason why an intelligent mystifier could not have foreseen such arguments and added some 'untypical' elements as indispensable to a successful mystification." Quesnell continues: "Smith tells . . . [that Arthur Darby Nock . . . ] refused till the day he died to admit the authenticity of the letter, suggesting instead that it was 'mystification for the sake of mystification.' " And, Quesnell goes on, " 'Secret Gospel' is written 'for the one who knows.' Who is 'the one who knows'? What does he know?" Discretion certainly can account for Quesnell's sage reluctance to answer his own questions; but plenty of others did so privately, and the entire quest for the historical Jesus fell under a shadow for some time to come: if this, then what is impossible?

I do not mean to suggest that scholarship on religions, including their histories, ought merely to paraphrase the texts — far from it. But I do think that scholars owe that upon which they work a measure of dignity, and owe themselves a moment of esteem. Much is to be done with the sources on which we work, including a labor of historical refinement, without our placing ourselves in the position of judgment upon the faith of other people. Ours is, after all, not a theological task; but if we make it so, then other rules, besides those of skepticism, doubt, and militant unbelief, must operate. It is the simple fact that people may say whatever they wish about "the Jesus of history," there being no appeal to a common court of evidence, method, argument, rational exchange of opinion; if anything goes, then nothing can go right. But Meier and Crossan explain and defend their work, as we shall see, on blatantly theological grounds, never asking what has Voltaire to tell us about Jesus Christ or Ranke about Matthew, Mark, Luke, and John!

Still, Meier's and Crossan's are magnificent and successful efforts to rehabilitate a field of learning that had fallen in disgrace. Their books should be read as valiant efforts in the face of the ridiculous and absurd to establish the rationality and reputation of a failing enterprise. And each, in its own way, forms a monument to intelligence, learning, judgment, and sound taste. Meier's book is a masterpiece of scholarship bridging the gap between the expert and the lay reader. It is a beautiful piece of writing and research, and it is difficult to imagine a finer presentation of the state of questions, beginning to end. Anyone who values learning will read the notes first. The text is clear and undemanding, the notes superb and enlightening. Meier sets forth the evidence, the issue of method, and then what he thinks we can know about the life of Jesus before his public career (volume two will proceed from there).

Meier leads us through the path toward "the Jesus whom we can recover by using the scientific tools of modern historical research." He offers these criteria for deciding what comes from Jesus: the criterion of embarrassment (the church later on will have been embarrassed by a saying, so it must be authentic); the criterion of discontinuity (the same approach, now discontinuity from Judaism); the criterion of multiple attestation; the criterion of coherence; the criterion of rejection and execution (he did something to alienate powerful people). Meier lists as dubious criteria those of (1) traces of Aramaic, (2) the Palestinian environment (what would fit into that time and place), (3) vividness of narration, (4) tendencies of the developing synoptic tradition, and (5) historical presumption. This last point shades over into theological debate: "This criterion brings us squarely into the debate about where the 'burden of proof' lies: on the side of the critic who denies historicity or on the side of the critic who affirms it?" This brief summary of the first half of the book — more than two hundred pages — gives no adequate appreciation of how beautifully Meier expounds each problem in sequence, with a clarity in his text, a scholarly mastery in his notes, without parallel in the recent past. If you want to know whatever there is to know about what people think about the historical Jesus, you must start in this book.

And yet, with the masterful notes in hand, we form the strong impression that scholarship here consists of collecting opinions and commenting on them. The evidence is still what it is: religious faith forming the story of a unique person, "God with us," God incarnate, a man who was crucified and who rose from the dead. But scholars' opinions provide no primary evidence concerning the first century, only our own. Some years back I lectured at Boston University and was asked a question with no bearing on my lecture: "Tell me, what was it really like in the first century?" I replied, "I don't know, I wasn't there." But, it is clear, we deal with a field in which people take in one another's washing. Then why bother?

Meier forthrightly responds in this-worldly terms: "the quest for the historical Jesus can be very useful if one is asking about faith seeking understanding, i.e., theology, in a contemporary context. . . . Faith in Christ today must be able to reflect on itself systematically in a way that will allow an appropriation of the quest for the historical Jesus into theology." This is for four reasons. First, "the quest for the historical Jesus reminds Christians that faith in Christ is not just a vague existential attitude or a way of being in the world. Christian faith is the affirmation of and adherence to a particular person who said and did particular things in a particular time and place in human history. Second, the quest affirms that the risen Jesus is the same person who lived and died as a Jew . . . a person as truly and fully human . . . as any other human being. Third, the quest for the historical Jesus . . . has tended to emphasize the embarrassing, nonconformist aspects of Jesus." Fourth, the historical Jesus "subverts not just some ideologies but all ideologies." And, Meier concludes, "the historical Jesus is a bulwark against the reduction of Christian faith . . . to 'relevant' ideology of any stripe. His refusal to be held fast by any given school of thought is what drives theologians onward into new paths; hence the historical Jesus remains a constant stimulus to theological renewal."

Why do I maintain that in works on "the historical Jesus" we deal with theology, not history at all? Because, with the best will in the world, these apologia strike me as nothing other than constructive theology masquerading as history and in the name of a healthy religious intellect claiming the authority of reasoned, historical scholarship. Presently, when we consider Joseph Ratzinger's critique of much scholarship on the historical Jesus, we shall find just his insistence that, replacing theology as the arbiter of truth, history is given a weight hardly justified by even the pertinence of its methods — or even of its premises which, in context, are simply irrelevant to what is subject to discussion.[5] Why ask history to settle questions that Meier himself specifies as fundamentally religious, matters of not fact but faith? And since when do matters of fact have any bearing on the truths of faith? Real historians do not give reasons such as these for writing, e.g., lives of Hitler and Stalin. I look in vain in Allan Bullock's *Parallel Lives*[6] for a counterpart to Meier's (and Crossan's) explanation of their lives of Jesus, and the comparison between his explanation of his work and theirs of their biographies leaves no doubt that his is a historical, theirs a theological, agendum.

Meier says we are going to talk about the Jesus whom we can recover "by using the scientific tools of modern historical research." But concerning no other person or subject does scholarship yield the results that this "quest" is asked to provide. Three decades ago, when I wrote on the life of Yohanan ben Zakkai, Eliezer b. Hyrcanus, and a gaggle of named Pharisaic authorities, no one imagined that my task was to remind faithful Jews that

---

5. Yet, for the study of biography in antiquity, before the church fathers with their voluminous writings well preserved, we have few figures nearly so well documented as is Jesus. Take Judaism, for instance. Not a single rabbi represented in talmudic literature is given anything like a biography, let alone four of them; no rabbi left anything like "Q." All rabbis' statements are reworked into documents representing a consensus of their framers. Excluding only a handful, those who flourished at the end of the second century and are represented in the Mishnah ca. 200, not a single rabbi of antiquity is attested in a document that (we suppose) reached closure within so close a span of time after his death as is Jesus by the Gospels. That is the argument of chapter 1 above. By contrast, New Testament scholars searching for the historical Jesus happily introduce as fact sayings in the names of figures assumed to have flourished in the first century, even though those sayings occur in documents that reached closure anywhere from two hundred to a thousand years later. Culbertson, cited above, believes about the inerrancy of the Talmud when it comes to citing rabbis what he denies about the inerrancy of the Gospels when it comes to citing Jesus. Not only so, but New Testament scholars happily treat as fact concerning the first century any available pastiche of what Judaism said or did or taught or practiced, formed of sherds and remnants in writings over a period of a thousand years, even though these same scholars pounce with glee upon the slightest hint of anachronism, apologetic harmonization (who opens a "harmony of the Gospels" and tells us about Jesus Christ?), or other intellectual gaffes. Exemplary in every way, Meier is fully informed of the critical agenda of rabbinic literature and honors it, and in this, as in other ways, his book marks the coming of age of Gospels research in its encounter with "Judaism."

6. New York: Knopf, 1992.

"faith in the Torah is not just a vague existential attitude." Meier's claim that "the risen Jesus" is the same person who lived and died as a Jew falls entirely outside of his methodological strictures; only in the context of Christian faith does that statement bear any meaning at all. But Christian faith requires no mere historical Jesus, bereft of miracles and dead like any other man, having, after all, the entirety of Jesus Christ, God, son of God, God incarnate, and all the rest. What has that incarnate God to do with Meier's results achieved with "the scientific tools of modern historical research"? In the case of research on ancient rabbis or on the historical Socrates, for that matter, who ever heard of the requirement that the results emphasize "the embarrassing, nonconformist aspects," and what biography of Caesar Augustus subverts any ideologies? At stake for Meier are profoundly religious sentiments and experiences, and to these, historical facts are simply, monumentally, irrelevant.

John Dominic Crossan's *Historical Jesus* is a very different book, but an equally substantial one. For reading, it is more compelling; as scholarship, it is nowhere near so definitive as Meier's. Crossan writes better, but he tells his own story (which may be why his writing is more engaging.) While Meier concerns himself with issues of method, analysis of sources, and, above all, a broad account of the received scholarly literature, telling us where the field stands, Crossan wishes to present something other than a reference work. His is, rather, an account of how he wishes us to see things, an intensely powerful and poetic book by a great writer who also is an original and weighty scholar. Here is a book to be read for the text, not only or mainly for the notes, of which, in fact, there are none.

Here is a life of Jesus in the grand tradition: narrative, reflective, a pronouncement, not merely a protocol and account of learning as it is. Crossan begins with an account of the empire and its life, the faith and life of Israel, the categories into which Jesus has been cast: visionary and teacher, peasant and protester, magician and prophet, bandit and messiah, rebel and revolutionary. He moves us on to John and Jesus, kingdom and wisdom, magic and meal, death and burial, resurrection and authority. The upshot of this eloquent story is this:

> That ecstatic vision and social program sought to rebuild a society upward from its grass roots but on principles of religious and economic egalitarianism, with free healing brought directly to the peasant homes and free sharing of whatever they had in re-

turn. The deliberate conjunction of magic and meal, miracle and table, free comparison and open commensality, was a challenge launched not just at Judaism's strictest purity regulations, or even at the Mediterranean's patriarchal combination of honor and shame, patronage and clientage, but at civilization's eternal inclination to draw lines, invoke boundaries, establish hierarchies, and maintain discriminations....

Clearly, we are in the hands of a master. Crossan's book is personal; Meier's, on the other hand, is a definitive account of the state of pretty much every question he treats. If I had to recommend only one book on the historical Jesus, it would be Meier's. Anyone with time to read more than one will want them both — the one for its masterful, enlightened learning, the other for its passionate art.[7]

As a master, Crossan concludes,

This book...is a scholarly reconstruction of the historical Jesus. And if one were to accept its formal methods and even their material investments, one could surely offer divergent interpretative conclusions about the reconstructible historical Jesus. But one cannot dismiss it or the search for the historical Jesus as mere reconstruction, as if reconstruction invalidated somehow the entire project. Because there is only reconstruction. For a believing Christian both the life of the word of God and the test of the Word of God are like a graded process of historical reconstruction.... If you cannot believe in something produced by reconstruction, you may have nothing left to believe in.

How that apologia conforms to the rules of secular historical research I cannot say. How these particular issues emerge from secular, historical study, I do not know; I do not think these are historical questions at all, and I do not think that data adduced as facts about things that really happened have any bearing upon these questions. That is the very nub of the matter, and that brings us to a weighty critic of just this conclusion — that accounts of "the historical Jesus" ever are historical — who is Joseph Cardinal Ratzinger. In a variety of important and authoritative papers, such as his Ingersoll Lecture, he has made these points — quite properly,

---

7. The comparison is not entirely fair to Meier, since at this writing we have only his first volume, and it is in the second that he reaches the standard agenda of the historical Jesus: as he lived, did wonders, taught, died, and rose from the dead. So the two books are asymmetrical at this time. In any case, faced with a choice, I should not deny myself the pleasure of Meier's brilliant footnotes, nor the certainties of his reasoned, judicious, and prudent text, in favor of Crossan's more eloquent and personal prose.

in the setting of Catholic faith and in the context of the claim to
let not theological truth but merely critical historical knowledge
advance in the quest of the historical Jesus.[8] The method itself
dictates scandalous results: "The faith in such a context is not a
constitutive element of method [at all], and God is not a fact to
be taken into account in historical narrative." ("La fede non è un
elemento costitutivo del metodo e Dio non è un fattore di cui occorre tener conto nell'avvenimento storico.") At the same time,
exegesis forms an important requirement of theology: The more
prudent among systematic theologians seek to produce a theology
independent, so far as is possible, from exegesis: "But what value
can a theology have that is utterly divorced from its own foundations?" ("Ma quale valore può avere una teologia che si separa
dale proprie fondamenta?")

So, Ratzinger argues, it is necessary to raise the question of hermeneutics: "The explanation of the historical process should not
be more than one part of the process of interpretation; the other
should be the comprehension of the text in contemporary terms."
("la spiegazione del processo storico non sarebbe che una parte del
compito dell'interprete; l'altra sarebbe la comprensione del testo
nell'oggi. Di consequenza, occurrerebbe indagare sulle condizioni
del comprendere stesso così da giungere ad una attualizzazione del
testo che vada oltre una 'anatomia del defunto' puramente storica.") How, he asks, is it possible to come to a comprehension
that will not be founded on the arbitrary decisions of my own
presuppositions, "a comprehension that permits me truly to grasp
the message of the text, recovering something that does not come
from me myself?" ("una comprensione che me permetta veramente
d'intendere il messaggio del testo, restituendomi qualcosa che non
viene da me stesso?") The answer is a correct hermeneutics: "for
hermeneutics to become convincing, first of all, it is necessary to
expose a harmony between historical analysis and hermeneutical
synthesis." ("so l'ermeneutica' deve diventare convincente, occorre
innanzitutto che scopra un'armonia tra l'analisi storica e la sintesi
ermeneutica.")

In that context, Ratzinger's critique of Dibelius and Bultmann — the finest minds in the two-hundred-year quest, and the
most important ones — takes on substantial weight. At issue are

---

8. "L'interpretazione biblical in conflitto: Problemi del fondamento ed orienta-
mento dell' esegesi contemporanea," in Ignace de la Potterie, Romano Guardini,
Joseph Ratzinger, Giuseppe Colombo, and Enzo Bianchi, *L'Esegesi christiana oggi*
(Rome, 1992), 93–125. The several quotations all cite this important article.

the premises and presuppositions in play, along the lines of my opening remarks on the peculiarity of a reading of the Gospels that begins with the principle that the topics most critical to the Gospels lie simply outside of all discourse: miracles, resurrection, and the like. So I find it easy to concur: "To the contrary, in Dibelius and Bultmann, all has degenerated into an evolutionary pattern of a nearly intolerable simplicity.... *With such presuppositions, the figure of Jesus is predetermined*" (italics mine). ("Di contro, in Dibelius e Bultmann, tutto ciò è degenerato in uno schema evolutivo d'un semplicismo quasi intollerabile... *Con tali presupposti, la figura di Gesù è predeterminata.*")

To make my point, we need not pursue the details of the constructive program that Ratzinger lays out; it suffices to say that the italicized sentence raises a challenge to all those Protestant, Orthodox, and Catholic (and even Jewish) scholars, theologians manqués to a man, who deem "the historical Jesus" a truly secular, this-worldly, historical quest. Ratzinger makes the point, which is amply illustrated by Meier and Crossan, that at issue in the historical Jesus is the Christ of faith. Crossan's somewhat strident concluding sentences say so in so many words, and Meier's characteristically more prudent remarks make the same point as well. Meier and Crossan, masters of the craft, turn out to validate Ratzinger's point of insistence: let theology be theology, but also address issues of history.

After all, as head of the Holy Office, Ratzinger does not require Meier's reminder that "Christian faith is the affirmation of and adherence to a particular person who said and did particular things in a particular time and place in human history." Nor has Ratzinger forgotten Nicaea and Chalcedon, so he does not need Meier's historical results to affirm Jesus Christ (to use Christian language) as a person as "truly and fully human" as any other human being. If Nicaea and Chalcedon knew that, so, too, did the evangelists, and that is why they wrote what they did about Jesus. But it seems to me no Christian can agree that Jesus really "subverts not just some ideologies" since, after all, there still is Christianity, and Christianity does believe that Jesus stands not for the subversion of all false things but the foundation of the true theology of his church, whichever one among many it may be.

All of this, then, shows how disingenuous is the quest for the historical Jesus. Beginning, middle, and end, the issue is theological. The challenge is to mediate between theological truth and historical fact, if and when they meet. So let them meet as, in these two books, they do not meet. Certainly, a debate between Crossan and Ratzinger, moderated by Meier, would give us a splendid evening.

But now, it is time to get back to work. The quest for the historical Jesus is monumentally irrelevant to the study of history (in which those who pursue that quest are not engaged and by which they are not even motivated) or history of religion (in which many of us are engaged even when we come to Christianity in its initial century). The quest for the historical Jesus forms a brief chapter in Christian theology of our own times. That field of learning supplies data for the history of Christianity in the nineteenth and twentieth centuries — that alone — and, as we now know that quest, precious little information of high consequence about the first century. That is the context in which to address the question, "What do I have to know about rabbinic literature to study the New Testament?" And in that context, "But, then, I answer, what makes you ask?"

If people want to study from the perspective of the history and comparison of religions about earliest Christianity as one of the most complex, well-documented, and interesting examples of the beginning of a religion, then they will find in rabbinic literature a remarkably rich and germane corpus of documents. For rabbinic Judaism took shape in the same world and at the same time and among much the same people. So if people want to know about rabbinic literature to study the context in which the New Testament and other earliest Christian writings formed, then they have to know nearly as much about rabbinic literature in its context as they require about Christian writings in theirs. Any labor of comparative theology that crosses the boundaries between one religious system and another comparable one will delight in the sources produced by the ancient rabbis, whose media of theological thought and discourse are wholly other, yet produce remarkably congruent conclusions.

If people want to know precisely who was the Jesus of history and exactly what he said, as distinct from what the Gospels (all four) tell about Jesus Christ, God Incarnate, then I do not think the rabbinic literature will prove ubiquitously relevant to their work (though here and there, on an episodic and anecdotal basis, they may find some interesting bits of information). Whether the results are worth the effort to get at that information — which is to say, whether it is rewarding to do the work in the critical and rigorous manner in which the quest for the historical Jesus is carried on — is for others to decide. For my part, since in my view the quest for the historical Jesus is precisely as germane to the study of religion (except in the nineteenth- and twentieth-century liberal Protestant world) as is the quest for the historical Hillel and Shammai, I do not think important the question, "What do I have to know about the rabbinic literature to study the historical Jesus?" But out of respect to a world of colleagues whose methods I have adapted in the creation of my field of work, I have spent this book answering just that question.

I am not so naive as to imagine that the quest in the rabbinic literature for the historical Jesus from now on will be carried on in a manner consistent with the mode of that quest in the synoptic Gospels. People do what they want to do and, as we have seen in this book, only a few have enough decent respect for the opinion of colleagues even to explain and try to justify the results. In these pages I have dealt with my critics and have criticized the work of others as well. It is what one can do. It is all one can do. I cannot predict what will happen in the quest for the historical Moses, Jesus, Hillel, Muhammad, Buddha, Zoroaster, or any of the other figures that stand for the beginning of great religious systems.

I am certain of one fact. Whatever the state of the question and the character of the quest, the world's great religious systems will go on much as they did before the question was raised (if it was raised) and without regard to the discoveries of the historical quest. For the rest, God will decide, and God is known to spring surprises on us. The one thing that will not surprise me is that, in the future as in the past, Islam, Judaism, Buddhism, Zoroastrianism, and Christianity, in most of their various subsystems, will go on in accord with their own eternal rhythms. The reason is that religions speak of God, truth, and eternity, not of the here and now of the facts of the workaday world. The issue of Christianity is not the historical Jesus, it is why Christianity; not who was, but who and what is Jesus Christ. Christianity begins on the first Easter, because it is with the resurrection, not the crucifixion, that that religion commenced its history. At that moment in its faith, the historical Jesus becomes Christ the Lord.

But little that is said about the "historical Jesus" accounts for Christianity, only for some improvements of "Judaism" (variously portrayed, to be sure). Most of the results, like those of Sanders, make us wonder why anyone should have found surprising or remarkable a perfectly routine set of teachings, pretty much at home in Sanders's conflationary Judaism and the counterparts drawn by others. The question is not only: why crucify a Mediterranean peasant, a Galilean wonder-worker, a marginal Jew, a Pharisaic "rabbi," or any of the other this-worldly, essentially secular and naturalized Jesuses of history? It is, more to the point: why should such an agreeable but on the whole unexceptional figure have risen from the dead? Why the empty tomb? If any of these pictures of the historical Jesus told the whole story, then how can anyone make sense of Paul? By excluding to begin with all that is the transcendent and supernatural in the Gospels, none of the proposed historical Jesuses explains the advent of Christianity, but only a trivial reform movement in Judaism, such as Christianity never was. Beginning where they do, the diverse historical Jesuses expose a single flaw: each answers peripheral questions, and all ignore the critical and urgent one.[9]

---

9. That explains why, for my theological confrontation with Christianity, such as I promise in my *Telling Tales: Making Sense of Christian and Judaic Nonsense. The Urgency and Basis for Judaeo-Christian Dialogue* (Louisville: Westminster/ John Knox Press, 1993), I address the Jesus with whom a practicing Jew can argue: the one who says he has come not to destroy but to fulfill the Torah. That is the one Jesus who invokes the Torah, and so with whom an argument based on a shared body of divine law and theology may be composed. On that basis, I addressed myself to Matthew's Jesus in *A Rabbi Talks with Jesus: An Intermillennial, Interfaith Exchange* (New York: Doubleday, 1993). The historical Jesus is not the only foundation for Judaeo-Christian dialogue.

## Appendix

# Jesus' Parables — Their Judaic "Roots"?

In *Jesus and His Jewish Parables: Rediscovering the Roots of Jesus' Teaching*,[1] Brad H. Young presents an account of parables in general, and then turns to the Gospels' parables in detail. He covers these topics: parabolic teachings and the problem of hermeneutics; modern parable research; the parables and talmudic literature: parable, aggadah, and tradition; the parables and the Gospels: the synoptic problem; the parables and their context: reapplication and interpretation in the parables; the parables of the kingdom of heaven; Jesus, the Jewish sages, and their parables; prophetic tension and the temple: the parable of the wicked husbandmen; Jesus, the Jewish people, and the interpretation of the parables. The book proposes no thesis, pursues no line of inquiry, argues no sustained proposition. The author prefers, as he says, "an inductive approach," which "allows research into the wider range of meanings of the term which are so important for a proper understanding of the development and emergence of the parable as a well defined pedagogic technique" (p. 10).

The book appears to have been completed some time ago, perhaps as a dissertation at the Hebrew University, where the author studied for ten years. Omission of all reference to the important article by David Stern on the parable, published in *Prooftexts* a half decade ago, and of Stern's name in the index, points toward both conclusions since, in general, Jerusalem scholarship reads Jerusalem scholarship and not much else. Further evidence of the

---

1. Mahwah, N.J.: Paulist Press, 1989.

overseas provenance of the work is that the language of the book is somewhat strange, and at many points it looks as though we have a translation from Israeli Hebrew.

Clearly, the purpose of Young's research derives from an interest in the parables attributed to Jesus. Young directs us to the right issues: "We see that the rabbinic parables are preserved in a literature that was compiled some time after the gospels." He further distinguishes the parables that occur in some rabbinic compilations — many hundreds of years after the time of Jesus — from those that occur in the Gospels. The latter draw heavily on verses of scripture; the former rarely do. These observations then suggest that Young will systematically work out a thesis. But the presentation of his ideas is so prolix, rambling, and disorganized that no thesis emerges. Here is an example of his discourse:

> The fable is an important forerunner of the parable. No fables appear in the gospels. It must be distinguished from the latter in that it employs animals and sometimes plants, attributing human characteristics to them. The antiquity of the fable is not disputed. Perry noted, "In the early period of Greek literature, and in the Alexandrian age, fables might be the subject-matter of separate poems, but much more commonly they were used subordinately as illustrations in a larger context...." Hence Greek literature preserves fables in both prose and poetry. Also Schwarzbaum has stressed the antiquity of the fable: "It should also be pointed out that some of the antecedents of the so-called Aesopic fables are to be found...." Jacobs observed that many of the fables of rabbinic literature are paralleled in both Greek and Indian sources. Thus the fable was a widely circulated didactic mode. The well-known fable of the Oak and the Reeds appears in the Indian Mahabharata xii.4198, Avian and Babrius 64 as well as in talmudic literature. The oak is not pliable and breaks as it stands against the powerful wind. The flimsy reed however bends with the wind and thus survives the storm. Flusser noted that the fable is probably behind the words of Jesus in regard to John the Baptist, 'What did you go out in the wilderness to behold? A reed shaken by the wind?' (Matthew 11:7; Luke 7:24). John's uncompromising nature put him on a collision course with Herod Antipas.
>
> In Exodus Rabbah a fable is used by the Amora R. Judah bar Shalom (ca. 350 C.E.) to elucidate the predicament of Israel who in spite of their deliverer Moses still had to worry about Pharaoh....

What is wrong with all this is that, through the introduction of a vast corpus of vaguely relevant information, Young simply makes no point. But that is misleading. In fact there is something at stake here. The author wishes to appeal to rabbinic compilations to bring us *ipsissima verba* of Jesus, and he says so in so many words:

> After examining the editorial aspects of the parable [of the two builders] in Matthew and Luke, one can propose a Hebrew reconstruction which more closely reflects the *ipsissima verba* of Jesus or at least the hypothetical Hebrew Urevangelium which underlies the texts of the synoptic gospels. More philological study is needed to determine to what extent one should look for a Hebrew closer to biblical or mishnaic. Was the vav consecutive employed? It seems that in a popular story parable that the vav consecutive would have been considered too literary. Here the passage, "Saying Lord, Lord" has been attached to the parable because it appears in both Matthew and Luke and could be an original part of the text. Though this is true, it is possible that it was derived from a different context. Perhaps one of the more remarkable aspects of the parable is the phrase, "who hears my words and does them." The text stresses the teachings of Jesus. The phrase which refers to hearing and doing may allude to the passages from the Pentateuch which speak about the giving of the Lord.... (p. 255)

The passage runs on, a single paragraph covering a variety of subjects, but the main point is clear at the outset. It suffices to note that the story in the rabbinic version occurs for the first time in the Fathers according to Rabbi Nathan, a document of indeterminate date but probably within the ambiance of the Talmud of Babylonia, so, let us say, something on the order of five centuries after Jesus is supposed to have made use of the parable. It is attributed to Elisha b. Avuyah. Even if we take the attribution as fact, Elisha can hardly attest to the state of affairs of Jesus, since he is a figure of the second century. But of course we cannot take the attribution as fact, and, consequently, the rabbinic version of the parable can hardly be adduced as evidence of what circulated in the time of Jesus.

In this day and age, we can hardly expect Young to ignore such considerations, and formally he pays attention to these issues. This is his language: "Elisha b. Avuyah's examples and Jesus' Parable of the Two Builders have a number of common elements. I. Abrahams noted, 'All authorities are agreed that there can have been no direct, literary borrowing by the later Rabbis from the books of the New Testament.' Indeed, it seems unlikely that the parables of Jesus or of Elisha b. Avuyah could have directly influenced one another." So far, so good. But then we move back to *ipsissima verba,* by a circuitous route:

> It seems overly simplistic to consider only the question of dates between Elisha b. Avuyah and Jesus or the time of the final compilation of the gospels and that of Avot derabbi Nathan. Nor should the importance of the time difference be minimized. Nonetheless the parables are too close to one another to be completely independent. However, were Elisha b. Avuyah's parable a secondary development from Jesus' illustration one would certainly expect that the parables would be more similar to one another and for the rabbinic version to betray signs of embellishment. The rabbinic version is shorter and conforms to the other parables in this chapter.... Perhaps it is wise to recognize the fact that there is a third intermediate stage in the transmission of these parallel parables that connects the world in which Jesus operated with the sphere of the parable of Elisha b. Avuyah. Insufficient evidence has survived to speak with absolute certainty about this intermediate stage but it represents a common stream of Jewish thought that links Jesus with the world of rabbinic learning, the love of man and the love of his Creator. (pp. 257–58)

If this is more then mere gibberish, then what Young illustrates is pseudo-orthodoxy in the sense in which Smith defined it twenty years ago.

What he seems to wish to say is something like this. First, we cannot take account only of the difference of a hundred years between the time of Jesus and the time of Elisha. The inference is that if we did, for narrowly historical and biographical purposes, then we could not invoke Elisha's use of the parable to tell us anything about Jesus' use of the same parable. We also do not have to take account only of the fact that the rabbinic parable appears in a document that reached closure many hundreds of years after the time of Jesus. The inference is that if we did, we could not posit any relationship of a historical character to permit us to comment on the use of the parable by Jesus.

Now why do we not take account of these paralyzing problems? Because the two versions of the parable ("the parables") are like one another ("too close to one another to be completely independent"). So what? It would be nice to conceive that Elisha's use of the parable reflected knowledge of Jesus' use of the parable ("secondary development"), but the data do not suggest so. For Young what is at stake is only history, only biography, only finding out more about the setting in which Jesus lived and taught. He honestly believes that the rabbinic literature forms a corpus of facts that illuminate the life and teachings of Jesus. That is what is at stake, and that is all that is at stake. If his interest were in the study of parables, the issues of attribution and redaction would play no role. The phenomenon itself would suffice to permit comparative studies to go forward. It is solely the insistence on recovering what Jesus really said and meant that requires Young to worry about the accuracy of the transmission of sayings, the reliability of attributions, the veracity of what is attributed, the inconsequentiality of when documents reached closure, and other such ominous considerations. As with S. J. Cohen, the questions that one asks attest to the presuppositions one holds about the character of the evidence.

So there is this "third intermediate stage." Of what it consists we know nothing. But even without evidence, we know that "it represents a common stream of Jewish thought that links Jesus with the world of rabbinic learning, the love of man and the love of his Creator." How we know it I cannot say, and Young does not tell us. So we have on the surface affirmed the critical premises of contemporary scholarship but forthwith ignored them, a phenomenon that Morton Smith classified as "pseudo-orthodoxy," meaning the profession of critical principles accompanied by the practice of unalloyed fundamentalism. Still, if all that is at stake is the modifying language, "the love of man and the love of his Creator," then that "common stream of Jewish thought" has flowed directly from the Old Testament. In that case, why take the trouble to call upon rabbinic compilations, spread over so long a span of centuries and two distinct empires, the Roman and the Iranian, to tell us what was going on in an age of which their authors had no direct knowledge whatsoever?

More to the point, why in any event ask these same compilations to tell us anything about the thought of a protean figure, who put the stamp of his own unique personality upon everything he used? What is striking to those knowledgeable concerning rabbinic writings is not the points in common with the deeds and statements of Jesus, but the stunning contradictions between the "known" (the rabbinic) and the new. There is scarcely a saying or a story in the Gospels that does not astonish and amaze, and that is precisely what Jesus is supposed to have said over and over again: "You have heard it said ... but I say to you...."

So we are left with the well-established fact that a single simile or parable may be used in a variety of settings, both gentile and Jewish, both rabbinic-Jewish and other-than-rabbinic-Jewish (classifying the New Testament books written by authors who professed to be Jews as Jewish but not rabbinic). Young contributes nothing new to the recognition of that commonplace. His interest is in placing Jesus into the "common stream" of rabbinic Judaism. But that requires him at once to profess and to ignore the critical problems inherent in using rabbinic compilations in pursuit of the historical Jesus. These are:

1. Attributions of sayings to named rabbis are notoriously uncertain and can be shown as pseudepigraphic where they are not merely contradictory (the same saying given to two or more authorities, sayings manifestly invented out of logical inferences and then assigned to named authorities, and other routine fabrications).

2. Redaction of documents in the rabbinic corpus took place from two hundred to six hundred years after the time of Jesus, and any utilization of their contents to describe the state of opinion prior to the time of closure requires demonstration that the contents antedate the closure of the compilations.

Appeals to the reliability of processes of transmission rarely find support in systematic and sustained demonstration, and those who invoke the principle that "our sages would not lie" ignore a considerable corpus of scholarship, beginning with Y. N. Epstein's *Mavo lenussah hammishnah* (1954), which shows that veracity in a historical sense is simply beside the point.

In my opinion, then, Young's research is superficial, since he does not appear to have read many current and important works on his subject and on the documents on which he is working. As a matter of fact his knowledge of the rabbinic sources is parlous and unreliable; a long list of misunderstandings could have been compiled to show how little people in Jerusalem really know about these writings.

Nevertheless, Young's book has the considerable merit of showing us precisely how one approach to the use of the rabbinic evidence for the analysis of the New Testament is carried forward. Young succeeds in presenting a thesis and illustrating a method and presenting results for all to see. The claim upon "critical" standing set forth by pseudo-orthodoxy stands refuted in the pages of this book. If all we are to gain is Young's "third intermediate stage" (he obviously means, "a third, intermediate stage" and not that there were three intermediate stages), why bother? Here are no consequential results of an other-than-theological character and, as to theology, history and biography make no difference.

# Index